D1598821

Spain under the Bourbons, 1700–1833

History in Depth

GENERAL EDITOR: G. A. Williams

Available from the
University of South Carolina Press

Spain under the Bourbons, 1700–1833

A collection of documents

Edited and translated with a critical introduction by
W. N. HARGREAVES-MAWDSLEY, M.A., D.Phil., F.R.Hist.S.
Professor of History, Brandon University, Manitoba, Canada

UNIVERSITY OF SOUTH CAROLINA PRESS
Columbia, South Carolina

First published 1973 in Great Britain by
THE MACMILLAN PRESS LTD
London and Basingstoke

Published 1973 in the United States of America by
UNIVERSITY OF SOUTH CAROLINA PRESS
Columbia, South Carolina

Library of Congress Cataloging in Publication Data

Hargreaves-Mawdsley, W   N   comp.
    Spain under the Bourbons, 1700–1833.

    (History in depth)
    Bibliography : p. 282
    1. Spain—History—Bourbons, 1700–
—Sources. I. Title.
DP192.H27   1973   946'.054   72–12666
ISBN 0–87249–289–3
ISBN 0–87249–290–7 (pbk)

Manufactured in Great Britain

IN PIAM MEMORIAM
VICENTE DEÓ LAGÜÉNS
RECTE VIXIT ET FORTITER OBIIT

Contents

General Editor's Preface

Historical perception demands immediacy and depth. These qualities are lost in attempts at broad general survey; for the reader of history depth is the only true breadth. Each volume in this series, therefore, explores an important historical problem in depth. There is no artificial uniformity; each volume is shaped by the problem it tackles. The past bears its own witness; the core of each volume is a major collection of original material (translated into English where necessary) as alive, as direct and as full as possible. The reader should feel the texture of the past. The volume editor provides interpretative notes and introduction and a full working bibliography. The volume will stand in its own right as a 'relived experience' and will also serve as a point of entry into a wider area of historical discourse. In taking possession of a particular historical world, the reader will move more freely in a wider universe of historical experience.

*

In this volume, Professor Hargreaves-Mawdsley explores the history of Spain during its exciting, ambiguous and ultimately abortive eighteenth-century revival. This is the 'missing century' of much English-language work on Spain. Among Spaniards it is the locus of intense controversy; one powerful and until recently hegemonic school sees it as a monstrous aberration, the 'French' century of the heterodox; many as they circle endlessly around that elusive concept, the *genuine* Spain, the *autentico ser* of Spain, locate in it the first crystallisation of those celebrated 'two Spains' whose conflict is said to have characterised Spanish history since.

For the century of the reforming *ilustrados* ended in cataclysm.

> Castilla miserable, ayer dominadora,
> envuelta en sus andrajos desprecia cuanto ignora...

wrote Machado, victim of the last and bloodiest confrontation of the 'two Spains', and it was precisely this image of a Spain in decline, wretched in its rags and despising everything it did not know – 'black

Spain' to the thin ranks of the Spanish Enlightenment – which the reforming Bourbons, coming in at the lowest point of Spain's 'Decadence', were concerned to eradicate.

The measure of their success has been underestimated. Slowly at first but strengthening to a climax under Charles III, pulses of reform, centralisation, a measured, selective and *bien-pensant* enlightenment, revivified industry, trade, administration, jogged the immobilism and backwardness of 'traditional' Spain; the great Reglamento of 1778 opened the America trade and stimulated growth in the trans-Atlantic empire. Pitt's Board of Trade grew alarmed at the Spanish 'reconquest' of America, hitherto the economic fief of foreigners.

But the movement was riddled with contradiction and ran into an inevitable ceiling. No monarchy, however 'enlightened', could destroy its own social base; the thrust of economic growth registered in the periphery not in the governing centre, in Catalonia not Castile. Novel 'French' ideas provoked a reaction from traditional and clerical Spain; Madrid crowds rioted against 'progress' in the Esquilache troubles, aristocrats adopted the folkloric styles of *costumbrismo*, the Spanish, i.e. anti-French garb of Goya's *majos* and *majas*. And the simultaneous onset of the political degeneration of the monarchy under Charles IV and his favourite Godoy and the unhingeing challenge of the French Revolution exposed the essentially precarious achievement of the Spanish Bourbons.

Unable to achieve effective military or naval autonomy, Spain was driven into satellite status; Godoy struggled to survive among the increasingly ferocious struggle of factions. An important sector of the intelligentsia, groping for support among the slowly forming middle classes, abandoned hope and looked to a Buonaparte for regeneration; other reformers turned from the monarchy and sought regeneration in an historical myth of ancient Spanish freedom – the impulse behind the celebrated Constitution of 1812 (as, oddly enough, Karl Marx was among the first to indicate). Many more rallied around tradition and the Church. Ferdinand's plot against Godoy and his father set in train the crises of 1808, when a French king and a collaborationist establishment had to face a popular national uprising and a protracted war, the first guerrilla war of modern times, entirely ambiguous in character, with monks leading guerrilla bands 'black' enough in spirit to drive many of the *ilustrados* into exile and with Cádiz radicals producing a constitution democratic enough to make a Jacobin wince. The Spanish *ancien régime* foundered during the war; empire in America disintegrated; the restored Bourbons oscillated between reaction and compromise. With Ferdinand's affront to monarchical sentiment in his settlement of the succession, the shrunken Spain of the nineteenth century stumbled towards liberalism and endemic civil conflict. The year after Ferdinand's death the first churches were burned.

The story assumes the character of an historical tragedy; it shades into myth. The first essential is therefore to get a grip on a reality comprehended in historical rather than psychiatric terms. Professor Hargreaves-Mawdsley in his collection of newly-translated texts presents a panorama which is essentially political and roots us in the problems of a new, sensible, pragmatic, sufficiently effective but limited dynasty struggling to find a new course in the imperialist conflicts of the century. It moves with a quickening pace into the crises and turmoil which followed 1789 and includes Quintana's eloquent letter to Lord Holland in 1823, a characteristic heartcry from liberal Spain and a fitting epitaph to a time of hope.

In the sweep and particularity of this survey the reader can find his first footing in that measured Spain of the forgotten revival whose breakdown into tragedy produced in Goya, a painter whose personal dilemmas paralleled those of his country, an artist of genius who gave to the Spanish crisis a universal resonance.

GWYN A. WILLIAMS

Introduction

Spanish eighteenth-century history has always been a neglected field both by the Spanish themselves and by foreigners. It has been looked upon as a backwater, a stagnant age lying between the Golden Age and the turbulent nineteenth century. It is certainly not an age of outward vigour such as the sixteenth century, nor has it the interest of the age of Philip IV with its dramatic, poignant quality, a great proud edifice standing alone, besieged on every side. There is still drama in the reign of the 'bewitched' Habsburg Carlos II, in whom is to be seen the play of spectres until that time decently hidden behind screens. All the evils of religion become fear and superstition, the bad fruit of close intermarriage and of the feline intrigues of a cobwebbed court are to be heard in this last hideous Habsburg gasp.

In English-speaking countries Spanish history has too often been approached through literature and art with the result that it has become their handmaid, except perhaps during the period from 1492 to 1588, that is from the time of the discovery of America to the defeat of the Armada. Of course, trade rivalries leading to wars between Britain and Spain were an important feature of the eighteenth century, but the fact remains that Spain seems always to be regarded as the younger and weaker brother in the Family Compact with France and is never allowed to stand on its own. It is significant that in the English-speaking world between the end of Lynch's work on *Spain under the Habsburgs* (1700) and the beginning of Carr's *History of Spain* (1808) there is a gap which will not be closed for a considerable time. Those who might have been working in this direction have been seduced by the fashion, well supported by educational funds, for South America.

I am afraid that with the increasing invocation of relevance and utility in state-aided academic systems anything that occurred before 1789 or perhaps before 1815 is coming to be regarded, certainly in Anglo-Saxon countries, as out of date and study of it as a luxury to which harassed tax-payers should not be expected to subscribe. In Spain the Golden Age fixation remains, added to which are two new and strongly differing areas of interest, the first the Mozo-Arabic, the second the reign of Ferdinand VII, both of them manifestations of a wish to break with traditional historical values and perspectives, the protagonist of which is Vicens Vives. Even so, the majority of Spanish intellectuals accept the stressing of Spain's debt to Arabs or liberals with a wry mouth and withdraw as often as not into the false paradise of El Cid, Alfonso el sabio and Isabel la catolica, for it dies hard that Spain is the country chosen by Destiny to man the lines against the Moors and Voltaires.

The great and typical Spain for most of us is the Spain which, exclusivist to the core and cut off from outside influences, produced its mystics Santa Teresa de Ávila and San Juan de la Cruz, its Cervantes, its Lope de Vega, its Góngora and its Calderón, its Zurbarán, Velázquez and Murillo. These men are greater than history, but Spain's history must be called in to explain their lives and their work. Spanish history is rarely studied for itself. Charles I was certainly king of Spain also and far more successful in that capacity than as Emperor, but it is as Charles V that the world knows him, and he is studied as the hard-pressed titular ruler of an already disintegrating German Empire. On the other hand, Philip II is the only well-known Spanish king because he impinged on the Anglo-Saxon west.

The Spanish eighteenth century has been far less neglected in France where Sarrailh broke new ground with his great work on the *éclairissement* in eighteenth-century Spain. His example was followed by the American Herr's book, the only worthy work written in English on the subject.

It is natural that the French should be interested, if anyone, in Spain's eighteenth century, for it is the French century, that of the four Bourbons, who for good and ill set their seal on economics, art, architecture, dress, education and medicine, if not yet on law, which influences were to be intensified, if in other ways, as a result of the Napoleonic upheavals after 1807. Indeed this interaction of widely differing national characters and cultures is of enormous interest, and if Spain loses much of its exclusivist and typical quality in the process, it cannot be denied that the French enlightenment provided a goal after which politicians and intellectuals were to strive and are still striving. The eighteenth century was the last century in which 'the people' were of little account except to face the cannons and till the land. The nationalism produced by the French Revolution put an end to all that, and the country was converted

from one which eagerly accepted the great-grandson of Louis XIV
as the solution of all their troubles to one which by 1808 looked
with reason upon the French as those who had betrayed their confidence. It was the court of Charles IV led by Godoy which had
betrayed them. There was a fierce return to exclusivism, coupled
now with nationalism which eventually overthrew the liberal
governments of 1812 and 1820, and allowed Ferdinand VII to visit
liberalism with bitter punishments. Yet the work of Orry and
Patiño, of Aranda and Campomanes was not forgotten, and dawn
came in 1834, if only a partial one; for if the whiggery of Lord
Holland and the English Reform Act (since in politics France was
still out of court) prevailed, there was always a harking back to the
romanticised ideals of a Golden Age, although it had become by
this time as much a travesty of the reality as Teutonic dreams of
the Hohenstaufen. Spain must have it both ways, it must reverence
its archives of a great past with Hartzenbusch, it must analyse with
unprejudiced eye its narrow, its fanatical catholicism with Menéndez
y Pelayo, but at the same time it must preserve its *hispanismo*, its
typical 'Spanishness'. It must take what was new and good and
served its purpose from Europe, but be sure to withdraw into itself
again, thus preserving its integrity. For this the First Republic and
liberal monarchy was sacrificed (1868–73), since foreign wolves were
violating the Spanish sheepfolds, and the reign of Alfonso XIII has
shown how unfit was Spain to rule itself according to foreign
methods. Already in 1898, that year of the ruin of the imperial
pride, Joaquín Costa and Unamuno had called on Spain to open its
doors to Europe, the while preserving its essential qualities, but these
Aragonese and Castilian intellectuals, though aware of the two
opposing sides of Spanish life, love of tradition and the half-unwilling
desire to accept innovation, failed to apply their analysis to reality.
There has been sadly enough no middle way for Spain, nor is there
yet, and when faced with the violence of syndicalists and anarchists,
tamely allowed their way in the name of freedom by the sort of Giron-
dins that the Spanish liberals have been, the country naturally
reacted (what other resources had it?) to dictatorships which invoked the secure and certain benefits of 'the Spanish tradition'
which alone everyone knew.

Eighteenth-century Spain was a true period of reform, the loosen-
ing of the country from the Middle Ages. It produced that quest
for innovation, which though altered and forcibly prevented at
times, has never ended. If the influence of France is stamped upon
it, there is no slavish imitation to be found. As we see in the life
and work of Jovellanos, Campomanes and Floridablanca, three of

the greatest names of that age, while there is an acceptance of the
best results of reform then taking place in France and Italy, these
influences are received in no slavish way, but are accepted as of
right and commuted into a substance suitable for their needs. It is
not their fault that the nineteenth century took over French and
English ideas piecemeal and tried to make them fit where they could
not possibly do so. For example, the Spanish educational system,
which no one can surely be proud of, is founded on that of France,
the basis of which is the Napoleonic reform of 1810, while the content is for the most part that, laid down in the intervals of reaction
between liberal epochs, of an over-prejudiced piety. The result is a
curious and unfortunate compound which satisfies no one. Spain
is not France, it is itself and must remain so, and when it comes to
make its reforms let us hope that it turns for guidance to that
eighteenth century, that age of reasonable faith when the golden
mean was still preserved.

With the arrival of the Bourbons in 1700 Spain's political and
diplomatic course was much altered, while civil servants from Versailles, undermining the traditional power of the grandees and replac-
ing them by professionals, created an efficiency in administration unknown before, which led to economic revival. Philip V, however,
although dashing in war, became passively melancholy as soon as he
was secure on the throne after Utrecht, and allowed his second wife
Isabel Farnese to rule with disastrous results. The bad old times seemed
to have returned, and his reign ended gloomily in 1746. Yet Spain had
essentially changed, and a new generation of bureaucrats were still
at their posts when the war-smoke had blown away.

Philip's son by his first marriage, Ferdinand VI (1746–59), mis-
judged by many and remembered as a madman who cared for nothing
beyond his obese wife and music, at least had one virtue, he loved
peace. Although he could not prevent Spain from being totally un-
involved in the Seven Years' War, he yet managed to modify this
involvement; and when in 1759 his half-brother Charles III succeeded, he found much that was favourable to the enlightened policy
he was to pursue, and by means of which Spain was on the whole
better governed than at any other time before or since. He was succeeded at his death in 1788 by his son Charles IV, a man of complete
intellectual laziness, who was so dominated by his wife, a neurotic
sensualist, that it was not long before he made over the ship of state
to her lover, that irresponsible helmsman Godoy.

The result was that Spain, which hitherto had worked as a partner
(if not quite an equal) of France, pursued a dangerous path, seeking

at once to remain enlightened when the Age of Enlightenment was
over, to defy her regicide neighbour and to preserve her own integrity.
The result was invasion, an indignity which Spain had not suffered
for seventy-five years, and the humiliation of the Treaty of San
Ildefonso (1796), by which the country sold out to revolutionaries
and became France's hireling.

The eighteenth century therefore illustrates the influence of a restless and modern France on formerly static and traditionalist Spain,
of a people in less than a hundred years hurried into the welter of
new Europe. Here is the country of Unamuno, with its deep-seated
tradition and its half unwilling desire for innovation. When analysed
thus eighteenth-century Spain becomes not only a fascinating but
an instructive study, an example of that condition with which we
have grown very familiar during this century of ours, a country
of tradition, assailed economically, politically, socially by the spirit
of a new age, to whose aims and assaults it must accede or be
damned.

Looking at Spain from this point of view one can see how short-
sighted is the literary purist's view who, when having reached the
death of Calderon in 1681, the termination of the Golden Age, turns
his back resolutely on the literary figures of Spain's eighteenth century,
dismissing them as unimportant, and takes up the thread again in
the completely new age of the Byronic poet Espronceda and the
liberal journalist Larra. Yet if one is to look for the 'typical' Spain –
if we are always to look for this in the 'Spanishness' of the Golden
Age – is it by these canons to be found either in Espronceda or
Larra? The first is the child of Byron, Hugo and Lamartine, the
second of those exiles like Blanco White and Trueba nurtured in the
schools of London journalism. It is a fact that must not be overlooked that Santa Teresa, Lope de Vega and Góngora, to mention
these alone, owe much more to the Jews, Arabs and Italians than
those who talk of typically Spanish literature will allow.

They who turn their backs on eighteenth-century Spanish literature, close their eyes to Feijoo, Jovellanos, Cadalso, Meléndez Valdés,
Iriarte and the Moratíns, father and son, to name only a few.
These are not just 'frenchified' Spaniards, they are writers who,
looking beyond the boundaries of their country, gather in the new
experiences of Europe and enrich the thought and art of their
country by doing so. You cannot go on reproducing Tudor houses
in an age that is not Tudor, nor can you continue to produce new
autos sacramentales when on your doorstep the secular theatres of
Paris, London, Venice and Hamburg are throbbing with the comedy
of manners and the comedy of tears. It is an age of journalists, clubs

and salons of the new merchant society that is growing up on all
sides round you; if you remain isolationist you will wither and die;
so Feijoo works in the Encyclopaedist spirit as scientist, economist
and religious modernist instructing a nation which in the Golden Age
was cut off by the Inquisition, in the name of the monarch, from all
questioning thought, and Jovellanos teaches his countrymen what
the Italians Verri and Beccaria and the Frenchmen Diderot and
Rousseau (if not Voltaire) are doing in the realms of agricultural
economics and law reform, in the realms of literary art and social
criticism. Cadalso is not afraid to voice passion, Iriarte, in giving a
Spanish turn to the tradition of the *fabula* as old as Aesop, makes
it the vehicle of his social and political satires, while Meléndez finds
an affinity between man and nature which no Spaniard had done
before, and the Moratíns revolutionise the stage.

If the literary critics often believe that they can dismiss the
eighteenth century, the art critics at least have Goya to contend
with, but they are inclined to treat him as the great Spanish
phenomenon of a new age rather than as the pupil of Mengs and
Bayeu, two figures firmly planted in the Age of Enlightenment.
They in fact too often take him out of his environment. He is surely
the rebel against a formal society. The man who finds himself at
home with the peasant, the man who, like Rousseau or Beaumarchais,
feels that love and passion and simple human dignity have the right
to self-affirmation, that the great name of Alba shall be no
stumbling block to desires, that convents are not inviolable, that if
Charles IV wishes him to paint a king and his family he will do it
on his own terms and spare nothing. Goya proves that the Spain of
Charles III and Charles IV contained men seething within, who
realised the latent force of the simple world, proud, natural and
vivid, and contrasted it with the charade of court life at Aranjuez.
It would be these and the peasants and the simple priests who
would defend Spain's integrity when the grandees – or most of
them – had sold out to the French Emperor of Fontainebleau. Thus
Goya's fifty-four years of life in the eighteenth century anchor him
securely in an age still too little known, and we should not forget
that his portfolios of etchings and stacks of oils with their deep
social commentaries were extensive long before the nineteenth century opened. His remarkable series of portraits contain almost
everyone of note in the social, intellectual and artistic world of the
period from the 1770s to the 1790s. Goya in short belongs as much
as did Blake to the eighteenth century; his mental equipment was
provided and conditioned by living in that important watershed,
the second half of the eighteenth century, dividing the old world

from the new, that age of digestion of the scientific, intellectual and social studies of the seventeenth century, tabulated, put in order and held in position to become the instrument with which to forge a new age and way of life.

It will now be necessary to consider the important occurrences of Spain's eighteenth century, all of which have been supported by documents in the present volume, after which the documents which I have chosen for the purpose will themselves be discussed.

The Will of Charles II, the last Habsburg King of Spain, is a natural starting point and a convenient one, for it was this document issuing from the anguished and dying monarch in 1700 which led to the succession of the Bourbons and the threat to the rest of Europe of two closely associated kingdoms if not a unified one. At any rate Louis XIV has been credited with the boast that there were no longer any Pyrenees. The young Duke of Anjou, Louis XIV's grandson, now become Philip V of Spain, arrived in his new country in January 1701 and by the end of the summer had been crowned and had won the loyalty of not only the Castilians but the Aragonese and at least the acquiescence of the ever particularist Catalans. Peace at home, however, was counterbalanced by the threat of a European Grand Alliance with the Empire and England to the fore. For the first it was a case of wounded pride that the Archduke Charles of Austria should not have been crowned King of Spain; for the second it was a fight for her existence as a naval and commercial power, since the spectre of a closely allied France and Spain, which had haunted the English and Dutch for half a century, had now become reality.

By 1702 the English fleet was busy in the West Indies and off the north-west coast of Spain, and the first important engagement of the War of the Spanish Succession was a naval one off Vigo where the English fleet was successful. During that time Philip V had journeyed to Italy to make sure that the Spanish territories there were safe, and then returned to Spain. In 1704 came an intensification of war which had now entered the Iberian Peninsula. The Archduke Charles, proclaimed Charles III of Spain by the Imperialists, took up his headquarters in Lisbon and prevailed on the Portuguese to advance into Spanish territory, while Admiral Rooke with his English squadron took Gibraltar in August. By the following year the Imperialists and Portuguese had gained a foothold on Spain, and Cataluña opened its gates to the Allies. In 1706 Philip V's fortunes were at their lowest; his siege of Barcelona was a failure, and for a time the Archduke held Madrid itself. Then came Philip's victory at Almansa (April 1707), his first success, and although there were to be three years of hard fighting, with victory visiting both camps, Archduke Charles as late as August and September 1710 gaining the victory of Zaragoza and re-entering Madrid in triumph, the Bourbons had by the end of that year, thanks to the brilliant battles of Brihuega and Villaviciosa, made the outcome of the campaign inevitable. By 1712 the diplomats of Europe were thinking not of battlefields but of congress seats, and when Philip solemnly renounced his rights to the French throne and the Salic Law was promulgated, the Peace of Utrecht went smoothly forward. Only Cataluña, the Baleares, Portugal and the Netherlands remained opposed to the now uncontested king of Spain, Philip V; but peace with the Netherlands and the end of the Catalan revolt with the taking of Barcelona (1714), a treaty with Portugal and the reduction of Mallorca and Ibiza (Menorca in British hands) in 1715–16, made an end of even the remnants of the opposition.

The War of the Spanish Succession had been essentially dictated by two questions, that of commercial imperialism and that of the balance of power. For the Imperialists it was almost entirely the latter, since Austria had little interest in what happened in the Atlantic and in the New World nor was it in a position to, even had it desired, its navy being almost non-existent. For them it was the two centuries of fear that France would acquire so great a hold over Spain, if not absorb her, that she would become as grave a threat to the balance of Europe as in the palmy days of Louis XIV. The Peace of Utrecht had obviated that threat, but the commercial aspect was by no means fully resolved.

Since Utrecht had reduced the Netherlands for ever to the status of a second-rate commercial power, three giants remained, Spain, France and Great Britain. Spain the possessor of a vast Empire, improvidently managed and its rule incompetent because antiquated, was, as it had for so long been, the passive member of the trio of rivals, the owner of the rich Garden of the Hesperides at which the other two looked enviously. France and Britain saw that Spain must be watched, guarded and reproved when necessary, for in her keeping was the limitless commercial empire for which both craved.

Then came the comet Alberoni in 1717 with his wild schemes for a great and aggressive Spain in Europe, and Sardinia was conquered, thus upsetting the terms of Utrecht; but when in 1718 Sicily was attacked Britain came in, and in the sea-fight off Cape Passaro trimmed the Cardinal. The following year France stepped in and Spanish territory was violated when the French took San Sebastian and the British occupied Vigo.

By 1720 Spain had acknowledged defeat and Alberoni had fallen.

Philip V took rule into his own hands, Sardinia and Sicily were finally evacuated, the balance of power was restored, and the following year Spain, France and Britain were in alliance. As a compensation for frustrated ambitions in the Central Mediterranean Spain had already turned south to North Africa with the expedition to Ceuta in December 1720. Such Moroccan conquests were to be a preoccupation from then on down to our own times.

In 1721 Walpole's long ministry began in Britain, and five years later Fleury became Walpole's counterpart in France. Both men hated war and set their minds against it, Walpole because he believed in the *status quo*, peace and plenty, Fleury for conscientious reasons. Walpole wanted divisions neither at home, where he was busy uniting Whig and Tory interests behind the new dynasty, nor abroad; peaceful co-existence, with trade as the binding force of good relationships and interdependence, was the lodestar of his foreign policy. Both were then of the same mind, and during the period 1726–31 when Spain, given a new lease of life by such gifted finance and war ministers as Patiño and Ripperdá, reasserted itself, France and Great Britain joined forces to prevent it. At the Third Treaty of Vienna (1731) Spain acknowledged diplomatic defeat.

With the opening of the War of Polish Succession in 1733 came the first signs of a growing cleavage between Britain and France. Both were becoming impatient of a stalemate as regards the expansion of either in world trade, and British merchants, backed by younger politicians who resented Walpole's dictatorship, however benevolent, and who sought to cover up their personal ambitions by preaching imperialism, began to point out that if Britain did not infiltrate further into West Indian trade, then France would. Walpole's doctrine of peace at almost any price had been good in 1721 when Britain needed consolidation, but in 1733 this policy was no longer suitable. This view seemed self-evident when that very year by the Treaty of the Escorial France and Spain drew together in the First Family Compact. Spanish interests in the Mediterranean again appeared when Don Carlos, a son of Philip V by his second wife, that Isabel Farnese who had earlier abetted Alberoni's ambitious moves, became King of the Two Sicilies in 1734.

Five years later in 1739 Walpole's peace policy was finally upset when Britain, refusing any longer to temporise, declared war on Spain over his head and Admiral Vernon sailed with a large fleet to the Caribbean. A year later on the death of the Emperor Charles VI, the same who had been Philip V's antagonist in the Spanish Succession War, came a war which was to assume vast proportions, the War of the Austrian Succession, into which were thrown all the pent-up frustrations or energies which had been hanging in the air since Utrecht. Apart from troop movements in Italy, Spain was able to avoid the main blows of this war, but its most significant move was its drawing still nearer to France by the Second Family Compact signed at Fontainebleau in 1743, boding ill for the future.

On the death of Philip V in 1746 his son by his first marriage succeeded him as Ferdinand VI, a man whose moods of introspection and despondency inherited from his father gradually deepened into near insanity. In his early years he chose his ministers rather well and seemed interested in internal reforms, but these good signs were stifled by his increasing religious mania. Due to him and to his minister Ensenada is that concordat with the Papacy which still exists.

In 1756, after eight years of European peace, the Seven Years' War began, a war which was to be as conclusive as the Austrian Succession War had been inconclusive. Great Britain had not gained the prizes in the New World she had hoped for and looked for a final solution. In the very first months of the new war France took Menorca from Britain, thus depriving her of a much needed Mediterranean base, and in 1761 Charles III, who had succeeded his half-brother Ferdinand two years before, still further cemented the alliance between France and Spain by signing the Third Family Compact at Paris. Britain's answer to this was to declare war on Spain, and she was now free to attempt once more to wrest possessions in the New World from her. 1762 was a year of varying fortune; if she lost Habana and Manila, she won back Almeida and Sacramento. At the Peace of Paris (1763), which ended the Seven Years' War, Britain was, however, the outstanding gainer. By following the policy of the Elder Pitt, as laid down at the Treaty of Westminster (1756), that Britain while subsidising her Continental allies, above all Prussia, should not become involved in European land warfare, but should concentrate on her navy, thereby founding a world empire, the country had driven the French from Canada and India, the Spanish from North America, the while seizing islands and fortresses the world over.

The great interest of Charles III's reign from this year onwards lies in his domestic policy. With the outstanding statesman Aranda at his side he brought the new concepts of benevolent despotism, common by now to most of Europe, to bear on the vast social and economic problems of his country. The expulsion of the Jesuits in 1767 simply followed the pattern of the enlightenment in every country of Western and Central Europe. Not that the Jesuits were by any means reactionary; they were punished because they had lively political interests and power, and were the emissaries of a Pope, a foreign potentate, a well-knit society which was enabled to spy on every court of Europe. A benevolent despot must control his people, paternally but firmly, which would both increase his personal power and bring his people what he believed was their happiness. All the benefits of his rule must come from him alone.

Since 1763 Spain and France had been gnashing their teeth and biding their time, waiting for an opportunity to revenge themselves on that pirate Great Britain. When therefore the American War of Independence began to go badly for the old arch enemy Spain declared war on her (1779). Much of her energy was however expended on a fruitless blockade of Gibraltar, although Menorca, which had been returned by France to Britain at the Treaty of Paris, became Spanish for the time being in 1781, but that was nothing compared with Spanish success in the New World that same year, for Florida and Nicaragua, lost in 1763, were retrieved. At the Peace of Paris of 1783 Britain was humbled and Spain won back some pride in herself. Two years later peace had been concluded with Algeria, and on his death at the end of 1788 Charles III left a country which outwardly at least had never been in a better condition.

Unfortunately Charles IV, the son and successor of that spare, active, homespun father, was weak and at the best pleasantly fatuous. Like his equally weak cousin Louis XVI of France, whom he so much resembled physically, there was also something sly about him, but he lacked his French counterpart's religion, benevolence and sense of duty, which, however misplaced, one must acknowledge Louis to have possessed.

Fortunately the new king entered on his reign with such good ministers of his father's time as Aranda and Floridablanca still alive and active, but within a year the French Revolution had broken out and with it came new challenges which were first to shake the old Spanish regime of rococo enlightenment and finally destroy it. When Aranda as Secretary of State refused, or was unable, to face the startling new situation, the old guard was doomed. It was a time for desperate measures, a time also for a political adventurer Godoy, the Queen's favourite, to become virtually dictator. Vilified retrospectively, one must credit him with activity when it was necessary, and with enlightened views which weakened the Inquisition, whereas Charles III had never attempted to undermine it, and with deep interest in judicial and educational reform. Godoy's political influence on Spain was, however, catastrophic.

Spain declared war on revolutionary France in 1793 in answer to the execution of God's anointed, Louis XVI. It was the gesture of an *hidalgo*, a quixotic gesture, such as no other country in Europe made, for elsewhere, by and large, it was the threat posed by this *enfant terrible* to commercial interests which led the allies into the tumult. For this noble mien the country was to suffer heartily, although at first under the brilliant General Antonio Ricardos France was actually invaded and Arles-sur-Tech (Pyrénées-Orientales) taken, but after Ricardos' death early in 1794 the initiative passed to the French : Spanish mainland territory was occupied for the first time since 1719, Figueras was lost, and when in the summer of 1795 San Sebastian was taken, Godoy was glad to come to terms with the enemy at the Peace of Basel at the expense of signing away Santo Domingo.

Godoy had been wise to come to terms; it was in fact all he could do, but now created Príncipe de la Paz by a grateful king and puffed up with new pride, he threw discretion to the winds. He wanted to draw even closer to France, hoping that Spain might ride on the wave of the success of his ally, and at the Treaty of San Ildefonso (1796) he handed over Spanish forces and forts to the tender mercy of the French Directory behind which lurked the menacing figure of Bonaparte. This provocation drove Britain to declare war on a Spain which only a few years before had appealed personally to George III for his aid and friendship against the bloodthirsty revolutionaries.

Once more the British navy faced Spain, and in 1797 Jervis won the naval victory off Cape Saint Vincent, while although Nelson's attack on Tenerife was a failure, in the following year Menorca was once more in British hands. Just before this opposition to Godoy had become so formidable that he was forced into eclipse, but he was back in power in 1801, backed by Charles IV and the Court against adversaries who rallied round Ferdinand, Prince of Asturias, the future Ferdinand VII.

This then is the skeleton of Spain's eighteenth-century history, and it is now time to consider the documentary and other evidence, seventy-nine examples of which I have used to illustrate these hundred years.

In Nicolini's valuable *L'Europa durante la guerra di successione di Spagna* is to be found evidence based on hitherto unedited despatches of diplomats of various countries resident in the Republic of Venice, that very hive of information. Charles II's will is there, so are the various reactions to the will including above all that of Louis XIV, and the proclamation of Philip of Anjou, who, backed by the old French king, set in motion events which were to lead to the War of the Spanish Succession.

Valuable information as to the diplomacy of France and the Empire in regard to Spain in those early years will be found in *Copia de carta del rey christianissimo Luis Dézimocuarto, a la Reyna nuestra*

Señora y Señores del Gobierno (in MS in the Biblioteca Nacional, Madrid) and in Ubilla y Medina's *Juramento y pleyto omenage que los Reynos de Castilla y León ... hizieron ...*, dealing as it does with the ready acceptance of Philip V by the greater part of the nation. Of printed matter dealing with the early years of the century none is more comprehensive and valuable than *Historia civil de España y sucesos de la guerra y tratados de la paz* by Fray Nicolás de Jesús Belando, published in Madrid in 1740, and covering the history, fully documented (including the Orendain papers) of the first thirty-three years of the century. Of newspapers, as one would expect, the *Gaceta de Madrid* at this period and throughout the century is of the utmost value.

That the Inquisition could still claim its victims in 1724 can be seen from the depressing document entitled *Relación del auto particular de fe ... celebró en la Inglesia del Convento de Santo Domingo el Real...*, although it is noteworthy that there is some show of clemency which a century before would have been the exception.

Belando's history ends just about the time of the signing of the First Family Compact and the opening of the War of the Polish Succession, and from now on much information can be gained from the *Gaceta de Madrid* set against the voluminous and disorderly, though valuable, work of Esteban de Ferrater, *Código de derecho internacional* (1846). In this work the terms of the Second Family Compact (1743) are to be found.

The commercial war of Britain and Spain is brought clearly home to one in the official document *Diario de todo lo ocurrido en la expugnación de las fuertes de Bocachica, y sitio de la ciudad de Cartagena de las Indias* (1741). Such an incident was typical of so much of the fighting at this time.

For peace treaties of the period of the War of the Austrian Succession no source is better than the *Mercurio Histórico y Político* of Madrid. In fact during the late 1740s and the 1750s it is to be preferred to the *Gaceta de Madrid*, and its number for March 1753 contains in full the terms of Spain's Concordat with Pope Benedict XIV; but that there were grounds for dissatisfaction on both sides arising from the Jesuit question can be seen from 'Trasumpto de la carta que escribió al Nuncio' (1759), which remains in manuscript.

Again it was the *Mercurio* which in 1761 prepared public opinion for the outcome of the war with Britain. It had become the mouthpiece for officialdom, and its freshness of approach suffered in consequence. The compensatory Compact of 1761 is dealt with in full in the work of V. Palacio Atard (1945), who gathered together relevant documents with great skill.

An interesting commentary on the domestic condition of Madrid early in Charles III's reign (1761) is to be found in the ever useful *Mercurio*. It is a world such as this that that remarkable playwright Ramón de la Cruz Cano (1731–94) drew in his *sainetes*, those short one-act plays, such as *El fandango del candil* and *Manolo*, which tell us so much of the everyday life of the city.

For the closing stages of the Seven Years' War as it affected Spain, which really meant the operations of the British Navy in the West Indies and the Spanish Main, one turns once more to the *Gaceta de Madrid*, and for the Peace of 1763 one relies, as one is to do more frequently during the second half of the century, on that great official compilation carried out between 1796 and 1801 under Godoy's orders, which needs a great deal of working through, the *Colección de tratados de paz, alianza, comercio...*

That period of the reign of Charles IV, during which Godoy was influenced by such great thinkers as Jovellanos, gave forth also the *Novísima recopilación de las leyes de España* (1805). Such a collection of Spanish laws had first been published in 1567 under Philip II, while at its next publication in the reign of Ferdinand VI it was brought down to 1755. Fifty years later its scope was widened by the incorporation of decrees, orders and resolutions, carrying the whole remarkable collection forward to 1804. Charles III's reaction to the *Motín de Esquilache* (1766), and the influence on him of Aranda are clearly brought out in the decrees issued at this time. Much information on Charles III as an enlightened despot may be found in F. C. Sáinz de Robles' *Historia de Madrid*, Manuel Dánvila y Collado's *Historia de Carlos III* and the *Relación verdadera y circunstanciada de todo lo acaecido en la ciudad de Zaragoza*, published in Madrid in 1766.

In 1767 came the expulsion of the Jesuits, a fact so important as regards Spanish kingship and the influence on it of advanced contemporary ideas. The controversy between Pope and King is to be found in a valuable manuscript in the Biblioteca Nacional in Madrid (No. 10902) entitled *Carta del Rey al Papa dándole aviso del Extrañamiento de los regulares de la Compañía de Jesús...*

The North African wars which now become important are best discovered in the *Gaceta de Madrid*, a letter of Miguel Sanz written in Morocco and in V. Rodriguez Casado's *Política marroquí de Carlos III*; while Spain and the American War of Independence is treated in masterly fashion, making use of all available manuscript material, in Yela Utrilla's *España ante la independencia de los Estados Unidos*. Spain, while glad of this opportunity to revenge herself on Britain, yet had fears for the settlement of her American Empire and came to terms with Portugal. Here the *Colección de tratados de paz*, mentioned above is very useful. Other episodes of the war, such as the Florida question, Menorca and the boundaries of the newly independent American States are dealt with in three contemporary sources, *Diario de la Expedición contra la plaza de Panzacola, Relación de la toma del Castillo de San Felipe en Mahón* and Aranda's Diary respectively.

In 1782 came the apparent solution of Spain's relationship with the Muslim world, a commercial treaty with the Ottoman Empire, and the following year at the Treaty of Paris (Versailles) came the end of the American War of Independence. Again the *Colección de tratados de paz* gives one the evidence, while Charles III's efforts to make Spain a nation of working professionals, farmers and artisans – with the very Grandees taking an intelligent and active part in the life of the state – was put forth in the *Cédula del Consejo* of March 1783, and is to be found in the *Novísima Recopilación de las leyes de España* mentioned above. This revolutionary move against the *caballeresco* concept is very much in tune with the policy of Enlightened monarchs throughout Europe.

During the period between the end of the War of Independence and the breaking out of the French Revolution the main external interests of Spanish history are the still unresolved Moroccan and Algerian problem, fully chronicled in the *Gaceta de Madrid*, the full terms of the Treaty of 1786 with the Dey of Algeria being given in the indispensable *Coleción de tratados*, so much used already.

A great change for Spain was to come with the French Revolution, although it was not until 1793 that she was drawn into the Revolutionary War. The royal proclamation of March 1793 sends Spain into the war against the French regicides, but two years later, with a show of honour and not much loss of face, the two countries are able to come to terms, although it is disconcerting to read of the statement about 'friendship and good understanding' which Charles IV (prompted, of course, by Godoy) takes for granted. So the Treaty of Basel of 1795 joins the *Colección de tratados de paz*, as does that more significant and dangerous offensive and defensive Treaty of San Ildefonso of the next year. This move naturally provoked Britain into war, and the nation is prepared for the coming blow by an official announcement in the *Gaceta de Madrid*, which naturally seeks to put Godoy's irresponsible policy in its best light; but soon the *Gaceta* was proclaiming, albeit in muffled tones, the disaster of the battle of Cape Saint Vincent and the bombardment of Cádiz, and before long the century was to end in a catastrophe. It was fortunate indeed, and the only ray of hope, that there were a few men who kept alive the belief in a sane liberalism in such times. Such reasonableness was to be found in Jovellanos' dignified *Representación* addressed to Charles IV in 1798 on the vexed question of the Inquisition, that incubus which still lurked in the shadows.

It was originally my intention to end the documentary survey of eighteenth-century Spain at 1808, which seems to be the natural conclusion to the old regime, even though it had for the last dozen years lived out a merely twilight existence. The more, however, that I looked into the matter, the more it seemed to me that it would be necessary to go further and include that remarkable reign of Ferdinand VII during which eighteenth-century despotism fights a battle with liberalism, during which the South American Republics come into being, and during which for the first time the 'people' of Spain stand up to Napoleonic France which proffers the proud, fanatical nation of individualists, that strange concoction, enforced liberty. Bludgeoned into freedom by infidels who scorched the earth, used the firing-squad to maintain order and who destroyed half the colleges of the University of Salamanca, not unnaturally Spain refused these ministrations.

Unfortunately the Spanish people, forming for the most part such ideas as they had on what their priests chose to tell them, came to oppose everything liberal as French. One could understand the bitter resentment, even fanatical hatred of a nation that had lost its self-pride by being enslaved by that well-intentioned king Joseph Bonaparte simply because he was an alien planted on them by force. Men such as Jovellanos and Floridablanca, liberals though they were and who had eagerly supported Martín de Garay the Secretary-General of the Junta Suprema in his appeal to the nation in 1808, were not guilty of any compromise with the French, who, although their ideas had much in common with their own, were yet foreign invaders. Such men as these were dead when the Cortes of 1812 proclaimed its liberal constitution; if they had lived there is little doubt that they would have been in its ranks; but the fact remained that, as has always been the case in Spain, the professional classes were small, and found themselves uncomfortably pressed between the great landowners and the peasants, with the ever present influence of Army and Church behind them.

A liberal policy, such as had grown up in much of Europe during the past generation, had gained no true hold on Spain. It was an exotic, which shrivelled when Ferdinand VII cast the evil-eye on it, and his intrigues against the new constitution of 1812 undermined it and then destroyed it when in 1814 Ferdinand returned as absolute monarch, issuing the Decree of Valencia. *Afrancesados*, that is those

Spaniards who had taken office under, or sympathised with, the French, were outlawed within Spain, while those who had followed Joseph Bonaparte back to France had to remain in exile for good. Thus the younger Moratín, Marchena and Meléndez Valdés never came home, and Goya found life in Spain increasingly disagreeable and finally settled in France, where he died.

Ferdinand VII, like his French Bourbon cousins, had learned nothing from the fundamental changes which surrounded him. His empire was tumbling. Mexico had already made its bid for independence in 1810, in 1811 Venezuela declared it, and hard on this came the Argentinian revolution, while in 1818 the declaration of the independence of Chile took place. The king had not given one instance of constructive policy. By 1820 came a liberal revolution, powerfully supported this time by the army. The royalists fought back with ink, but were firmly answered by the new government which declared in the words of its President of the Cortes, no less a person than Luis de Borbón, Archbishop of Toledo, that the crown must be constitutional. The intrigues of Ferdinand continued, but the constitutional government remained firm until 1823 when it was brought down by a French Bourbon invasion, backed by Metternich's Europe. Quintana's letter to Lord Holland of November 1823 sums up the liberal position very clearly, and incidentally brilliantly assesses Spain's last half-century. It is written in the light of the fall of the constitutionalists, and the reassertion of benighted absolutism, for in 1823 the position of 1814 was repeated, only Ferdinand's severity was intensified. He was not going to be baulked again. Every act of the liberal government was annulled and the ultra-royalists were called in to support a savage autocracy. Nothing, however, could save the dissolving South American Empire, and by 1826 the last foothold on that continent had been lost.

Ferdinand was not to enjoy peace of mind even at home, for there now loomed up the vexed question of the succession. The king was determined that his elder daughter Isabel (for he had no son) should succeed him; but since the Salic Law was in force his brother Charles staked his claim. The spectre of civil war was threatening, so Ferdinand had recourse to a Pragmatic Sanction proclaimed in March 1830, and lest there should be any doubt of his intention the king on the last day of 1832 declared Isabel his successor, at the same time pointing out what dangers to the peace of Spain there would be if there were any popular support for the Carlists. Charles protested to Ferdinand about what appeared to him to be his disinheritance, but Ferdinand stood firm, and when Charles remained dissatisfied condemned him to exile. That was the king's last act. In

1833 he died, the age of absolutism was over, the liberals came out of exile, prison and hiding, rallied to the legitimist throne of the girl-queen Isabel, and faced the irresponsible Carlists, now assembling their forces, by appeals to ultramontanist clericalism and regional nationalism.

As to the documents supporting the history of these agitated thirty-three years, we begin with Lafuente's *Historia general de España*, the Barcelona edition being the best. One can consult in this the terms of the second Treaty of San Ildefonso of 1800, the Franco-Spanish offensive alliance against Portugal of the following year, and when war broke out again after that breathing-space the Peace of Amiens (1802), chronicled in the *Gaceta de Madrid*, one turns once more to Lafuente for the terms of the treaty of neutrality between France and Spain, the prime mover in the negotiations being Talleyrand.

Godoy was now forced to pursue the only path open to him, almost complete subjection to France, both in foreign policy and the use of armed forces. The first Treaty of San Ildefonso had been the fatal move (1796) and the net had been relentlessly drawn tighter year by year. Now in 1805 came the blow, Trafalgar, at which the Spanish navy was ruined, bearing the same fate as Villeneuve's French ships. The description of the battle taken from the *Gaceta de Madrid* is taut and concise, but nonetheless striking.

Godoy had shown after this some signs of trying to depart from that bear's-hug alliance, but in spite of an appeal to the nation, in which without doing more than implying Napoleon he denounced a tyrant, the pressures were too strong. The result of this was that opponents of the Court began to form a rival faction round the hopeful (or so it seemed) young Ferdinand, Prince of Asturias. Ferdinand, as the letter of October 1807 in Llorente's *Memorias*, a translation of which made by Llorente himself from the original publication in the Paris *Moniteur* of 5 February 1810, is included in Conde de Toreno's *Historia del levantamiento, guerra y revolución de España* (1835), proves, was himself playing a double game. Here he makes a bid for recognition by the Emperor he hated as the only alternative to his effete father Charles IV as ruler of Spain.

Then came a few days later in that disastrous October of 1807 the infamous Treaty of Fontainebleau, the terms of which are recorded in Barado's *Museo Militar*, the sum total of it being that Portugal and probably Spain itself were to be eventually ceded to France, while Godoy was to be given valuable estates in Spain and Charles IV was to go to South America as Emperor.

Lafuente again leads the way through the intrigues which followed: the arrest of Ferdinand, his pardon and contrition, and with the fatal year 1808 comes Charles IV's address to the nation, published in the *Gaceta*, counselling calm in the face of certain invasion by French armies. That official publication implacably takes all in its stride, mouthpiece that it is of whichever party controls Spain. Impartially it announces Godoy's imprisonment and by March Charles IV's abdication. The throne of Spain is now Napoleon's, and in a letter recorded in Toreno's *Historia del levantamiento* he looks about for a member of his family to occupy it. Meanwhile the Emperor keeps Ferdinand at bay (Ceballos, *Exposición de los hechos y maquinaciones que han preparado la usurpación de la corona de España*, a contemporary publication of great value). Now that Spain has shown her opposition to the Imperial will in the rebellion of Aranjuez, his presence is a provocation to further and greater disorder; he must go.

The incident at Aranjuez in March is only a prelude to greater things; at last the nation takes matters into its own hands, and Madrid blazes out in open rebellion on 2 May. The French are there already, and two days later seven savage articles against the rebels are published in the *Diario de Madrid*. A few days afterwards Ferdinand in Bayonne renounces the throne under pressure, and a week later this is published in the *Gaceta*, while Charles IV, as a document preserved in an appendix to Toreno's work relates, also at Bayonne attempts to play his last cards. Charles's bid fails and, as the *Gaceta* records shortly afterwards, he too is forced to take the path to political oblivion.

Northern Spain is now clearly at war, and the raw material of revolt is organised and addressed by the Junta General of Asturias. The documents of this period, including the first communications with the British government, are to be found most conveniently in Rodriguez Solis's *Los guerrilleros de 1808*, while Lafuente and the *Gaceta* illustrate Napoleon's attempt to win over the Spanish by fair words and his conferring of the Spanish crown on his brother Joseph, who himself on his arrival in Spain in June issues a proclamation in the *Gaceta*.

Meanwhile the war against the French invaders has spread to the South. In the *Demostración de lealtad* Seville declares for Ferdinand, and the great moment comes when what was apparently a rabble of nationalist peasants under General Castaños turns into a great army to defeat the French insurgents at Bailén. In Toreno's work one finds the terms which that victory led to, but the tide turns in 1809 against the loyalists with the capitulation of Zaragoza, and enables Marshal Lannes to make a show of magnanimity in a document also preserved in Toreno.

The Junta Suprema with men like Floridablanca and Jovellanos now becomes better knit and more efficient. In a letter to General Sebastiani from Seville, Jovellanos points out with dignity that Spanish and French aspirations can never coincide, and at the first meeting of the Cortes of the Junta Suprema Martín de Garay upholds loyalty to Ferdinand VII. Toreno provides both these documents.

Now begins the period of the great battles between the British and French in Spain, with the Spanish forcefully aiding their British allies by every kind of harassment with which they could visit the enemy. Canga Argüelles' *Documentos pertenecientes a las observaciones sobre la historia de la guerra de España* (1835) is a primary source of the utmost value.

Meanwhile the Spanish Empire in South America was breaking up. For Mexico Riva Palacio's *México a través de los siglos* contains documents not easily found elsewhere, while for Venezuela and Argentina much information is to be gleaned from the *Gaceta Extraordinoria de la Regencia de España e Indias* and from Daniel O'Learey's *Bolívar y la emancipación de America*.

By 1812 a united and disciplined war-effort, discussed by Toreno with documentary evidence as to Wellington's command, was being directed by an efficient constitutional government which issued an important definition of the Spanish state contained in the *Colección de los decretos y órdenes de las Cortes generales y extraordinarias* (1820), and in that same compilation is the famous decree in which the Cortes sitting in Cádiz abolished the Inquisition (1813). Within a year Ferdinand VII was back in power and all the reforms of the liberal government were undone by the Decree of Valencia, reproduced in Melchor Ferrer's *Historia del Tradicionalismo español*.

Still the members of the South American Empire fall away. In 1816 Bolívar at the Assembly of Angostura declares the complete severance of Venezuela from Spain with the formation of 'an independent, free and sovereign' Republic (Gil Fortoul's *Historia Constitucional de Venezuela*), and two years later Bernard O'Higgins announces the independence of Chile (Carlos Calvo's *Anales históricos de la Revolución de la América*).

Again the tide turns in Spain, and this time in favour of liberalism and against Ferdinand when revolution against the arbitrary crown is declared by the Army of Cádiz and published in the *Correo Universal de Literatura y Política* (April 1820). In that same periodical Ferdinand fights back, but to no avail, and in May, again in the *Correo* that great advocate of constitutional monarchy Luis de Borbón,

Archbishop of Toledo signs the Manifesto of the Junta Provisional. Soon there appears in the *Correo* Ferdinand's hopeless appeal to recalcitrant South America. It becomes the mouthpiece of the nation until in 1822 the *Gaceta de Madrid* takes up the train of events with its lively report on the royalist attack on Madrid which was repulsed.

The days of the Constitutional government were, however, numbered, and Lafuente in his *Historia general* traces the stages by which the Holy Alliance of Austria, Prussia and Russia with France, now taken into their confidence as a willing associate, decides at the Congress of Verona to interfere and put an end to dangerous liberalism by intruding that savage autocrat Ferdinand on Spain, and it so far succeeds that in 1823 as in 1814 the acts of the constitutional government are made null and void by a vengeful king (Ferrer's *Historia del Tradicionalismo español*).

One more glimpse of a now irrevocably lost Empire is contained in the remarkably candid letter from Javier de Burgos to Ferdinand, cited in J. Becker's *La independencia de América*, and then come the last acts of the dismal reign turning on the succession, documents supporting which are to be found in Lafuente and Ferrer.

N.B. Although in the Introduction anglicised spellings of proper names are employed where there might be ambiguity, in the Documents Felipe, Carlos and Fernando are used as preserving more of the flavour of the original. The Archduke Charles of Austria is, as being non-Spanish, referred to by his assumed title of Charles III of Spain, which also has the virtue of removing any ambiguity there might otherwise be about the Bourbon king, who is always called Carlos III. An attempt to preserve in the translation something of the character of the original may be seen in certain archaic turns of phrase.

I

Will of Carlos II

1700

'Recognising, in accordance with various counsels proffered by Our Ministers of State and Our Judiciary to the effect that the reason which has compelled the Lady Anne and the Lady Marie-Thérèse, both of whom were Queens of France, the one Our aunt and the other Our sister, to renounce Their respective rights to these Our Realms was none other than fear of the consequences for Spain which might ensue from union with the Crown of France; and recognising that, while this cause for concern is no longer a valid one, the right of the closest relative to succeed to the Throne still subsists under the laws of these Realms, and that this claim can now be entered on behalf of the second son of the Dauphin of France, We do herewith, in due observance of these laws, appoint as Our successor (in the eventuality of God calling Us to Himself while We are yet childless) the Duc d'Anjou, second son of the Dauphin, and We do name Him heir to all Our Realms and all Our Domains without any exception whatever. And We do command and direct Our subjects and vassals in whatever part of Our Realms and territories that, should We be called away from this life while We are yet denied lawful issue, they shall take and recognise the said Duc d'Anjou as their rightful King and Natural Lord and shall straightway grant Him possession of the said territories, as soon as He has taken the customary oath of observance of all the laws, charters and customs of these Our Realms and domains. And it being Our intention that, in the interests of the peace of Christendom and of all Europe and of the well-being of these Our Realms, this Crown and that of France shall ever remain sundered, We do declare, with reference to the stipulations made above, that, if the said Duc d'Anjou should die before We are Ourself called to God, or should He accede to the Throne of France and prefer to wear that Crown rather than that of these Our Realms, then the said Crown shall pass to the Duc de Berry, His brother, and the third son of the said Dauphin, and that all the conditions set out above shall pertain in this eventuality;

and that, should the Duc de Berry die before We are Ourself called, or should He accede to the Throne of France, We do declare that it is Our will that this Our Crown pass to the Archduke, second son of Our uncle, the Emperor, passing over, for the same reasons that We have listed above, – and because of the same concern We showed above for the common-weal – the firstborn of the Emperor, Our uncle; and should the Archduke die before We are Ourself called to the life hereafter, We do declare that is Our will that, in such an eventuality, the Crown pass to the Duke of Savoy and to His heirs. This is Our will and We do command Our subjects that they observe this to the letter and not suffer it to be altered one whit, for it is thus that their own well-being and the orderliness of their own Realm are best served, and We do charge them not to permit the slightest dismembering of this Our Realm nor to permit any lessening whatever of the greatness of this Monarchy which basks in the glory and renown earned by Our forefathers in its service. And, since We do so fervently desire that peace and union subsist between the Emperor, Our uncle and His Most Christian Majesty, and since the peace of Christendom hangs upon this, We do exhort Them and beg They may be pleased to cement the bonds of friendship that do bind them together, by joining the Duc d'Anjou and the Archduchess in Holy Matrimony, and grant Europe thereby the peace She so desperately needs.

In the event of Our dying without issue, the said Duc d'Anjou shall succeed to all Our Realms and domains, both those attaching to the Crown of Castille and those that do pertain to Aragón and Navarre, and, indeed all of them, both within and without Spain; to wit: in particular the following lands that do attach to the Crown of Castille: Castille itself, León, Toledo, Galicia, Seville, Granada, Córdoba, Murcia, Jaén, the outposts of Algeciras, Gibraltar, the Canaries, the Indies, the mainlands and island both on the far shores of the Atlantic in the Americas, and in the South Seas, the Philippines, and all other islands and lands discovered either now or at any time in the future, together with all other rights of whatever kind attaching to the Realm of Castille; and the following that do attach to the Crown of Aragón: Aragón itself, Valencia, Catalonia, Naples, Sicily, Majorca, Sardinia and all other territories and rights of whatever kind that do attach either to the Crown of Aragón or to the Realm of Navarre, together with all lands that belong or shall belong at any time in the future to it in the Low Countries, and all rights and other privileges that have redounded to Us in virtue of Our succession to that Throne. And it is Our will that, when God is pleased to take us from this present life, the said Duc d'Anjou shall be called to the Throne and crowned King of all the said lands and territories, all Acts of Abdication and all other legislation to the contrary notwithstanding, (all such acts being held as without foundation and, accordingly, declared null and void). And We do hereby charge all Dignitaries of Our Church, Our Grandees, Dukes, Marquises, Counts, and Gentlemen of quality, and all Our Priors, the Knights-Commander of Our Orders of Chivalry, Our Knights, the Captains-General and Judges in Our colonies, the Governors of Our castles and Our country-seats, Our Nobles, and all the Members of Our Councils, Justices, Mayors, Bailiffs, Aldermen, Municipal Officers, and all the Yeomen of these Our cities, towns and villages, in all the lands pertaining unto these Our Realms and Domains; and all Our Viceroys and Provincial-Governors, the Governors and Wardens of Our castles, Our Captains and all those Officers who guard the frontiers of Our Kingdoms both here in Spain and overseas, and all Our Ministers and all those who hold office both in the civil service and in both branches of Our armed forces throughout Our Realms, in Castille and in Aragón and Navarre, in Naples, and Sicily, in the Estates of Milan and the Low Countries and in all other lands that do attach to Our Crown, and all Our subjects, vassals and all the indigenous peoples in Our territories, of whatever rank and station, and wherever they reside, who find themselves bound by their duty as vassals and subjects; to accord this Our Will and Decree the obedience which they owe to it, as loyal subjects of a King who is their Natural Lord, in virtue of the oaths of loyalty and allegiance which they have sworn to Our Royal Person and which it was their duty to swear, in which it is decreed that whensoever God is pleased to call Us from the cares of this present life, that they shall take the said Duc d'Anjou as their lawful King and the rightful Lord of all Our Realms, domains and possessions, and cleave to Him, should it come to pass that We die without issue; and We charge them, as soon as they shall know of Our death, to comply with the laws of these Our Realms, Domains and Estates, by raising banners for their new King and carrying out all the public Acts prescribed by precedent and custom in each Realm and Province, giving every sign and outward show, performing every ceremony and executing every rite that is in their Realm and Province a token of the loyalty, allegiance and obedience which as vassals and subjects they are in duty bound to afford their King and Natural Lord. And We do hereby command the Wardens of Our fortresses and castles and the Governors of our country-seats and their lieutenants in all the cities, townships and villages of our Realms and all the uninhabited places therein to pay

homage to the said Duc d'Anjou as is laid down in the Laws of the
Realm and the ancient rights and privileges of Spain, Castille, Aragón
and Navarre and all the lands pertaining thereunto; and We do command that this be likewise performed in the Estates of Milan and
all other Domains and territories under Our Crown in accordance
with the traditions and customs of the particular provinces in honour
of the Duc d'Anjou, and to keep the said tokens of homage and
fealty for as long as they are commanded to do so and then to hand
them over to the person appointed, whose name and identity shall
be communicated to them either in writing or by word of mouth.
All this do We command them to perform without any departure
whatever from the letter of this Our Will, and to do so, on pain of
the grim fate that befalls all traitors to the State and all those who
are unheedful of the wishes of their Sovereign and Natural Lord
and who break and shatter oaths of loyalty and allegiance and disregard those acts of homage to which they have pledged their faith.

   This tallies with the originals of the Will of Our Lord, the King
(R.I.P.). Madrid, second day of November, seventeen hundred.
   Don Antonio de Ubilla y Medina.
   This copy tallies with the one from which it was taken and which
I handed to His Excellency Don Manuel Arias, Governor of the
Council of State, to which fact I, Don Rafael Saenz Maza, secretary
to His Majesty and senior clerk to the Council, do hereby bear
witness. Madrid, third day of November, seventeen hundred.'
   (Nicolini, *L'Europa durante la guerra*, vol. I, pp. 167–8.)

2

*Proclamation of Felipe V. An account of 16 November
missing the phrase 'il n'y a plus de Pyrénées'*

1700

'Last evening, the Court returned to Versailles from Fontainebleau,
and this morning, during the "levee", the King seemed most satisfied within Himself, and, after the ceremony was over, he sent for
the Spanish Ambassador and, some time later, for the Duc d'Anjou.
He received them in his study, and it was not long before the
Ambassador emerged into the antechamber where, with the emotion

showing in the tears that coursed down his face, he announced to an audience of courtiers, gentlemen of quality and foreign ministers ... that His Most Christian Majesty had been pleased to accept the stipulations contained in the will of Carlos II, and that Spain had, as of a few moments ago, a new King, Felipe V. The Ambassador announced that he had had the good fortune to be the first of the subjects of the new King to take an oath of allegiance to Him ...

... the Imperial Ambassador contended in the Antechamber that this same will was null and void, and that the decision taken by Louis XIV ... would evoke some violent reactions both in London and in The Hague. (This His Most Christian Majesty declines to believe.)

Felipe V, as the Duc d'Anjou is now known to all, is seventeen years of age. Of average height, He has very pale skin and wears His hair long, spurning the wig. His face and his whole bearing show Him as a born King. His lower lip, with its trace of the blood of the Austrias, betrays the heritage of His grandmother and great-grandmother on His father's side. He is of an affable disposition, has been most excellently educated by the Duc de Beaullier* and is naturally inclined to gratitude and to generosity.'

(Nicolini, L'Europa durante la guerra, vol. I, pp. 180–1.)

3

There follows the text of the letter in which Louis XIV accepts the Spanish Crown on behalf of His grandson

1700

'To Her Most Powerful and Most Excellent Highness, the Princess, Our dearly beloved Sister and Cousin; to Our dearly beloved Cousins and to all other Members of the Council of State for the Government of all the Realms and lands throughout the world, that do attach to the Crown of Spain: We are in receipt of the letter penned on the first day of this present month, and bearing Your Majesty's signature and, indeed, those of all of you, the which letter was handed to Us by the Marquis of Castel dos Rius, Ambassador of His Most Powerful

---

* Duc de Beaulieu.

and Most Excellent Highness, Our dearly beloved Brother and Cousin, Carlos the Second, King of Spain, on whose memory the sun shall never set. This Ambassador did at the same time entrust to Our Royal hands a copy of the will made by the late King, his Master, containing the names and order of precedence of those He appointed His heirs and successors to the Kingdoms and Estates of the Crown of Spain, and setting out all the other prudent measures which he bequeathed in order to ensure the wise government of those same Realms right up until His successor should attain his majority. The keen sorrow which the death of a Ruler, whose abundant gifts and whose close kinship with Ourself necessarily awoke in Us feelings of true friendship, is infinitely deepened when We contemplate this tangible proof of His justice, and of His love for His faithful subjects, who were His chief concern even as He lay dying, and of His preoccupation with the peace of Europe and the well-being of His Realms for which He has legislated even from beyond the grave. For Our part, We do also wish to contribute in like wise both to this peace and to this well-being, and to do justice to the implicit trust He chose to place in Us by ensuring that each and every one of the stipulations He made in this His will, which Your Royal Majesty and all of you did send to Us, are indeed carried out. We shall accordingly spare no effort to ensure the said foundations of peace and that She shall henceforth ascend to a pinnacle of glory and renown, the height of which has never hitherto been seen. We do hereby in the name of Our grandson, the Duc d'Anjou, accept this will of the late King of Spain, and so in like fashion is it accepted by Our son, the Dauphin. He knows no impediment to His renouncing all rights thereunto enjoyed by His Mother, Our late and dearly beloved Queen and those invested in the late Queen, that most honourable Lady, Our Mother, all of which, in the opinions of the various Ministers of State and Members of the judiciary consulted by the late King of Spain, were established beyond dispute. And He is willing to sacrifice His own interests to ensure that the Crown might once again shine with all the brilliance which it knew of yore, a Crown which the late Catholic King willed should pass to Our grandson. We shall accordingly give leave to the Duc d'Anjou to depart forthwith for Spain that His subjects might straightways be afforded the consolation of receiving a King who recognises full well that, since God has been pleased to call Him to the Throne, it shall be His prime duty to reign with justice and with proper regard for the obligations placed upon Him as a Christian Prince, to make His first priority the happiness of His subjects, to bring fresh glory and renown to this most powerful of Realms, to delegate authority to those (from among a Nation as renowned for Her prudence as She is for Her valour) who shall serve Him faithfully in all His undertakings both in matters temporal and in matters spiritual, and to reward them handsomely. We shall tutor Him in His duties towards subjects who are unswerving in their loyalty to their King, We shall school Him in the dictates of His own honour; We shall exhort Him never to be unheedful of His own ancestry and We shall entreat Him always to love the Country whence He came, that there shall ever be between Our two Thrones the perfect harmony and understanding that is imperative for the mutual happiness of Our two Nations. It has ever been Our most fervent desire that such good relations should exist and if, in the past, We have not always been permitted by circumstances to allow this desire to come to the surface, it is Our wish that this great event shall now change things in such wise that We shall every day be afforded fresh opportunity to give voice to Our regard and Our attachment for the entire Spanish Nation. In the meantime, Your Most Powerful and Most Excellent Highness and our dearly beloved Sister and Cousin, We do pray God, who is the fount of all consolation, He may vouchsafe You comfort at this time of Your grief; and We do assure you, Our dearly beloved cousins and Members of the Council of State for the Government of the Spanish Nation, of the particular esteem and affection in which We do hold you all. Given at Fountaynebleau, on the twelfth day of the month of November, 1700. Your Majesty's loving Brother and Cousin, LOUIS. Colbert.

[Written on the back:] To Her Most Excellent and Most Powerful Highness, the Princess, Queen of Spain, our dearly beloved Sister and Cousin, and to Our dearly beloved Cousins and Members of the Council of State for the Government of the Realms and Estates attaching to the Crown of Spain.'

(B.N. s.l.s.f. – *Copia de carta del rey christianissimo Luis Dézimocuarto a la Reyna nuestra Señora y Señores del Gobierno.*)

4

The new King leaves Paris

1700

'The decision having been taken at the Royal Palace at Versailles, that the Duc d'Anjou, now His Catholic Majesty Felipe the Fifth, should leave for Spain as soon as possible, as His subjects were impatient to receive Him, it was agreed that the departure should be fixed for the fourth of December, come what may.

So it was that, at eleven o'clock in the morning, Our King set out from Versailles in the company of His Most Christian Majesty, His grandfather; His Highness the Dauphin, His father: His Excellency the Duke of Burgundy and Her Excellency the Duchess of Orléans. They travelled in a richly decorated state carriage drawn by eight horses; a spectacle altogether befitting such an occasion ...

... First of all, the King is most gracious in His person and in His bearing; He is very much the gallant and looks extremely Spanish. His hair is His own, very fair and he wears it in ringlets as is now the fashion. It is generally believed, however, that He will adopt a wig before He finally leaves French territory. He has a noble forehead and full eyebrows, soft and arched. He boasts large eyes, but His lower lip is a little prominent, betraying the blood of the Austrias. His face is very pale and his general expression grave yet kindly. He has a strong arm and an iron grip, having no great difficulty in bending a silver plate double. His hands are almost like leather from reining in His horse and from playing at the "jeu de paume", with which sports and His riding to hunt, He has built up the strength of His body.

He is a person of such goodly habits that, had He not been chosen as a great King by birth, then He would surely have merited such honourable estate on account of them. He is most devout and always inclined to piety and to the Faith. He is magnanimous, and strives always to be true to His word. He has a good hand, indeed a very fine and clerkly one, and He excels in Latin studies, in Philosophy and as a painter as well as having a highly trained ear for music. He dances well and in horsemanship he has no peer in all the Realms of France. Highly skilled at the quinteyne * and "cabezas",† He has on occasion picked one target up on his lance and simultaneously another on the point of his sword, to the amazement of all who beheld Him do so.

His upbringing might well be taken as a programme for the education of a Christian Prince. At eight sharp He dresses, and at a half past eight He takes a light breakfast. At a half past nine He accompanies His grandfather to Mass, which is always sung. At a half past ten He has a lesson in the Spanish language. At eleven He takes exercise on His horse or reads History. At a half past noon He attends formal luncheon. At two He rides to hunt or plays at the "jeu de paume", or else does distract Himself at painting, for He is most adroit with brushes and palette. At seven he takes some light refreshment of a simple kind. At a half past nine He joins the Royal Family for formal dinner. He retires at a half past eleven.

It was originally decided that the party would leave Versailles on the first of December, but their departure was postponed until the fourth in order so to arrange their journey that Christmas would come upon them when they were in a large city. They chose Bordeaux. His Majesty will reach the boundaries and border of France in forty-one days, and will make Madrid in a further twenty; and, barring any unforeseen occurrences, He will be in His Palace by the fifth or sixth of February.

He is taking fewer than twenty Frenchmen with Him on His journey into Spain, together with His confessor and his deputy, both Jesuits, and most of these are members of His household. He has also taken His governess, whom He could not bring Himself to leave behind and to whom He is so deeply indebted. He has already adopted the insignia of the Order of the Golden Fleece of which He is now Grand-Master, and it is not yet known whether He will choose to leave off the habit of the Order of Saint-Esprit, since there is no stipulation preventing Him from wearing the insignia of both. His Majesty was effusive in His welcome of the Spanish Ambassador and his family who, since they were the only Spaniards then at Versailles, begged leave to kiss His hand, and there is no doubt but that they have been graced with favours accordingly ...'

(*Primera relación extraordinaria de la salida del Rey* ... pp. 3 ff.)

---

* Quintain: a sport of tilting at a post set up as a mark and often provided with a sandbag to swing round and strike an unsuccessful tilter.

† 'Cabezas': an equestrian sport involving a number of wooden objects, traditionally imitation heads, at which the contestant rides at full gallop, and which he attempts to pick up on the point of his lance.

5

Felipe V swears to observe the ancient laws of the Spanish Realm and is accepted as King

1701

'Thy Majesty: As King of the Realms of Castille, León and Granada and of all the other Realms and Domains attaching to the Crown of Castille, Thou shalt herewith place Thy right Hand upon the Holy Gospels and pledge Thy solemn troth to God thereon, that Thou shalt give Thy Royal Word before those cities and towns whose Commissioners are here present, and before all other cities, towns and villages in these Realms, which are here represented, and to each and every one of them, to the same effect as had they been named herein every one, that Thou shalt keep and safeguard the patrimony of all these Realms, and all the lands pertaining thereunto, as is specified in the Ancient Laws of Castille and all other Statutes of these Realms (and in particular the Laws of King Juan promulgated at Valladolid) wherein is provision made that these Realms shall suffer no dismemberment, not of cities nor of towns nor of villages; that neither shall any boundaries be altered nor shall any lands under their sway be sundered therefrom, that no rents nor any tithes nor any dues attaching thereunto shall be allowed to relapse; and that the patrimony of all those lands attaching either now or at any time in the future to the said Crown shall be in no wise subject to any defalcation whatsoever, and that should any such defalcation be occasioned by the gift of any part thereof to some other person, that act of cession and that gift shall be null and void and of no lawful import whatever, and that the person profiting therefrom shall not thereby acquire any right of tenure whatsoever to the lands and patrimony so bestowed upon him; so help Thee God and the Holy Gospels in this Thy resolve, Amen. And, moreover, Thou shalt confirm all the said cities, towns and villages in their immunities, exemptions, enfranchisements and privileges, confirming both those consequent upon their inherence in the Patrimony of Thy Royal Crown and in those adhering to them in respect of all the other prerogatives they do enjoy; to wit: all those lawful privileges and godly customs, all those rightful practices and all the statutory rights to which they have proper entitlement, and all estates and rents, lands and territories which they do hold and possess in virtue of and in accordance with the Laws of these Realms; and Thou shalt herein give Thy pledge that these lands shall not be lost to them nor shall they suffer any defalcation therefrom, that run contrary to those same laws, neither now nor at any time in the future, be such loss or defalcation occasioned by Thee or Thy Royal Decree or be it occasioned in any manner whatsoever; and Thou shalt hereby command that all the said rights and privileges be observed by all men exactly as they are stated in their various deeds of entitlement, and that no man presume to act in any manner whatever that run contrary to all the stipulations contained therein, nor to any part thereof, neither now nor at any time in the future, nor in any manner nor at any time whatsoever, on pain of Thy displeasure and those sanctions contained and set down in the said deeds of entitlement. To all of this Thy Majesty, Thou shalt, as King and Sovereign of all these Realms, hereby entreat the Commissioners of the said cities here present, to witness Thy attestation, pledge and solemn oath, and Thou shalt again confirm this and repeat it.

As soon as this Charte had been read out, the Cardinal-Archbishop of Toledo did make his way to His Majesty, and standing up and baring His head, did stretch out His right hand and placed it on the Cross which lay on the missal the Archbishop held in his hands, and did say, somewhat loudly: We do hereby solemnly swear to obey and uphold this Charte and all the stipulations contained therein. He thereupon resumed His seat and the Archbishop returned to the place allotted him.

Thereupon the King at Arms sprang to his feet, shouting, Oyez, Oyez, Oyez. Pray silence for the Oath of Allegiance and Act of Homage of Their Lordships the Prelates, Grandees, Nobles and Knights, and The Worshipful Commissioners of Madrid and of the other cities of the Realm, here present at the Royal Command, to His Christian Majesty Felipe V, recognising Him as Lawful heir and successor to these Realms and Domains and as King and Natural Lord therein.

When the King at Arms had once more resumed his seat, Don Juan De Layseca and those same Ministers as before came forward once again and took up the positions they had occupied during the reading of the previous Charte, whereupon Don Juan de Layseca read the following Oath of Allegiance.

Oath of Allegiance of Their Lordships the Prelates, Grandees, Nobles, and Knights and Their Worships the Commissioners of Madrid and the other cities of the Realm:

All those here present, do you now witness that Their Lordships the Prelates, Grandees, Nobles and Knights and The Worshipful Commissioners and Deputies of Madrid and the other cities of the Realm, here present at the Royal Command do, in the Name of these Realms, and all together, and of their own free will and volition and spontaneously, each one in his own name and in that of his successors, and the Commissioners in their own Name and in that of those they represent, in virtue of the powers invested in them (which have been held as sufficient unto the day) by the city of Madrid and by the other cities of these Realms; and I, in their name; and in compliance with the duties imposed on them by the rightful Laws of these Realms, and in compliance with the dictates of their own loyalty and fealty, and in true observance of the traditional oaths of allegiance which in days of yore the Princes, Prelates, Grandees, Knights and the Parliamentary Deputies from Madrid and the other cities of these Realms did make to their Sovereign, and, wishing to follow and to keep this tradition, do declare that: They do recognise, uphold and receive His Catholic Majesty Felipe V (here present) as King and Natural Lord of all these Realms of Castille and León and Granada and of all other Realms and Domains attaching thereunto, and of all those acquired in gift, or acquired by any other means and of all others incorporated therein, and pertaining thereto; and that they do undertake to maintain Him as King and Lawful and Natural Sovereign thereof, and that they do hereby offer Him their allegiance and do hereby promise Him their obedience, reverence and unswerving loyalty; as, in virtue of the Laws and Ancient Statutes of the Realm, they are as goodly subjects and natural vassals in duty bound to do so, and that they do hereby pledge themselves ever to serve Him and ever to discharge their duties and obligations towards Him. In virtue and confirmation thereof, and in order that all the aforegoing shall enjoy full and legal effect, their Lordships the Prelates, Grandees, Nobles and Knights of these Our Realms, in their own Name and in that of their successors and of those that shall come hereafter; and Their Worships The Commissioners of Madrid and the other cities of the Realm, in the name of the Realm and in the name of those they represent and of those that shall come hereafter, and in virtue of the powers invested in them by those same people they represent, do all state of one heart and with one voice that they do swear by Almighty God and by Mary, His Mother, and by the sign of the Cross and the word of the Holy Gospel which is written in this missal which they do see open before them, and with their right hands on this Holy Gospel, that, in their own name and in the name of those they represent and in that of those who shall

come hereafter, that they do take the said Sovereign, His Catholic
Majesty Felipe V, to be their lawful King and Natural Lord and
shall proffer Him all the obedience and reverence which, as subjects
and vassals, they are obliged to render Him; and that they shall obey
every last part of these stipulations and shall never, neither directly
nor indirectly nor for any reason whatever, nor from any manner
of cause, in any way go against, contradict or fail to comply with
them. Do you swear this, so help you God, both in this world and
that to come, wherein you shall dwell far longer; and do you state
under oath that it is your solemn wish that, should you at any time
and in any way prove false to this your oath, it shall cost you right
dear, as is wont to come to pass with those that take the name of
the Lord their God in vain. And, moreover, that, in such an eventuality, you do desire you shall be held as villains, perjurers, men of
little faith and blackguards and thereby incur all the penalties reserved
in the Laws and Ancient Statutes of these Realms for traitors and
rebels to the State, and set down therein. To all the which stipulations
Your Lordships the Prelates, Grandees, Nobles and Knights of these
Our Realms, in your own name and in that of your successors and
of those that shall come hereafter; and Your Worships the Commissioners of Madrid and the other cities of the Realm in your own
name and in that of those you represent and of those that shall
come hereafter; do you all pledge your troth and render your homage;
once, twice, thrice, once, twice, thrice as is ancient law and custom
of Spain, at the hands of Don Francisco Casimiro Pimentel, Count
of Benavente, who shall from each and every one of you take and
receive in the Name of and on behalf of His Catholic Majesty, Felipe
the Fifth, this your oath and homage, which you do hereby swear
that you shall keep and remain faithful to in every last part, and
shall never, for any reason whatsoever, nor from any manner of
cause, in any way go against, contradict or fail to comply with, on
pain of incurring the aforementioned penalties and all those sanctions to which any person that prove false to the homage formally
rendered and given to his King and Natural Lord, does make himself
liable? In token of this your pledge you shall now, and with all
proper obeisance and respect due to a King and Natural Lord, kiss
His hand.

Once he had read out this Oath of Allegiance in full, Don Juan
de Layseca resumed his place, together with the Ministers who had
been with him.

The King at Arms then rose to his feet, and after making the
customary bows, he turned to where the Grandees were seated and
did cry out loud: Rise, Count of Benavente and take this written

homage. For the King had appointed him to this honour the previous day and had sent His Private Secretary to him with a letter, written in the Royal Hand, informing him of this.

Having gone through the pretence of not wishing to perform this office, and having made the customary bows, he took his place beside the altar, alongside the epistolary and next to the Cardinal's seat. He remained standing there, his head uncovered.

Thereupon the Patriarch and the other Prelates went down into the body of the Church and took their places on the bench set aside for them.

This same King at Arms then stood up once more and called: Come forward Cardinal Borja and take the oath and render homage.

The Master of Ceremonies thereupon approached the bench on which the Cardinal was sitting and accompanied him to the altar, where he knelt down and, with his hands on the Cross and the missal, did deliver up his oath at the hands of the Cardinal-Archbishop of Toledo in the following form, as did all the others after him.

Oath of Allegiance
Thou dost swear to have and to hold all the stipulations contained in the Charte which I have read out to thee, so help thee God and the Holy Gospels?

I do, Amen.

When Cardinal Borja had taken the Oath of Allegiance, he approached the Count of Benavente and, still standing, placed his hands in those of the Count and recited the following Act of Homage, as did all those present after him.

Act of Homage
Thou dost hereby make an Act of Homage, once, twice, thrice, once, twice, thrice, once, twice, thrice, and dost give thy bounden word to have and to hold all the stipulations contained in the Charte which I have read out to thee?

To the which question, he replied: I do.

When Cardinal Borja had made the Act of Homage, he approached the King and kissed His hand. And The King did take the Cardinal's hat from off his head.

When Cardinal Borja had returned to his place, the King at Arms once again rose to his feet and cried: Come forward Their Lordships the Prelates and take the Oath of Allegiance and the Act of Homage. And the Patriarch, followed by the other prelates, did come forward, take the oath and render homage, whereupon they each in turn did kiss the Royal Hand.

Then the King at Arms once again rose to his feet and cried: Come forward Their Excellencies the Grandees and take the Oath of Allegiance and make the Act of Homage. And they straightways came forward in the order in which they had been seated, and with due regard for all the ceremonial attaching to these their actions, they did take the oath and render homage at the hands of the Count of Benavente, whereupon they each in turn did kiss the Royal Hand and return to their places forthwith...

Then the King at Arms once again rose to his feet and cried: Come forward Their Worships the Commissioners and Deputies of the city of Toledo and take the Oath of Allegiance and make the Act of Homage. And they did do so. They then approached the screen where Don Juan Alfonso Guerra, alderman of that city, did briefly address His Majesty and entreat Him to bestow upon that city all manner of favour and all nature of honour, keeping all its privileges inviolate, confirming them and ever increasing their number. His Majesty replied: This We shall be pleased so to do. And thereupon this Commissioner did entrust to His Majesty his warrant from that city and, giving thanks, he and his compeer did kiss His Majesty's Hand and did beg leave to request a written confirmation of the ceremony and the content thereof, and His Majesty was pleased to order that this be done.

When the Commissioners from Toledo had resumed their places, Don García de Guzmán, Equerry to His Majesty, came forward from where he had been seated behind the screen and, making obeisance in the same manner as those who had gone before, he did approach the Master of the King's Horse who did hand him the Royal Sword of Justice. This he held while the latter did take the Oath of Allegiance and render homage and did kiss the Royal Hand, whereupon he did retrace his steps and take back the Royal Sword of Justice, and Don García de Guzmán did return to his seat.

After the Master of the King's Horse had taken the Oath of Allegiance and rendered homage, the Lord High Steward did cross to where the Count of Benavente stood and the latter did turn to face the altar and did make proper genuflection, and thereupon did take the Oath of Allegiance and make the Act of Homage at the hands of the Lord High Steward, who thereupon returned to his seat. The Count resumed his rightful position and the Cardinal-Archbishop did then rise and cross over to the seat beside the epistolary, where he was disrobed, and then, making proper genuflection at the altar and due obeisance to the King, and bowing to those present, he did cross to the gospel-side where Cardinal Borja was seated. Cardinal Borja did then, observing the same ceremony as the Cardinal-Archbishop, cross back over to the seat beside the epistolary where he did assume the pontifical robes of the other and did approach the seat lately occupied by the other before the alter, and there sat down.

And the Cardinal-Archbishop did straightways step forward in the company of the Master of Ceremonies and there take the Oath of Allegiance on his knees before Cardinal Borja, whereupon he did move over to where the Count of Benavente was standing and at his hands did make the Act of Homage. He then approached the King and did kiss His Hand. And the King did take the Cardinal-Archbishop's hat from off his head. The Cardinal-Archbishop then returned to the seat beside the epistolary, and the Count of Benavente came forward, and, genuflecting to the altar, did step down from the dais and take his rightful place on the bench where sat the Grandees.

The Marquis of Campollano, Secretary to the Royal Chamber, making proper genuflection, thereupon came forward, together with the Clerk to the High Court of the Realm, and did ask in a loud voice:

Thy Majesty: As King and Natural Lord of these Realms and as lawful heir and successor to the Throne, dost Thou accept the Oath of Allegiance and Act of Homage and all other ceremonies here performed in accordance with Thy Majesty's Will, and dost Thou command Rafael Sanz Maza, Clerk to the High Court of the Realm, to make faithful written testimony thereof, and dost Thou command him to go to each and every one among the Prelates, Grandees, Nobles, Knights and all other persons who do on such occasions as this take the Oath of Allegiance and make the Act of Homage, and receive at their hands this same Oath of Allegiance and Act of Homage? And to this His Majesty was pleased to respond: We do accept all these acts and do so command.

Thereupon the senior Commissioner from Burgos did step forward from the place allotted him and addressed His Majesty in the Name of the Realm:

Sire. The Realm does kiss Thy Royal Feet in recognition of this great mercy Thou hast been pleased to bestow upon It by pledging Thy Royal Oath of Loyalty to It. And I do hereby beg Thee to command that a copy thereof be made, and that Thou do sign that copy and do hand that copy to the city, for which great boon we shall be eternally grateful.

And His Majesty was pleased to reply:

We do thank thee for thy speech and do hereby command that the copy thou dost so request be granted thee.'

(Ubilla y Medina, Antonio de, *Juramento y peyto omenage que los Reynos de Castilla y León por medio de sus Capitulares y los Prelados, Grandes, Títulos y otras persones, hizieron el día 8 de mayo de 1701.*)

6

European Reaction to Carlos II's will. The Empire, England and the Low Countries join forces to combat the excessive might of a united France and Spain

1701

'Basis of the Grand Alliance, concluded at the Hague on the seventh day of September, 1701, between the Emperor, the King of England and the Estates-General of the Low Countries.

The Emperor enters a claim that the succession to the Throne of Spain does rightfully belong to His illustrious House, now that Carlos the Second, on whose memory the sun shall never set, has died and left no issue, yet these rights notwithstanding, His Most Christian Majesty has taken possession of the entire legacy of the late King and the whole Spanish Realm in the name of His grandson, the Duc d'Anjou, claiming that the Crown does lawfully belong to the said Duke in virtue of some will or other made by Carlos II, and has, by brute force, occupied the Spanish possessions in the Low Countries and the Duchy of Milan, equipped a Fleet which is in a fit state to leave Cadiz harbour, where it is presently anchored for any part of the globe, at a moment's notice, and has already despatched many men-o'-war to guard the Spanish colonies in the Indies; all this to such effect that it is now the case that the fates of the Kingdoms of France and Spain are so intimately bound up in each other that it will not be realistic henceforth to think of them save as one and the same, a single, unified Realm; and this being so, one may confidently assert that, if the necessary steps are not taken to prevent this happening, His Imperial Majesty shall never again be in a position to entertain any real hope of seeing his lawful claims recognised, and that the Roman Empire will lose all its rights, both over the lands it possesses in Italy and over those Provinces of the Low Countries that are presently part of the Spanish Realms. Likewise, English and Dutch shipping shall never again enjoy the freedom of the high seas and the trade they have enjoyed hitherto both in the Indies, in the Mediterranean and elsewhere. The United Provinces of the Low Countries shall see the security they have hitherto enjoyed as a result of having the Spanish parts of the Low Countries between their own lands and France as a buffer state, cruelly denied them. In short, this union of France and Spain shall, before very long, make them so enormously powerful that they shall be able, at will, to force the whole of Europe to bow down under the yoke of their wretched tyranny. For indeed we have only to glance at what is happening at this moment as a direct result of this act by the King of France: His Imperial Majesty has been constrained to send an army to Italy to defend both his own lands and those belonging to the Imperial Fiefs; His Majesty the King of Great Britain has been forced to withdraw some of his auxiliary forces from the Low Countries and the whole situation is just as though war were openly being waged; and the Estates-General of the Low Countries have accordingly been forced to take every measure at their disposal to defend themselves, as though they had actually been attacked during a war, for with the threatened collapse of the buffer state protecting them from France, all their frontiers will be suddenly exposed to view, naked and unprotected. Since all Europe is in a state of panic and doubt, which is more perilous even than any real war, and since France and Spain are daily making every effort they can to strengthen their alliance and bind themselves in harness one to the other, making common cause to throw Europe into fetters of their own forging and to wreak havoc with all the trade She daily enjoys, His Holy and Imperial Majesty, and His Godly Majesty, the King of Great Britain, and Their Powerful Highnesses the Estates-General of the Low Countries find themselves forced to take every measure within the bounds of possibility and the limits of Their Forces to forestall and obviate all the hurts and injury that could be done by them by this present peril, and have accordingly resolved to form a Confederation and Alliance among themselves for their mutual defence against this mighty peril.'

(Belando, Fray Nicolás de Jesús, *Historia civil de España...*', Part One, pp. 47 ff.)

7

Felipe V declares war on the Allies

1704

'WE, THE KING ...

War is the ultimate Court of Appeal for the sovereigns of this world, and They may honestly and openly have recourse to it, but as its hearings are often bloody and even horrendous, placing terrible burdens on the Realm and inflicting grievous torture on those who dwell therein, it is only right and proper that these subjects should be afforded the comfort which derives from a full knowledge of the reasons that make an appeal to this Tribunal inescapable. Our Own lawful accession to this ever venerable Throne was made public, and all the world was invited to see that We were called to bear the burdens of the Realm because of Our blood-ties with those who had worn this Crown hitherto. This kinship was recognised by Our uncle, His Catholic Majesty King Carlos the Second (Requiescat in pace) when He named Us as the only lawful heir and successor to that Crown. All Our Realms acclaimed Our accession to the Throne, they received Us as their King, and took a solemn Oath of Allegiance to Us; His Holiness, who is Father of all the peoples of Christendom, recognised Us; Our Lord and Grandfather, His Most Christian Majesty, the maritime Powers, England and Holland, the most powerful Rulers and Republics of Italy, the greater part of the Northern Nations, and the King of Portugal, all heralded Our elevation to the Throne and have continued to afford Us tangible proof of their support for Our inheritance throughout the four years of Our reign; and not even the war which the Emperor and his faction have declared on Us in Italy and in Flanders has tempered the loyalty of Our Realms and of Our subjects one whit. Almighty God had been pleased to bless Our righteous cause with great victories and We have faith that He will continue to come to Our aid. But We have observed of late that certain malign persons have insinuated themselves into Our Realms and attempted to undermine the innate loyalty of Our beloved subjects, and have caused The King of Portugal not only to fail to comply with the obligations incumbent upon Him in virtue of the mutual Defence and Offence

Alliances that is binding between Our two Countries, but even to stoop so low as to declare Himself a neutral in the present conflict, and, He then instructed His Ministers, who connived at this with Him, to make this neutrality public, and, repudiating His solemn avowals of support for Our cause, entered into new alliances with the Emperor, and with England and Holland, offering them troops and agreeing that the principal Provinces of these Our Realms should be sundered one from the other as a result of this present war. Under cover of procuring the well-being of Europe and the liberty of all her Nations, He is party to a plot to put Archduke Charles of Austria on Our Throne and to make over to Him all the rightful possessions of this Our Crown, always scheming at the same time to increase His Own Realms by inducing this same Archduke to make a number of cities and provinces over to Portugal in perpetuity; to wit: the city of Badajoz, the townships of Alacantara in Extremedura; Bayona, Vigo, Túy and la Guardia in Galicia; and all the lands on the far banks of the River Plate, thereby making this river the effective border of Spanish possessions in the Indies. His design is to avail Himself of troops which are enemies of both Realms; His plan is to throw open the doors of all Our sacred churches, thus exposing them to the sacrilegious outrages which do even now threaten their ruin; His aim is to welcome this Archduke into Our Realms: acts of treachery and acts which are in open contravention of International Law, since, having pledged Himself to Our cause and having not declared war on Us, He has made unwarranted attacks on Our shipping and prejudiced the interests of Our subjects.

These reasons of such great moment have led Us to place Ourself at the head of Our armies, there to do battle to defend the honour of Our subjects, – that honour which is theirs in virtue of their many glorious feats of arms and in virtue of the unswerving loyalty which has won them fame and renown throughout the world; – there to fight and to be the envy of all Nations, there to prove an impenetrable wall against which the enemies of Our peoples shall dash themselves and their ambition; there to stand, the valiant champion of Christendom, the sheet-anchor of this mighty Realm and the inspiration of Our illustrious subjects, who do take up arms in Our cause; and We do therefore now declare war on those who conspire to destroy Our Realm, and do unsheathe Our sword in the Name of Our Realms, of Our Faith, of Our Crown and of the honour of Our Fatherland, We do accordingly declare the King of Portugal, Archduke Charles of Austria, and all Their allies to be Enemies of Our State, and We do herewith entreat, exhort and command Our subjects to join forces with Us in defence of the Cause, to spurn the honeyed wiles of all those who would wage war on Us, motivated more by the odium in which they hold Our Faith, than by any other interest they assert.

That the purport of this Our resolution may be known to all, We do hereby command that it be published throughout the length and breadth of Our Realms, and We have authorised all steps that prove necessary to the proper fulfilment of all the stipulations contained therein to be taken. Given in Plasencia on the thirteenth day of April, in the year seventeen hundred and four. We, the King. Don Antonio de Ubilla y Medina.

This is a faithful copy of the Royal Decree, a part of a copy of which survives among those documents in my possession at the Admiralty Office. It bears the signature of the Marquis de Ribas.

Don Francisco Daza.'

(*Razones de la guerra del Rey Católico* ...)

8

*Imperial version of
the attack on Gibraltar and its fall*

1704

'No single incident worthy of mention befell the Fleet from the 25th June until the surrender of Gibraltar: largely because, as soon as he had word that the Lisbon squadron had put to sea, Admiral Rook[e] ordered his ships back through the Straits to rendez-vous with that squadron in Lagos Bay (which he had chosen especially for this operation) and to take on the supplies which they so sorely needed. This was duly effected in the first few days of July, but, loathe to lie idle, Admiral Rook[e] immediately put out again, and, eager to find some action in which he could afford tangible proof of his gallantry and zeal in the Allied cause, he set course for the Straits, which he approached towards the end of that same month. Here he called his colleagues and officers together to discuss their plans for future operations, and it was decided to attack and take the crucial stronghold of Gibraltar, come what may; which they duly did most successfully at the beginning of August as can be seen from the following account.

On Friday, the first of August, the combined fleet hove into sight of Gibraltar. The English and Dutch had between them amassed a mighty force: 69 ships of the line, 7 of 96 cannon, 5 of 80 or 84 and the rest of 60 or 70, and sixteen frigates of between thirty and fifty cannon in addition. That same day the fleet entered the harbour, and, although they came under fire from the fortress known as Nuestra Señora de la Europa, no damage was done either to vessels or to personnel. That same day, an hour past noon, under cover from the fire of the frigates, they put ashore three thousand men from the combined armies, a cannon-shot off from the Land Port. One hundred and fifty enemy horse attempted to prevent this landing, but they were peppered with gun-fire and forced to withdraw. The English and Dutch troops who were encamped in the fields immediately below the town-defences and the walls and consequently within range of enemy fire, set about digging trenches for themselves as protection. That same day, the Prince of Darmstädt sent a message to the Governor of Gibraltar, painting a grim picture of the results of any defence he might offer, and pointing out that he could not possibly hope to put up a resistance against such a greatly superior fleet. The Governor, however, was of the opinion that he certainly could stage such a defence, since the town was both by its natural position well-guarded against attack, and had been most skilfully constructed to boot, and he accordingly sent a reply to the effect that while there was still a single shell remaining in the town that could be fired in its defence, he would not fail to do his duty.

On Saturday the second of August all the small outlying forts trained their guns on the fleet and began to rain fire down upon her. She, however, did not fire a single round by way of response, nor were our ships in any way scathed by the fire directed at them. Thereupon a detachment of eighteen ships, twelve of them English and six Dutch, together with three Dutch sloops each of two small cannon and capable of firing carcasses,* broke away from the main body of the fleet and formed up in a line below the main defence battery and a musket's-shot off from the defenders. There were two French vessels in at the quay, one a corsair † and the other a merchant-ship; the Admiral ordered an attack to be made on the former from ten or twelve armed launches, the attack being covered by musket-fire from the other ships, and then his orders were that this

* A kind of fire-ball.   † A privateering vessel.

vessel was to be fired. More than a hundred French from these two ships were taken prisoner. All this time the defenders kept up a constant hail of fire on the fleet. The Prince ordered our guns to make no reply to the town batteries until he had sent once more to the Governor with the same message as before. The Governor gave the same reply, and even seemed strengthened in his resolve.

At dawn on Sunday the 3rd of August, the detachment of eighteen ships and three sloops began to bombard the town with such fury and with such virulence that, in the space of five or six hours, they fired twenty-five thousand rounds at the town and sent five hundred carcasses hurtling at the defences. This savage attack opened a sizeable breach in the first of the outlying Spanish forts, the one right alongside Nuestra Señora de la Europa, and, when the Admiral observed this, he sent word to all the vessels in the fleet that they should each one lower a long-boat and man it with both soldiery and marines. These long-boats were then to make for this breach and take the fort. This order was carried out to the letter. Three thousand men, from both branches of the services, were put ashore and they advanced on the said fort, and taking the breach, ran up the colours of the two Nations, the Dutch at the same time capturing the next fort along, which is the second of the three that stand in a group above Nuestra Señora de la Europa. This operation was not an unqualified success, however, for, as the first wave of our attack poured in through the breach that we had worked in the defences, the whole fort quite suddenly burst into flames and in the panic and turmoil more than a hundred of our men either perished or sustained injuries and several of our launches were sunk by the rubble that poured down upon them. In the resulting confusion, we were not able to discover the cause of this sudden fire that favoured our cause so ill: some thought it must have been a mine which the enemy had laid there, others were of the opinion that a bomb had struck the castle's magazine. This sad event was not enough to persuade the two Nations to desist from their attack, and when the Governor realised this, he sent out a signal for the hostilities to cease, running up a white flag on a castle that stands atop the mountain right inside Gibraltar, which now lay open and defenceless. The guns fell silent and the enemy agreed to surrender, on one condition however; that the surrender should be made to His Majesty the Prince who was in command of the expedition and that he should first garrison one of the gates to the town and give his word that all agreements would be honoured.

On Monday the fourth, two gentlemen rode out from the town to the open ground that lies behind, and two gentlemen from our own lines rode into the town as surety for the safety of the others. This is an ancient custom and one still practised among the arts of war when a fort surrenders. The Commander-in-Chief received the delegation with all the ceremony and magnanimity that is characteristic of his princely nature, inviting them to dine at his table. Two hours past noon, the whole camp accompanied the Prince to garrison the Land Port and there the following terms of surrender were duly signed:

I.   The garrison officers and soldiery shall be permitted to keep their arms and all necessary equipment, and the soldiery shall be herewith granted leave to take with them everything they can carry on their backs; those officers that own horses shall be permitted to take their horses with them and vessels shall be provided to transport those who have equipment of their own.

II.   They shall be herewith granted leave to take with them three brass pieces of ordnance of different calibre, together with twelve kegs of powder and a corresponding number of balls.

III.   They shall be given bread, wine and meat sufficient for six days' journey.

IV.   No search shall be made of baggage, trunks, coffers and the like belonging to the Officers, aldermen and other gentlemen of quality. The garrison shall be out of the town within three days, and any clothing that they cannot manage to take with them at this time shall remain in the garrison, and they shall send for it at their earliest convenience. There shall be no embargo placed on the use of carts to transport belongings out of the town.

V.   With respect to the inhabitants of the town and those Officers and soldiers who choose to remain there, they shall be afforded the same rights and privileges that they enjoyed during the reign of Carlos the Second, and no alteration whatever shall be made either in the stipulations regarding religious practices or in the administration of justice, on condition that they all take an oath of allegiance to His Majesty, Charles III, their lawful king.

VI.   All stores of powder, all supplies, both armaments and provisions, and all arms remaining in the town shall be produced for examination.

VII.   All Frenchmen and all subjects of His Most Christian Majesty shall be exempted from the above stipulations, all their goods and effects being made over to the occupying forces and they themselves being detained as prisoners-of-war.

All the above Articles were signed by Prince Georg, Landgrave of Hesse-Darmstädt and by Don Diego de Salinas, Governor of the city. The army thereupon occupied the town and found there more than ten cannon, a great quantity of armaments and provisions and two hundred horses.

Fifteen days before they took Gibraltar, the fleet had taken an envoy of the King of Morocco on board so that he could observe their operations along the coast.

Meanwhile, the application to duty and the fervent zeal of His Majesty the Prince of Darmstädt in the common cause have made him indefatigable in his efforts on its behalf, and in particular does he spare no pains in organising the defences of Gibraltar, nor in persuading the Spaniards of the justice of our cause, and in this he is signal both in his liberality and in the good fortune that graces his enterprise, for many of those who fled in fear of those first days of our occupation of that town have now returned, their confidence restored by the kingly and courteous treatment with which the Prince has commanded they shall be regaled, and do now realise that they have no cause to fear that they will be treated with violence or be trodden under the heel of tyranny, provided they do fulfil their duty as good Spaniards and true and loyal subjects of a King as gentle and as predisposed towards them as is Charles the Third. And it is to be hoped that in the light of this treatment received by those who have come back into the fold, many more will be guided by their example and join our glorious party, and that the righteous cause which we all do serve shall carry all before it in triumph as these happy events do augur that it shall.'

(*Diario de la Expedición de las armadas inglesa y holandesa al Mediterráneo* ...)

9

Barcelona rises for Archduke Charles – and with him at its head staves off the first siege by the Bourbons. An Imperial account of the action

1706

'The ancient and noble city of Barcelona was among the first to succumb to the Moors and among the first to be won back for Christendom. In the era of the Moorish invasions, more battles were fought and more blood spilt over her than any other city. Once she had shaken off the Mohammedan yoke, and was free once again, she not only gave generously of herself in the victories she won for the freedom of Catalonia, – and with the freedom of Catalonia, the release of both Valencia and Mallorca, – but, with her own glorious Counts and Sovereigns at her head, she played a vital part in restoring the ancient Monarchy of the Goths to both Aragon and Castille. She continued to lead her subjects along this victorious path right up until the reign of Felipe III of Aragon, or IV of Castille. From those times until the reign of King Carlos II, known as His Catholic Majesty throughout His realm, she found herself beset with powerful foes, but now, it seems, she shall, with God's help, once again emulate those glorious deeds in which she did rejoice from birth, and, by dint of heroic struggles, once again reveal herself in all her glory. Such greatness and such glory are augured indeed in the valiant opposition she staged during the attacks, intrigues and plots with which France did assail her, and, in particular, during the grim siege of 1697 when she fell victim to the ambitious designs of the partisans who betrayed their own characters when, on the death of King Carlos II, they did debar our beloved Monarch Charles III* and His August Family from Their birthright of the Spanish Throne. At that time, beset in every quarter with enemies and bereft of her rightful forces, she could not requite her passionate desire nor slake her raging thirst for the gentle government of her true and venerable Monarch, whose Hand does today guide her as she journeys on to fame and renown, but, now, with God's help, and the advent of His Catholic Majesty Charles III, she is once

* Charles, Archduke of Austria, afterwards Emperor Charles VI, 1711–40.

again beginning to cloak herself in all her pristine glory. Her lawful
King did land with a whole host of troops recruited from the French
armies and from those of their allies, at Barcelona on the 22nd of
August 1705, ensuring with His arrival both His own safety and
independence and that of the Principate, which, having already,
of the love and affection she bears towards His Majesty, sworn true
allegiance to His arms, was there to welcome Him in the person of
her nobles and her people, who thereupon did pledge themselves
to uphold His Majesty's cause, and to do great and glorious deeds
in its defence, that His banners might be carried in triumph into
other Realms where those who envied her feats in arms and the
laurels of victory that garlanded her brow, were plotting to bring
her low and to blot out the memory of her glories. Yet once again
she did prove her mettle in a time of crisis and, waxing in strength
at the very moment that she saw herself pitted against enormous
odds, she was successful, with God's help, in resisting the enormous
forces which the Duc d'Anjou had mustered from both France
and from Castille, and did bring here this very year, 1706, persuaded
that He might humble her by siege. And, although the garrison was
sadly depleted, comprising but 1,330* men – 250 foot from the
Queen Anne regiment and 1,700 from Royal Catalan Guards, 250
horse from Count von Seckendorff's Regiment and 130 English
dragoons – it managed, with the assistance of its revered Monarch,
to stand up to the enemy and to beat them off as they attacked
Montjuich. That they did so was in great part due to the inspiration
provided by the King, who unfearful of the imminent peril arising
on account of the small size of the garrison, and betraying no concern for the breach which the enemy forces had made the previous
September in the city-defences, and blithely unheedful of the un-
prepared condition of the city, and the dilapidated state of her
defences, not only at Montjuich, but all round the city walls and
her batteries, and trusting in the steadfastness and loyalty of His
subjects, did make the dashing and magnanimous resolve to remain
within the city and share as a fellow-soldier all the labours of her
defence and all the rigours of a terrible siege. And all this time it
seemed that the King and His subjects were engaged in some
manner of rivalry, each bettering the other; His Majesty to bestow
as many blessings as possible upon his subjects and they to proffer
Him as many services as possible, now that they had at the session
of Parliament convened by command of His Majesty this same
year, rendered Him due homage as rightful Sovereign and lawful
Monarch of Spain and paid no attention whatever to the claims

* The number that follows amounts to 2,300.

of His rival whose threatening footfalls could be heard outside the city. His Majesty was so pleased at the favour thus granted Him that He did address the final session of the said Parliament and there did pledge Himself ever to strive for its well-being and good fortune. So it was that they were fired by enthusiasm for this gentle Monarch and fervently desired that He should ever be their King, and this was the inspiration that sustained them through all the days that followed and it was thus that they took heart and succeeded in their resolve to hold off the enemy until the allied fleet should arrive to relieve them. The glorious way in which they achieved this shall now be related as faithfully and as briefly as possible, and to make this our account the more intelligible there follows a description of Barcelona.

... On the thirty-first of March 1706, in the knowledge that the enemy were hastening from East and West to effect their design of laying siege to Barcelona, and that their army was considerable – 37 regiments of foot, each 500 strong, thus making a total of 18,500 men; and 25 squadrons of horse together with 300 horse of the Duc d'Anjou's private guard: a total of 3,800 – His Majesty convened a Council of War of all His advisers and military chiefs so that they might all discuss together what should be done in this time of grave crisis to safeguard the public interest and the well-being of His Majesty's loyal subjects. They debated this great issue long and pondered it deep, weighing all the probable consequences of the various courses of action open to them, and it was their general feeling that His Majesty should not lay himself open to the dangers and perils of the siege that the enemy were threatening both from the landward side and from the sea, especially in the light of the many several siege-engines and other horrible inventions which it is the practice to use in war against those resisting a siege; and that His Majesty should seize the opportunity to get out of the city which He still could, and then do everything within His power to bring forces to relieve those still inside.

His Majesty was deeply moved by the Council's resolve, and, while yet a conflict raged in His pious breast between His wish to remain with His beloved subjects and His concern to bring reinforcements to relieve them in their plight, He bowed before their reasoning and did accept this their resolve, determined to leave the city the following day.

That night Mr Mitford Grove, Ambassador-Extraordinary of Her Majesty, the Queen of Great Britain, did leave the city bound for Valencia, there to beg the Earl of Peterborough, Commander-in-Chief of Her Majesty's Armed Forces and who had overall command of the allied forces, to come to lend assistance, and, hearkening to this request, he did order some of his cavalry to leave immediately for the outskirts of Barcelona.

On the 1st of April, the day on which He had resolved to leave the city, His Majesty felt it imperative that He should make this His resolution known to all the people in the city, to the City Fathers and to the Military, and explain how He had come to this decision, and also that He should deliver to them a stirring exhortation that they might prove steadfast in the crisis, the severity of which He judged they would appreciate when they saw that it demanded such a desperate remedy. He accordingly did pen three letters in the Royal Hand giving expression to His own disinclination to leave those He loved at such a time, and assuring them that He would leave no stone unturned in His efforts to provide them with reinforcements and furnish them succour.

... His Majesty straightway began to issue instructions for the defence of the city (which had no more than 1,330* soldiers, was short both of provisions and of military supplies, and had many of its defences incomplete and, commanding some of His Royal Ministers to go forth and supervise repairs to the defences, he ordered a number of persons of quality to ride through the length and breadth of the province, organising levies and armed bands of citizens which they were to lead in the forthcoming action, and also getting in touch with all those Commanders at present outside the city and concerting with them their various campaigns in the mountains, the story of which we shall, in due course, relate.

One hour before noon on the 2nd the enemy troops were sighted. Under the command of the Duc de Noailles, they were coming down from the Ampurdán† and were already at San Andrés, a small village about ten hours' march from the city. Orders were given that 100 horse from Count von Seckendorff's regiments, some of the English troops, and 200 rifles under Don Antonio Desvalls should sally forth from the city and make an estimate of their strength, keeping them under close observation. This they did, coming within pistol-range of them, but not one of them ventured to leave his lines ...

... The enemy installed one of their batteries below the Santa Madrona convent so that they could prevent us from putting the finishing touches to our battery which we were in the process of setting up on the wall that runs from the San Antonio gate right

* See previous note.
† Ampurdán: a region to the east of Gerona, roughly that area between the Pyrenees and San Feliú de Guixols.

round to San Pablo, and also so that they could subject the outlying buildings of the city, which already lay in ruins, to a constant deluge of incendiary balls.

At eight that evening, the enemy began an intensive shelling of the castle, and 1,500 grenadiers under Lieutenant-General Asfelt took this as their cue to mount a concerted attack on the Sierpe flank, where we had but 50 men of the Catalan Guard under Lieutenant-Colonel Don Antonio Meca y Cardona and Don Francisco Puig y Sorribes, who, seeing the overwhelming odds, found themselves obliged to retreat, which they did, coming off with very few losses. As soon as the enemy had taken this post, they advanced on the Buey flank, where Don Antonio Puig had a force of 60 men, and on the orillion there, which was defended by a further 20 under Don Felipe Armengol. These staged a stout resistance to the first enemy attempt to storm this redoubt, but this only served to irritate the attackers who, joined by reinforcements, now began a series of blistering assaults, and, had not Lord Donegal, the Commander-in-Chief, arrived on the scene with the English troops and reinforced our men with their singular valour and courage, then the enemy would have taken all the new defence-works at Montjuich, leaving the far extremity of the Sierpe flank as the only fortifications still in our hands. Among our dead and wounded figured a number of non-commissioned officers, but enemy losses were far greater, for the number of their dead and wounded o'ertopped 500. The action lasted until midnight with the entire enemy assault being directed by Field-Marshal Count von Wolfeld [?] and General Santaman.

The enemy kept up their shelling of the fort on Montjuich all that night right through to dawn, and they had ample reply from our troops, who subjected them to a steady stream of mortar-fire, wreaking grave losses among their number. At dawn they began to set up a battery on the Sierpe flank to which the bulwarks of San Felipe lie naked and exposed.

... At seven in the morning on the 22nd, a large band of honest citizens, their patience exhausted and their minds ill at ease on account of the misfortunes we had suffered the previous night when we had lost to the enemy an important position inside the new fortifications on Montjuich Fort, did consult among themselves and, fired (albeit excessively) with ardent zeal, by their loyalty and love for the Royal Person of His Majesty the King, and by the love they bore Him and the Fatherland, they decided that they boasted courage and dash enough to recapture that vital post, and so accordingly they did betake themselves, their arms at the ready, to the San Pedro convent, where they were admitted into the Royal Presence and there did eagerly lay before Him this their gallant resolve. They many times asserted that it was their wish that they might shed their blood and die in defence of the Realm, and they therefore did plead with His Majesty that He would deign to issue the necessary orders that they might waste not a moment longer in putting this their resolve into effect, and they did furthermore request His Majesty that He be pleased to command that the Standards of St Eulalia and St George, the patron saints of the city, be given into their possession, for thus might as many citizens as possible be induced to join their band, and stating that with the protection that these standards would afford them, they would be certain of success in this enterprise. The King, our Lord, fully recognising that this petition grew from no other seed but the desire of these people to fight in the defence of His Royal Person and to ensure that His good government should be ever vouchsafed them, did accede to their request lest yet greater hurts be occasioned by a refusal, and the sixth Chancellor grasping the standard of St Eulalia, and the Military Governor laying hold of the standard of St George, they did walk in procession down to Montjuich, followed by all the Members of the Military Council and the Royal Chamber and some officers of the Municipal Benches, and did there place the standard of St Eulalia in the old fort and the standard of St George at the point where the lines of communication branch out of the new workings to link up with the old fort. That the whole action might be given purpose and direction, His Majesty appointed Don Jaime Puig de Perasita and his son, Don Francisco, to lead the attack. Recognising that many citizens were unaware of this gallant undertaking, and wishing to gather as many of them together as swiftly as possible, some persons did take themselves off to the Cathedral and to the parish churches of San Jaime and the Pino and there did ring the bells. It was decided, however, that such a din served no purpose and, indeed that it might prejudice the whole enterprise, and accordingly the First Chancellor Don Francisco Nicolás de San Juan and a number of other worthies, intending to put a stop to it, did climb the Cathedral Tower (for at that moment this was the only place where the bells were ringing) and succeeded in silencing them; when they returned to the body of the Cathedral, however, three unidentified men passed them and began to climb the far tower (where it is too dark to recognise anybody) saying that the other bell must be rung, and when the Chancellor ordered them not to ring the said bell, a shot rang out and the Chancellor fell dying. There on that very spot he passed away, having received absolution and the Extreme Unction, and, to keep the news of his death from the people (who might have reacted in a manner detrimental to our cause), his body was hidden in a corner of this same Tower, until that night when, under cover of darkness, it was removed and given proper burial.

No sooner had this force been mustered under the command of those appointed to lead it, than they all began to rush upon the enemy position, and although instructions had been issued that they should there await the detachment of regulars that was to support their assault, they could restrain themselves no longer and, brooking no delay, hurled themselves headlong at the enemy with such great force, and, letting off their guns in every direction did cause many of the enemy, appalled at this sudden horde, which heedless of its own safety, swarmed up at them, to snatch the three standards which they had set up on the fort, and turn tail, fleeing in panic, and sustaining heavy losses as a result. Seeing this great throng of people seething up the mountain-side, the enemy concentrated all their strength in an effort to reinforce their counter-attacks, but in the ensuing struggle they could not dislodge our noble citizens from the positions they had lately taken, and by the time they finally pulled their forces off, after battling from nine in the morning until two hours past noon, leaving some of their dead and wounded where they fell, the enemy had sustained many and grievous losses.

... At first light on the 8th, the enemy fleet disappeared from view, and our own frigates which put out from Mataró, Vilanova, Sitges and Vinarós managed to take three French fishing-smacks, capturing a Colonel and several other Frenchmen who were coming from the East, nine horses, a good deal of baggage, some wheat and other supplies.

Our Fleet hove into sight in the estuary: 52 ships of the line and a whole flotilla of supply vessels. This was a welcome spectacle for those within the city, for the enemy had already taken the counter-scarfe on the San Antonio bulwarks and were already before the breach. In recognition of this timely intercession of Divine Providence, His Majesty commanded that the Holy Sacraments be exhibited in San Pedro church and to that Church did He make His way, together with all the Court, there to sing the Te Deum and in solemn Mass to offer up His thanks to God.

The allied Fleet put in at Barcelona: the Commander-in-Chief the Earl of Peterborough and his two English colleagues, Baron Walsenar* and General Wils†, the Dutch Commander, the Count of Noyel, his compatriot, General Palm and 3,000 infantry. His Majesty rode out of the city to where they landed (as a token of the importance He attached to their having sailed to relieve Him), and then the whole

---

* Lord George Carpenter (1657–1732).   † Charles Wills (1666–1741).

party did proceed to the Ramblas, whence His Majesty did take measures to ensure that the new arrivals had proper escort as far as the defile and breach against the possibility of the enemy's attempting some kind of attack upon them, and as they made their way up into the defences, they were regaled on every side with wild demonstrations of acclamation from the people, from the soldiery and from all the inhabitants.

At that time, the enemy could be seen striking camp over between San Andrés de Palomar and the Gracia convent, and abandoning their positions to join up with the main body of their army which was in Sarriá and Sans and on Montjuich mountain. Six deserters from their ranks informed us that the enemy had given themselves up for lost, finding that their squadron had abandoned them and in its place there lay our own very powerful Fleet.

All that night our ships continued to put our forces ashore until the number of those landed was 8,000. These were straightways stationed in the Ramblas in case the enemy should attempt an attack. The enemy went on firing from their batteries and hurling the occasional bomb at us, but in reply our men kept up a constant mortar-fire and our muskets crackled unflaggingly.

As soon as the enemy had disappeared from view, a great crowd of people surged out of the city to see what they had left behind, and they did marvel at the equipment, munitions and provisions they found there. They did take especial notice of all that the enemy had abandoned that they might give His Majesty a detailed account of the spoil, and the figures they gave, and which were later to be confirmed by the military commanders, were: 106 bronze cannon complete with mountings, twenty-seven bronze mortars – some of these still having their iron housing, more than 5,000 kegs of powder and 500 panniers of rifle and musket-shot, a great quantity of lead, bombs in excess of 2,000, 10,000 shells, countless hand-grenades, 8,000 picks, shovels and spades, more than 40,000 cannon balls, sixteen thousand sacks of flour, vast quantities of wheat and oats, more than 10,000 pairs of shoes, many several iron stoves and a plentiful provision of medical-stores for the sick and the wounded, over 500 of whom they had abandoned in the Gracia convent: all this and many other supplies and pieces of equipment besides, and every day we find more, hidden here and there; in all so much that, had we not witnessed it with our own eyes, we would never have given it credit. All this vast treasury of supplies and equipment the enemy abandoned is incontrovertible proof of the fear and the ignominious haste with which they decamped from the city.

On the 13th, the enemy troops continued on their way, heading for the Ampurdán, burning, sacking and laying waste whatever they found in their path, even the churches. They devastated the whole countryside, deliberately spilling all the wine and oil and smashing every other single thing which the honest labourers had left in their houses when they took to the mountains, both to shelter their families from the marauding troops and to swell the numbers of those who took it upon themselves to harass the enemy's rearguard, which they did untiringly, occasioning them great losses and forcing them to abandon many of their supplies, carts, cannon, and in one case, a mortar, which they had to leave behind at the Villa de Celoni.

This retreat was very costly to the enemy in both men and supplies until they reached the comparative sanctuary of the Ampurdán...;
... Between Barcelona plain and Figueras, they lost 4,000 men either dead or wounded, which, added to those that perished in the siege of Barcelona, amounted in the general concensus of opinion to some 8,000 dead or wounded. Some put the number as high as 12,000 while His Majesty's glorious victory had but cost Him 2,000 men either dead or taken prisoner, and this figure includes the civilian dead...'
(*Diaria ye verídica relación de las operaciones y sucesos del sitio de la ciudad de Barcelona...*)

10

Official account of the Battle of Almansa addressed by Felipe V to the University of Salamanca, stressing the religious nature of the war

1707

'To Their Excellencies, the Venerable Rector, Director of Studies and Staff of the University of Salamanca:

Gentlemen: God, of His Divine Mercy having graced this Our righteous cause, as ever He has done hitherto, and having watched over Our armies and those of His Majesty, Our grandfather, and having granted that they should enjoy complete and crushing victory in the field at Almansa on the twenty-fifth day of April last, routing the enemy utterly and exacting just vengeance on his infantry, killing approximately 6,000 of them, capturing all their artillery and equipment with a great number of banners, standards and drums, and taking more than 10,000 prisoners, not counting the 800 officers, five commanders, many several colonels and officers of higher rank who did also fall into their hands; We have determined that, in recognition of these singular favours granted Us by the Almighty and of the great glory redounding therefrom to our gallant and loyal subjects, and, desirous of giving the fullest and most fervent demonstration of Our beholdenness to His Divine Goodness, there shall be held throughout Our Realm public services of thanksgiving for this great and important victory, and public prayers shall be offered up to the Virgin Mary, the Protectress of Spain, that She may intercede for Us and obtain the great boon of God's Divine Mercy until the enemy shall have been utterly destroyed, the peace of Our Realms re-established and Our Holy Faith cleansed of those that would attempt to sully Her. Thus we do look to ... your loyalty, devotion and zeal in the service both of God and the King and do hereby charge you to bring to this matter all the loyalty and fervour you have shown Us hitherto and which you are in duty bound to afford Us. – Buen Retiro Palace, 15th May, 1707. We, the King. By command of His Majesty, the King, Don Lorenzo Vivanco y Angulo.'

('Carta del Rey Nuestro Señor Dn. Phelipe 5 escrita al claustro y universidad de Salamanca ...')

II

Felipe V abolishes Aragonese and Valencian privileges

1707

'Considering that the Realms of Aragón and Valencia and all those who dwell therein, by dint of the rebellion they did raise against Us, thus travesting the solemn oath of allegiance they did swear to Us as their lawful King and Lord, have voluntarily resigned all rights, privileges, exemptions and liberties which they did enjoy and which We, following in this the example set by Our magnanimous predecessors on this august Throne, were pleased of Our own bounty to grant them; and considering that to the rights which We do enjoy as lawful King of the said Realms of Aragón and Valencia are now added the rights of a conqueror freshly garlanded by those Our armies that did quell the said rebellion; and considering also that one of the principal offices and rights that attach to Kingship is that of Law Giver, wherein are comprehended both the prerogative of creating new laws and that of rescinding old ones, and that We are accordingly empowered to alter the Statutes of the Realm as circumstances themselves do alter, and that We should enjoy this Our right even had We not been given the ample justification for so doing which the Realms of Aragón and Valencia have lately afforded Us; We have deemed it opportune, both for the reasons set out above and because it is Our will that all the Realms of Spain shall obey the same laws and statutes, and observe the same customs and practices as one another, and that each shall be subject to the Laws of Castille which do merit the highest of praise and are worthy to be disseminated throughout the globe, that all the said rights and privileges presently attaching to these same Realms of Aragón and Valencia shall forthwith cease to have effect, and We do hereby decree that they shall henceforth cease to have the said effect and that these Realms shall forthwith be subject to the Laws of Castille and to the customs, practices and institutions therein pertaining, and that the laws and tribunals in these said Realms shall be in every way identical and at one with those pertaining in the Realm of Castille ... In consequence of which We have resolved that the Council of Deputies which does represent Valencia and that which does represent Aragón shall be in every way a faithful model of the Courts of Chancery of Valladolid and Granada, and that all those same rules, laws, pacts, ordinances and customs which do govern the rule of these last shall in every way govern the rule of those of Valencia and Aragón, without any difference nor departure whatsoever, save in all controversies and points arising concerning the jurisdiction of the Church, in the which cases all those practices that have pertained hitherto shall continue to be observed hereafter, because the Concordats with the Holy See are binding upon Us. We have determined to inform Our Council of this Our resolve that they may not remain ignorant of it. Buen Retiro Palace, 29th June, 1707.'

(Belando, *Historia civil de España...*, Part One, pp. 316 ff.)

12

French defeats in Flanders have repercussions on the
Spanish war-effort. They produce a sharp reaction in the
Imperial camp, and after taking Zaragoza, the Archduke
enters Madrid. An Imperial account of these actions

1710

'Having won a laudable victory against the forces of the Duc
d'Anjou on the twentieth day of August in the vicinity of Zaragoza,
due both to its own strength and equally to the military genius of its
most loyal commanders, the army of His Majesty Charles the Third
(whom God preserve) did straightways march on to the noble city of
Zaragoza itself and did take the city and with it the whole of the
Realm of Aragón, part of that of Navarre, the cities of Tudela, Corella
and Agreda and several smaller townships; and its triumphal progress
was everywhere acclaimed with wild paeans of joy by the Aragonese
people who now could look forward to the restoration of their time-
honoured Courts, laws, Privileges and other prerogatives vouchsafed
them of old By His Majesty's august and illustrious predecessors of
this noble Throne, and they did celebrate that this their Realm and
these their rights were once again unassailable by addressing warm
words of welcome to the troops and by offering them aid, both in
money and in men. His Majesty and His victorious host did then
march on in triumph into Castille, passing through the cities of
Sigüenza and Guadalajara on their way to Alcalá de Henares where
they arrived on the 20th to a tumultuous welcome from both City
and University and where, much fêted with bonfires and with the
whole city lit with torches in His honour, His Majesty resides at
present and shall stay until He comes here to the capital, which He
shall do in the very near future.

On the 21st, His Excellency, Mr James Stanhope, Lieutenant-
General of His Majesty's Armed Forces and British Ambassador-
Extraordinary and Plenipotentiary, betook himself with a large
detachment of horse to Madrid where, as soon as they heard that he
had come among them, the Municipal Authorities in the capital
appointed four honourable gentlemen to ride forth and, in the name
of the city, prostrate themselves at His Majesty's feet. These Com-

missioners, Don Jerónino de Miranda, Don José Domingo de Goz, Don Juan Cristóbal de Barcos and Don Manuel Manrique, sought an audience with His Excellency Lieutenant-General James Stanhope, who issued an authority that they be escorted to Alcalá where His Majesty was graciously pleased to receive them and did show them great kindness, and where they did have the honour of kissing His hand. That same afternoon, many gallant young officers entered the city and the aforementioned detachment of horse pitched camp, down in la Florida along the banks of the Manzanares, and straightway a number of edicts were published to the effect that grave penalties would be invoked to deal with any person found molesting or in any way interfering with another, and that any enemy soldiers harboured either in the houses of private citizens or in the hospitals should give themselves up, or send some third party to announce their presence in the city within twenty-four hours, on pain of death. Orders were then issued that all political prisoners should be set free at once; although for the time being no criminal was granted his liberty ... In the same way, His Majesty caused a Decree to be promulgated throughout the city and affixed in all the usual public places proclaiming His own kindly disposition, the justice of His cause, and the triumphs both of His Christian Armies and of those of His noble allies.

This City has remained peaceful and orderly, thanks to the circumspection of His Worship the Mayor, Don Antonio Sanguineto, who has shown great capacity for administration and has accordingly made sure that the life of the city has continued as normal, taking the precaution of ensuring that supplies of food-stuffs have ever been plentiful and maintaining a careful surveillance in all public places to prevent any breaches of the peace. In this he has been ably supported by the Municipal Council, who have rivalled him in omitting no expedient that could be conducive to the maintenance of law and order.'

(*Gaceta de Madrid*, 24 September 1710.)

13

*Another version of the Archduke's reception in Madrid.
The Author, a supporter of Felipe, emphasises the cold-
ness of the population towards Him and the anti-Catholic
nature of the allied troops*

1710

'As soon as news reached the capital of the disaster that befell His
Majesty's armies in the field at Zaragoza on the 20th of August, the
city echoed with despondent talk that Their Majesties would soon be
constrained to leave the city and betake Themselves to Valladolid,
and as soon as reports reached us that the enemy was already near-
ing Cuenca, They did indeed leave for the north in the morning of
the 9th of September. It was a most heart-rending spectacle for all
Their loyal subjects and indeed it did seem to mirror another such
flight of which Scripture has painted a picture known to us all. All
the Members of the Royal Council and all the Grandees and Nobles
attached themselves to Their Majesties' train, and there was none
that stayed behind and pleaded poverty nor any that did shelter in
the skirts of age or infirmity. Some of the ladies accompanied Her
Majesty the Queen, others left in company with their husbands; yet
others sought the shelter of a convent. Apart from a few ex-Ministers
of the Council who had lost their posts under the last régime and
therefore did not now hold office or seek preferment – and this was to
prove their downfall – there was not a soul remaining in the city or
its environs. This same day His Excellency the Duke of Veraguas,
Grand-Master of the Orders of Chivalry and Member of the Council
of State, passed on, and his son, the new Duke, did not even wait for
the funeral, so great was his rush to follow Their Majesties.

Madrid was left a turmoil and desolation which can be easily imag-
ined, and this chaos did reign until the 21st when Lieutenant-General
James Stanhope, the English Ambassador Extraordinary, arrived and
approached the Municipal officials asking that they take an oath of
allegiance to the Archduke, and four of their number did ride to
Alcalá so to do; the same afternoon that they did take the oath, the
edict published in Zaragoza on the 21st was promulgated in Madrid.

The purport of this was as follows: That the Archduke did, of His great bounty, promise to observe and uphold all those rights, privileges and prerogatives granted them by His great Predecessors, the Kings of Spain in the House of Austria, and moreover, that He would be graciously pleased to bestow upon all those who followed the dictates of duty and prudence and did take an oath of allegiance to Him, the handsome and ample honours befitting such exemplary conduct, threatening at the same time that any such persons who obdurately persisted in the errors of their ways and, unheedful of this His proclamation, abstained from taking this same oath of allegiance, and had not done so before October was out, would be for ever "personae non gratae" and ever be spurned and banished. That same day there appeared three more edicts: the first that no person should molest or in any way interfere with another; the second, that all soldiers from the armies of Felipe V harboured either in the houses of private citizens or in the hospital should give themselves up or send some third party to announce their presence in the city within twenty-four hours, on pain of death, this same sentence being applied also to any person disobeying the first of these edicts: the third, that all political prisoners should be set free at once.

Stanhope set up his quarters in la Florida next to where his men were encamped along the banks of the Manzanares. For three nights in a row the candles burned before the Blessed Sacrament, the lights in the churches were turned down low and the bells muffled, for the sacristans were mortally afeared of the English heretics and, with their eyes glued on the chalices, they spent their days and nights convulsed with terror.

On the 22nd a detachment of sixty horse under the command of a corporal did go down to the convent of Nuestra Señora de Atocha and there took out the flags and standards of the allied nations which Our King had offered in tribute to this the greatest of all Queens, and did hand them over each to the particular nation to which it had originally belonged. A troop of Grenadiers then paraded them through the streets of Madrid and bore them out of the city to Canillejas. For heretics to take these trophies from the very feet of Our Lady was surely an ill omen and one which did indeed give us a foretaste of the bitterness that was to come. From that day forward the robbery and looting were destined to know no respite: both by day and by night the streets and even the main squares witnessed assault after assault, theft after theft and the authorities did nothing even to restrain the common rabble among the soldiery from committing these outrages. The looting and sacking raged unremittingly through the city and accordingly the terror of the people knew no bounds. That same day Don Antonio Sanguineto y Zayas, whom His Majesty had appointed Mayor during His absence, instructed Stanhope to issue an order to the effect that, on pain of death, all moneys of all denominations, both coins of the Spanish Realm and all foreign currency, should be declared legal tender both in Madrid and elsewhere, and that all exchange should be effected at the rates of interest hitherto pertaining, and he fixed the rate of exchange for all currencies using that of Portugal as the standard.

On the 26th, the army pitched camp out near Canillejas and the Archduke moved his quarters to the estate belonging to His Excellency the Count of Aguilar which lies one league without the city from where He did send orders that the city should be lit on the 28th in His honour. On that day the Archduke did betake Himself to hear morning mass in the Church of the Virgin Santísima de Atocha, making His entry into the city along the Calle Atocha, thence through the Plaza Mayor and under the Puerta de Guadalajara. Continuing along the Calle Mayor, He did leave the city by the Puerta de Alcalá, little satisfied by the scant and luke-warm welcome He had received at the hands of the people of Madrid.

On the first of October, the same day on which the Archduke attained 27 years of age, there was held a ceremony of Kissing of The Hands. It was attended by very few and these obscure. There was besides a Meeting of the Municipal Officers, presided over by Don Francisco Alvarez Guerrero. The following were elected: Don José Sotelo, Don Andrés Pinto de Lara, Don José Palacios, Don Agustín de Cárdenas, Don Luis de la Revilla and Don Pedro Infante. Don Pedro Ramírez attended in his capacity as Attorney-General. As many as 40 Officers of the Peace were appointed, all of them very able and well-deserving of the honour. Those ladies who had taken shelter in convents were requested to return to their homes, and warned that, if they did not do so, their houses would be turned over to billets for the military.

On the 4th, the camp out at Canillejas was struck and the whole force moved to El Pardo, and it was about this time that the persecutions began against the Frenchmen resident in Madrid and all those who had remained loyal to His Majesty. They were all condemned to exile until the city was emptying so fast that these persecutions had to cease, although in the meantime many were driven underground by fear.

On the 6th, the Marquis of Palomares took over his duties as Mayor. On the 7th, the order was given to stage a bull-fight for when the Archduke should make his entry into the city, and all those who owned horses were commanded on pain of death to present them for inspection as it had been decided to form a new cavalry regiment and Colonel Bonifacio Manrique de Lara was appointed to be its Colonel-in-Chief. This order was obeyed, although no payment was made to those who did display their horses. It was also decided to form two new Infantry regiments, one, to be known as the Toledo, with the Count of Puebla de Portugal as Colonel-in-Chief and the other, the Guadalajara, Don Antonio de Villarroel commanding. Both these officers were promoted to the rank of Colonel-in-Chief from that of Lieutenant-General.

On the 12th, all ladies of the first rank were instructed to remove themselves to Toledo within four days: those who wanted to, obeyed this order; those who did not, stayed at home. On the 14th, a guard was placed on the Palace, and on the 15th, all Frenchmen were ordered out of Madrid on pain of death, that an effective halt might be called to all relations between their country and our own. On the 17th, there was another edict: that all fire-arms should be handed in, on pain of death, to Quincoces, the Lord Mayor's henchman. On the 18th, it was publicly explained that this only applied to those arms which were government supply.

On the 19th, a letter, signed by Don Ramón Vilana Perlas, was sent to all heads of religious houses instructing them to present all goods and effects entrusted to their safe-keeping by courtiers who had left Madrid with His Majesty, to the bailiffs for inspection. On the 22nd, there was a hurried meeting of jurists and theologians to discuss how best to lay their hands on all such goods and effects deposited on holy ground, and the result of this meeting was that a thorough search was instigated of all such sanctuaries and even tombs were ransacked. With reference to this, it comes to mind that Don Francisco de Parga (God rest his soul) who was curate of the parish church of San Ginés and absolutely devoted to His Majesty, was sent a letter condemning him to exile that day after they buried him: this is an example of the blind fanaticism to which these people were prey, and I am sure this is not an isolated case. In fact, Don Bonifacio Manrique de Lara, the new Military Governor of the City, reiterated the edict that no person was to have any dealings with those loyal to His Majesty, on pain of death. At the end of October, a proclamation was issued to the effect that all persons found in the streets, in doorways, in inns, or in private houses who had come from Valladolid or elsewhere without written permission, whether they bore sealed documents or no, should be straightways condemned to summary and ignominious death, without it being necessary for any proof to be entered against them save that they had been arrested or turned in. This was the great work that Farruco does relate in his sad and sorry tale.* All those banding together or discussing affairs of state, the position of the allies or the strength of their forces would be condemned to ten years penal servitude, were they of noble blood, a not unkind sentence, and were they from the common people, they would receive two hundred lashes and be banished from the city. These same punishments were to apply also to all those who did go out of the city to make some estimation of the strength of the troops there stationed, to all who visited the hospital to assess the number of the wounded, and to all those who did visit and tend the sick. All women committing these crimes would be imprisoned for life, and, should any person under sentence of banishment return for whatever reason to the city, he would be publicly hanged, and should any person of noble blood commit this crime, they would, irrespective of their sex, be sent to the garrote. Finally, any person caught shouting "Long live Felipe V", or even muttering the same under his breath, would be shot there and then, and would not be permitted to make any statement in his own defence.

On the 20th, Don Francisco de Quincoces promulgated a decree ordering that all those soldiers now prisoner and all others who had served in His Majesty's Armed Forces should come forward within 24 hours on pain of summary trial and confiscation of property, and that all those harbouring such soldiers should be subject to these self-same punishments. A third part of all the properties so confiscated would go to any person denouncing such soldiers. A great number of men in holy orders, both clerics and monks, were either threatened with exile or actually banished, and in the first few days two Dominicans, Father Blanco and Father Atienza, the Superior of San Bernardino and Father Cardoma were all expelled from the city.

... Throughout this period, one could see people selling chalices, patens and ciboria and every class of sacred vessel that the heretics had looted from nearby churches. It is estimated that they ransacked above seventy such sacred places, in some cases dashing everything they found on to the floor and in others selling off that which cannot be mentioned without weeping (the Host). They also sacked the houses of many prominent private citizens, including those of Ministers who had left with His Majesty, and almost all those owned by Frenchmen; and it was pitiful to see country labourers, with no clothes to cover their backs, trooping into the city laden with their babies and children, only to find that the situation here was as miserable and as wretched as the one from which they had sought escape.

On the 2nd of November, an edict was published forbidding any person from leaving the city, on pain of two hundred lashes. On the

* Identity of this Farruco?

5th, when there was no more flour in the public granaries and the stocks that had been taken from all convents and flour-mills and all the private dwelling-places had given out, bread began to be in short supply; there was a shortage of meat and wine, fish was scarce, and vegetables could not be had. As a result, all kinds of crimes were committed by people desperate to obtain something to eat, and yet, despite all this, the order was given that all citizens should take their pigs, chickens and vegetables out of the city and into the country, on pain of being declared traitors to the state.

On the 18th, Don Francisco de Quincoces did order three decrees to be published; the first, that all military presently in the city should give themselves up within 24 hours on pain of death, which penalty would apply also to all those who did harbour them; secondly, that all military uniforms should be handed in, along with all powder, balls and other military paraphernalia, and the third, once more stating that artillery equipment, fire-arms, rifles and carbines should be surrendered to the authorities, and investing authority in the officers of law and order to arrest any soldier found in the streets after dark.

On the 9th of November, the festival of the Blessed Virgin, the Patron Saint of the City, all the recently formed Councils were ordered to betake themselves to Toledo, since the absence of troops in Madrid had led to their authority being openly mocked and derided by all the street-urchins, and on the 11th they did leave for Toledo, travelling part of the way with the army, which was bound for Ciempozuelos; and it was a baleful picture indeed that they did paint, with not even enough she-mules and plasterer's asses to carry them all.

On the 12th, a small detachment of His Majesty's troops appeared in El Angel...

On the 23rd, the two Pignatelli regiments of horse and the Santiago regiment, under Field-Marshal Don Feliciano de Bracamonte, began to withdraw. On the 24th, the anniversary of the proclamation in the city of Madrid of His Majesty, Felipe V as king of Spain, these same troops did reverse the procession that the Archduke had made on the 28th of September, with far more joyous acclamations from the people than on that previous occasion. They did enter along the Calle de Atocha, by which route he had left in September, and then did process along the Calle Mayor, through the Puerta de Guadalajara and along Calle Atocha, finally leaving, as he had entered, through the Puerta de Vallecas. That same day His Majesty was pleased to confirm the appointment of Don Antonio de Sanguineto y Zayas as Lord Mayor.

And lastly, on the feast of St Francis Xavier,* at three o'clock in the afternoon, His Majesty the King did arrive at the convent in Atocha and, after giving thanks to the Blessed Virgin and singing the Te Deum laudamus, he did mount his horse and, in company with His Highness the Duc de Vendôme and the other Princes of His house, the Grandees, the Nobles and the Royal Bodyguard, He did make His triumphal entry into the city. I shall leave the tale of the ceremonies and the pageantry, the ornament and the tumultuous welcome that did greet Him to another pen more able than mine. I ask only: Have those that were present ever known a greater day? And here I shall desist from my narrative so little blest with the soft phrase of peace, and lay my quill to rest with but one last thought: I do beseech and pray to God that he preserve and watch over His Catholic Majesty, Felipe V, our King, that He might ever be the scourge of heretics and the stye in the devil's eye.'

(*Relación diaria de todo lo sucedido en Madrid* ...)

14

Britain makes Her position clear: There is only one obstacle to her agreeing to a peace settlement; Her fear that the Crowns of France and Spain might be united. Felipe V decides to sweep this obstacle away and renounce all His rights to the French Throne

1712

'Instrument of renunciation made by His Catholic Majesty, Felipe the Fifth.

Felipe, by the grace of God, King of Castille, etc., etcetera. That this, Our instrument and avowal of renunciation and relinquishment, shall be made known and shall ever be remembered, We do herewith publish and declare to all Kings, Rulers, Potentates, Republics, Societies and to all private persons, both those that now are and those that shall come hereafter, that, one of the most signal peace-treaties involving this Our Crown of Spain, that between France and England, being dependent upon this Our resolve, We have determined, both

* 3 December.

to establish this treaty on a firm footing and to spread the boon of peace, thus ensuring the good of all people and the peaceful balance of power with Europe,... to accede to the representations made by England and approved by His Majesty, Our Grandfather, and, so that it shall henceforth never come within the realms of possibility for this Crown to be wed with that of France, to agree to renounce, in Our own Name and in that of all Our descendants, all rights to the French Throne, which renunciation shall be matched by an equal and opposite renunciation...; ... with the assurance that, ever adhering to this fundamental maxim that the balance of power within Europe shall be maintained, all steps shall be taken to guarantee that at no time shall this inheritance fall to the House of Austria, for, should this happen, this House, even without the domains and territories attaching to the Empire, would be made formidably powerful, a factor which in the past made the superation of the hereditary estates enjoyed by the House of Austria from the body of the Spanish Realms a laudable enterprise. It has accordingly been agreed between Ourself, His Majesty the King of England and His Majesty, Our Grandfather, that, in the event of Our dying without issue, or of Our line being for any reason interrupted and not enjoying due continuance, the heir to this Our Throne shall be the Duke of Savoy and His sons, born of lawful wedlock; and that in the event of this His line being for any reason interrupted and not enjoying due continuance, the heir to this Our Throne shall be the Prince Amadeo di Carignano and His sons, born of lawful wedlock; and that in the event of this His line being for any reason interrupted and not enjoying due continuance, the heir to this Our Throne shall be the Prince Tomasio di Carignano, His brother, and all His sons, born of lawful wedlock; who, being the descendants of the Princess Doña Catalina, daughter of His Majesty Felipe the Second, and being expressly nominated as successors, do now have clear and incontrovertible rights to the Throne. It is our dearest wish that, given the friendship and the permanent alliance which shall and must now be sought with the Duke of Savoy and his descendants on this Throne, these Our precautions shall secure the balance of power which all Realms do now so amicably seek among Themselves, and that We shall thus preclude all the trials and tribulations and all the uncertainties that are born of war, there being none among the Powers that shall be entitled to change any part of these Our stipulations and agreements for ensuring the balance of power in Europe, neither by any act of renunciation nor by any act of secession, for indeed right reason does persuade us of the need for their permanence and of the motives which have occasioned them, and they shall accordingly henceforth and for ever be a fundamental and unalterable law governing the rights of succession.

We are therefore resolved, both for the reasons We have set out above, and on account of Our love for the Spanish nation, and Our recognition of the love they do bear Us, and the many several avowals of allegiance and fidelity which they have sworn to Us, and also that We may in some small wise repay Divine Providence for the great boon she has bestowed upon Us in elevating Us to this Crown and granting that We may rule over subjects so illustrious and so deserving, to abdicate in Our own Name and in that of all Our heirs and descendants, all rights of succession to the French Throne, fired in this by a desire never to part company with these Our beloved subjects while We do yet live, and it being Our fondest wish that We may be granted leave to die among them and bequeath to all Our heirs and descendants this great bond that shall link them to the love and fidelity of this Nation; and also because it is Our fervent desire that there may hereby be removed one of the principal motives for the wars that have hitherto scarred the face of Europe. We, Felipe, by the Grace of God, King of Castille, with this present instrument, motu proprio, of our free will, and spontaneously, in Our own Name and in that of Our heirs and successors, do hereby renounce, relinquish and forswear for ever, Amen, all rights, claims and entitlements which We, or any of Our heirs or successors, have made in the past or which shall be made hereafter, to the succession to the French Throne; ... It is Our will and desire that henceforth any such rights and claims invested in Us or Our heirs and descendants shall be deemed to have passed and been transferred to the person of Our brother, the Duc de Berry and to His male descendants born of lawful wedlock; and should that line be in default and not enjoy its due continuance, that all these rights and claims shall be deemed to have passed and been transferred to the person of Our Uncle, the Duc d'Orléans, and to His male descendants born of lawful wedlock; and should that line be in default and not enjoy its due continuance, that all these rights and claims shall be deemed to have passed and been transferred to the person of Our Cousin, the Duc de Bourbon, and to His male descendants born of lawful wedlock; and so on through all the Princes of France in the order that They shall be called to the succession by the precedence of Their birth, for ever and ever Amen. ... And that this Our Act of Abdication of all those rights and entitlements that do attach to Us and to Our heirs and descendants in respect of the Crown of France may enjoy full and complete effect and be held as law, We do specifically renounce and foreswear all those inherited rights which do attach to Us in virtue of the letters-patent and instrument in which His Majesty, Our Grandfather did appoint Us sole lawful successor to the said Crown of France, and which were issued at Versailles in the month of December, 1700, and passed, approved and sanctioned by Parliament; and We do hereby declare that it is Our wish that this instrument shall in no wise entitle Us to the said succession and We do here refute the stipulations contained therein and do declare them to be null and void and of no legal standing whatever and do command them to be cancelled... And that this Our Act of Abdication and the stipulations contained therein may enjoy full and complete effect and be held as Law, We do here again pledge Our Troth and give Our Royal Word, and do solemnly swear by the Holy Gospels on which We do here place Our Hand, that We shall ever keep, observe and prove faithful to this Our Act of Abdication and Renunciation; and We do make this solemn pledge both in Our own Name and in that of Our heirs and successors; and We do swear that We shall observe all the stipulations contained therein in the light of the most literal, natural and obvious interpretation of them, and that We have never sought nor shall ever seek to be released from this Our Royal Oath, and, that should any third person seek such release in Our Name or should it be granted Us without Our having sought it, We shall never avail Ourself of it...

... We, the King.... Madrid, 5th November, 1712.'

(Belando, *Historia civil de España...*, Part One, pp. 542 ff.)

15

Peace-Treaty of Utrecht. England shall keep Gibraltar and Minorca as well as her trading rights in the West Indies

1713

'Peace-Treaty between His Catholic Majesty Felipe the Fifth & Her Highness Anne Stuart, Queen of England.

The English negotiators were The Bishop of Bristol and the Earl of Stratford; the Spanish, the Duke of Osuna and the Marquis of Monteleón. They did unanimously compact the following Peace-Treaty comprising twenty-five Articles:

I. There shall be a binding peace between the two Sovereigns and

Their successors, and each shall endeavour to ensure that His subjects observe this peace.

II. That all fears that the Realms of France and Spain might ever be conjoined in one Person shall be allayed, and that the peace herein convened between the two Powers shall be firmly established and the proper balance of forces ever guaranteed and peace thereby ensured, His Catholic Majesty does here reiterate and reaffirm the abdication of all His rights to the Crown of France. Hereto were appended the Act of Abdication, the resolution of the Cortes, the Royal Decree naming the House of Savoy as lawful heirs and successors to the Spanish Throne, the Acts of Renunciation made by the French Royal Family of all Their claims and rights to the Throne of Spain, and the epistle of His Most Christian Majesty.

III. All those acts of hostility occasioned by this present war shall now pass into the annals of history and no more shall men remind themselves of them.

IV. All prisoners-of-war shall be straightways set at liberty upon the ratification of this present Treaty.

V. His Catholic Majesty does hereby solemnly pledge Himself to recognise the limits placed on the succession to the British Throne, with respect to the House of Hanover.

VI. His Catholic Majesty does hereby enter into a solemn undertaking that He shall henceforth never commit any act of hostility against Her Majesty the Queen of Great Britain nor any of Her line who do succeed her.

VII. All the Tribunals and Petty Sessions shall once again be established and convened, that all subjects of either Monarch shall be entitled to seek satisfaction at law in respect of all their claims and allegations.

VIII. Both parties shall enjoy all shipping concessions and rights and permission to trade freely the one with the other, as is their wont in time of peace, and as was the inviolable rule during the reign of King Carlos the Second; and all such freedoms shall apply to the trafficking in negroes as is set out in Article twelve.

IX. Each and every subject of the one Realm shall enjoy the same privileges and enfranchisements as do the subjects of the other, and do those subjects of the French Realm and all members of all other Nations whatsoever.

X. His Catholic Majesty does hereby cede all rights to the township and stronghold of Gibraltar to the Crown of Great Britain; yet with the proviso that the cession and granting of such rights shall in no way imply the granting of any territorial jurisdiction and that it shall in no wise be taken to include any rights whatever to open com-

munication with those Spanish cities and lands that do surround the
said township and stronghold; and Her Britannic Majesty does hereby
enter into an undertaking that no Jews nor any Moors shall enjoy
the right to be elected to positions of authority in the said township
and fortress nor to reside therein, and does pledge Herself to exclude
all Moorish men-o'-war from the said port and harbour. She does
furthermore hereby grant licence to all inhabitants of the said township to practise whatever Faith they do profess.

XI. His Catholic Majesty does hereby in like wise cede to the
Crown of Great Britain the island of Minorca together with the
harbour, city and fortress of Mahón, on the same terms as those
stipulated above in respect of the cession of Gibraltar, with the proviso
that, should the said Crown at any time wish to relinquish these
same rights, she shall not do so to any third Power without first offering them to the Crown of Spain.

XII. His Catholic Majesty does hereby cede to Her Britannic
Majesty and the Company* of her subjects for the period of thirty
years from the first day of May, 1713, exclusive rights to import
negroes into His colonies in the Americas, on the same conditions as
those hitherto applying to the similar rights enjoyed by the Crown
of France, and on the terms set down in the Treaty of Settlement
drawn up in Madrid on the 26th of March in this present year, 1713,
which Treaty shall be deemed to be included herein word for word,
precisely as though it had here been inserted in its entirety.†

XIII. Seeing that Her Majesty the Queen of Great Britain does
intercede on behalf of the inhabitants of Catalonia and does beseech
that they be granted pardon and the restoration of their ancient
rights and estates, His Catholic Majesty shall be pleased to grant not
only that these rights and estates be fully restored unto them but
that they shall henceforth enjoy also those privileges that do attach
to the inhabitants of the two Castilles.

XIV. His Majesty does also hearken to the entreaties of Her
Britannic Majesty and does herein admit Her request that the
Realm of Sicily be ceded to His Royal Highness Victor Amadeo,
Duke of Savoy, and Her Britannic Majesty shall undertake to use
Her every good office to ensure that, should the male line of the
House of Savoy at any time cease to enjoy proper continuance, this
Realm shall revert to the Crown of Spain; and She does hereby enter
into an obligation to guarantee that the said Realm shall never be
made over in gift to another Head of State, for whatever reason and
whatever pretext, unless that other person be His Catholic Majesty
the King of Spain or one such among His heirs and successors.

* The South Sea Company.   † This is the famous *Asiento* clause.

XV. Their Royal Majesties do hereby reiterate all Peace-Treaties and all Pacts of Confederation and all Trade Agreements compacted hitherto between Their two Crowns, and do reaffirm them, save that they be in contradiction of the Articles contained herein; and Her Britannic Majesty is pleased to recognise all rights and privileges claimed by the Basque peoples and by other subjects of the Spanish Crown to fish in the waters that do surround the Island of Newfoundland, and is pleased to ratify them.

XVI. All the provisions for requital and restitution contained in the Cease-Fire Treaty agreed on the 22nd August between His Most Christian Majesty and Her Britannic Majesty, and prorogued until the 22nd of April of this present year, shall have full and lawful effect.

XVII. Should any subject of either Monarch flout any of the stipulations contained herein, this shall not be sufficient and necessary cause for hostilities to be renewed, but rather shall any such felon be punished in accordance with established law.

XVIII. Should some stroke of fate occasion a renewal of hostilities (God forbid), there shall be a moratorium of the persecution of individuals of either Nation such that they shall be vouchsafed six months during which they may either remove or sell all the property and interests they do possess on the soil of the other.

XIX. All those Rulers named in this Treaty and all those which shall be named herein by mutual consent within six months of the date of this Treaty, shall be deemed to have concurred with all the provisions contained herein.

XX. All the Articles of the Peace-Treaty which is about to be concerted between His Catholic Majesty and the King of Portugal shall be deemed to form part of this present Treaty and Her Britannic Majesty does hereby constitute Herself guarantor of this.

XXI. All the agreements reached on that same day between His Catholic Majesty and His Royal Highness, the Duke of Savoy, shall be deemed to form part of this present Treaty and Her Britannic Majesty does hereby pledge Herself to observe all agreements so reached.

XXII. His Majesty the King of Sweden, His Highness the Duke of Tuscany and His Highness the Duke of Parma, together with their subjects and all their rights and liberties shall be admitted with due solemnity as co-signatories to this Treaty.

XXIII. The Most Serene Republic of Venice shall be deemed co-signatory to this Treaty.

XXIV. It is furthermore the avowed wish of Their Majesties that the Most Serene Republic of Genoa be deemed co-signatory to this

Treaty and that Her subjects enjoy all those trading rights which were ever theirs during the reign of Carlos the Second, King of Spain.

XXV. The City of Danzig shall be deemed co-signatory to this Treaty.

XXVI. This Treaty shall be ratified within six weeks.

... This same Peace-Treaty was confirmed by Her Majesty, the Queen of Great Britain in Kensington on the 31st day of July of this same year, and by His Catholic Majesty in Madrid on the 4th of August; peace thereby being established between Their two Crowns, to the great joy of all Their subjects.' (10th July, 1713.)

(Belando, *Historia civil de España*..., Part One, pp. 650 ff.)

16

Barcelona, abandoned by both friends and allies, stands alone against Felipe V

1713

'Having had right counsel from Military Command on the 6th of this present month, that we should persist in this our great resolve to defend the Principate not only because we should thereby guarantee that to the benevolent hand of the Emperor, Our King (may God preserve Him) should ever be entrusted the guidance of this great ship of state, and that His righteous cause, sanctioned by His Holiness and expounded to all of Europe in the First Resolution of the 1706 Cortes, should thereby wax mightily in strength, but also that we should by such an act of stalwart resolution uphold the Liberties, Privileges and Prerogatives bought by our ancestors with their glorious blood and which it is our bounden duty to maintain and defend – for they were accounted as but little by the Treaties of Utrecht and Hospitalet where all emphasis was directed to establishing peace throughout Europe (a peace which We must regard with no little suspicion, and one, moreover, which does pay but little heed to His Majesty, Our King and His righteous cause) – and, lastly, that we might forestall the grim repercussions that could well echo throughout the world in the wake of a surrender by Catalonia; we, the Council, have determined, having once rendered up our prayer that the Patron Saints intercede for us with the Almighty and we

thereby obtain Divine Protection for this our noble enterprise, to
issue a public Proclamation to the effect that the whole Nation now
prepare to defend itself; and, word having reached us that the enemy
have busied themselves distributing leaflets exhorting the people to
declare themselves for the Felipe faction (that self-same people whose
interests shall ever be uppermost in our hearts), we do request and
charge the Justices, Consellers,* Pahers* and Consuls and all the
citizens of this our Realm to honour and obey His Majesty the King
for as long as they are able... The Council is abetted in this its resolve
by the loyalty and constancy of all the people of this Realm and is
confident that they will observe and comply with all the tasks we
have allotted them in the light of the importance of these same tasks
for the common weal and the preservation of the Realm. May God
watch over...

Barcelona, 12th July, 1713. Dr José Vilar. The Members and
Deputies of the General Council of the people of Catalonia that do
reside in Barcelona.'

(Sampere y Miquel, Fin de la nación catalana, p. 154: this has
been translated from the Catalan.)

17

*And now, finally, Peace with Holland. Note the important
Trade-Agreements contained in this Treaty*

1714

'Peace-Treaty between the Spanish Crown and the Estates-General of
the Low Countries.

This Treaty boasts forty Articles, which may be summarised as
follows:

I. There shall be a binding peace between His Catholic Majesty
and the Estates-General.

II. All those acts of hostility committed by subjects of either Nation
during this present war shall now pass into the annals of history and
no more shall men remind themselves of them. All possessions and
honours lost on account of the said war shall be restored to their rightful owners.

III. All goods confiscated from the subjects of either Nation as a

* Both titles of administrators in Catalonia.

direct result of the said war shall be restored to those subjects, without such subjects being obliged to go to litigation to secure the satisfaction due them therein.

IV. All subjects of either Nation shall be entitled to demand all those goods and effects taken into custody as a direct result of the said war.

V. The subjects of His Catholic Majesty shall not accept from any Ruler at War with the Estates-General any commission involving the sale of armaments or the issuing of letters of marque and reprisal to the detriment of the said Estates-General; and the Estates-General shall be subject to the same restrictions in like matters touching upon the security and prosperity of His Catholic Majesty.

VI. There shall be strict codes of conduct regulating all matters relating to prizes taken at sea by ships of the one Nation from ships of the other, both in the oceans of Europe and in the distant colonies.

VII. All letters of marque and reprisal issued hitherto shall be hereby annulled and specific regulations shall be devised to govern their issue in the future.

VIII. The subjects of His Catholic Majesty shall not be arrested, nor their goods detained against debts owed by the Spanish Crown; nor shall the subjects of the Estates-General receive such treatment in respect of the truancies of their Government.

IX. There shall be every effort made by both signatory Parties to foster and foment good relations between His Catholic Majesty and the Estates-General.

X. The Treaty of Münster shall serve as the basis of this present Treaty, and the stipulations of the said Treaty of Münster shall be valid and binding in so far as they do not suffer direct contradiction by the Articles of this present Treaty.

XI. There shall be good relations between the subjects of His Catholic Majesty and those of the Estates-General.

XII. It shall likewise be lawful for subjects of the one Nation to possess on the soil of the other private dwelling-houses and warehouses wherein to store their merchandise without their being liable to greater imposts and duties than the subjects who have erected such dwelling-houses and such warehouses on the soil of their own nation; and neither shall the warehouses of such subjects be searched by the officials of that Nation wherein these persons do trade, save that such a search be consequent upon the said officials being in possession of tangible proof that these persons are involved in fraudulent practices or do traffick in contraband goods.

XIII. Merchant shipping of the one Nation shall enjoy free access to the ports and harbours of the other, and shall be permitted to trade therein with whomsoever they choose.

XIV. All such shall be subject only to the tariffs imposed upon the nationals that do trade therein.

XV. That no official nor any Minister may contravene the stipulations of this present Treaty by exacting heavier dues than are countenanced herein, all tariffs shall be levied only at those places where it is presently the custom for the said tariffs to be imposed.

XVI. Once any such subject shall have paid all harbour dues at the point of entry and all tariffs as set down above, he shall not be required to pay any further duty on his goods, even though he transport them from one part of the country to another.

XVII. All subjects of the Estates-General shall be treated with particular favour in the lands pertaining to the Spanish Crown, in such wise that they shall enjoy especial advantages in virtue of this Treaty; and such shall also be the reception afforded all subjects of His Catholic Majesty when they do travel to the lands under the sway of the Estates-General.

XVIII. No such merchants, no ship-owners, and no pilots, nor any that do sail in the said vessels, shall be subject to arrest and detention born of concern for national security, all proclamations and civil directions alleging debt and insolvency notwithstanding.

XIX. Should any such merchant vessel belonging to one of the Nations find herself driven by storms on the capes along the other's coasts, or compelled to put in for any cause whatever in the harbours that do there abound, she shall not be obliged, in virtue of this, to discharge cargo there, nor shall she be constrained to sell her merchandise to the local tradesmen nor to pay any extraordinary dues therein, but rather shall any such tariff be exacted only on that portion of her cargo that she does choose so to disembark or sell.

XX. Similarly, both Nations shall enjoy such privileges in the case of men-o'-war, and shall enjoy free entrance to ports and harbours and shall be permitted to remain there for as long as they shall require. Neither shall they be boarded and searched, though they shall conduct themselves discreetly and in a manner such that their presence shall not give rise to suspicion.

XXI. All men-o'-war of either Nation, and those of their allies, shall be at liberty to convey their prizes wheresoever they choose, and neither shall they be liable to pay any dues nor excise.

XXII. The Consuls set up for the succour and protection of their compatriots shall enjoy the same exemptions and immunities in the one Nation and in the other, and these exemptions and immunities shall be lasting and inviolable.

XXIII. All subjects of either Nation shall be at liberty to appoint lawyers and attorneys of their own choosing to conduct any litigation on their behalf in the courts of law of both Nations.

XXIV. The said subjects shall not be under any obligation to produce their registers and accounts for inspection, save when this is required to substantiate or disprove any accusation against them and thereby avoid taking them to law. These said registers and accounts may not, however, be impounded nor may they, on any pretext, be retained by the authorities.

XXV. The subjects of His Catholic Majesty shall all be entitled to inherit property bequeathed them by subjects of the Estates-General, whether or no such a legacy is attested by a written will; and the subjects of the Estates-General shall likewise be entitled to inherit property bequeathed them by subjects of His Catholic Majesty.

XXVI. All goods, merchandise, documents and papers belonging to subjects of the Estates-General who meet their death in the lands of His Catholic Majesty shall be forthwith declared the rightful property of those heirs that are in those lands, or of the dead man's executors; and this same rule shall be observed in the case of subjects of His Catholic Majesty who do die in lands attaching to the Realm of the Estates-General.

XXVII. It shall straightways be decreed, in the Name of His Catholic Majesty, that there shall be, in all important trading-posts, a particular place set aside for burying all those Dutchmen who do die on Spanish soil, on the pattern of that already established in Cadiz.

XXVIII. That trade between the two Nations shall henceforth flourish, His Catholic Majesty shall issue the necessary orders to ensure that all the trade regulations shall be observed in all dealings with the subjects of the Estates-General, all the time that the peaceful implementation of these regulations does not lead to any fraudulency and public outcry, and the Estates-General shall issue similar orders with respect to the trading on Their lands with subjects of His Catholic Majesty.

XXIX. His Catholic Majesty hereby undertakes to maintain as hitherto persons in authority to represent and safeguard the interests of the Dutch community within His Realms.

XXX. All those duties placed upon merchandise originating in the Low Countries as a result of this war shall cease to have effect immediately that this present Treaty shall have been signed and sealed.

XXXI. His Majesty hereby undertakes to follow the stipulations of Spanish Law and not to permit any foreign Nation to send a fleet to the Indies, nor to trade therein, save that traffick in negroes set down in the Asiento contract.

XXXII. All subjects of the one Nation presently held prisoner in the other shall forthwith be set at liberty, and no ransom shall be demanded for their release.

XXXIII. That trade and traffic between the two signatory Powers shall be best served and duly fostered, it is hereby agreed that the Naval Treaty concluded at The Hague in 1650 be here restated and reaffirmed.

XXXIV. If it has been stated in the aforegoing Articles that there shall be free trade between the two Nations, and that all subjects of the One shall be permitted to reside in the territories and cities of the Other, and that they shall all enjoy mutual shipping rights in the ports and rivers of the Other's Realm, it is hereby stipulated that this shall only have application in all those lands belonging to the two Powers on the continent of Europe.

XXXV. If any of the Articles of this present Treaty be at any time contravened by either or both of the two signatory Powers, this shall not be sufficient and necessary reason for that clause to cease to have effect, but rather shall it subsist and shall all reparations occasioned by this same breach of the Treaty be straightways accorded.

XXXVI. Should there ever be (God forbid) any rupture between the Crown of Spain and the Estates-General, there shall be a moratorium on the persecutions of the individuals of either nation such that they shall be vouchsafed a twelvemonth and a day from the date of the said rift during which time they may remove all those properties they do possess on each other's soil.

XXXVII. The Crowns of Spain and France shall ever remain sundered and never shall they be permitted to be conjoined in one Person.

XXXVIII. All rulers named by mutual consent within a certain time of the date of the Treaty, which period shall be concerted by the two signatories, shall be deemed to be co-signatories to this Treaty.

XXXIX. To ensure that all the clauses and Articles of this present Treaty shall enjoy full and lawful effect and shall become common knowledge, it is hereby agreed that this same Treaty shall be recorded by the legislative bodies in the usual fashion, published throughout the two Realms, and affixed in all the public places therein.

XL. This Treaty shall be approved and ratified within six weeks.'
20th June, 1714.

(Belando, *Historia civil de España*..., Part Four, pp. 48 ff.)

18

Fall of Barcelona

1714

'James, Duke Fitz-James of Berwick, etcetera ... Ambassador Plenipotentiary and Commander-in-Chief of the Army of the Two Crowns
in Catalonia.

Although the city of Barcelona has been exceedingly tardy in
approaching His Majesty and beseeching Him to show clemency
towards it, Field-Marshal the Duke of Berwick is of his very disposition so kindly that he is loath to have recourse to all the rigours
permitted him by the Articles of War, and has been graciously
pleased to spare the lives of all the people and inhabitants of Barcelona
and of all those who do presently there abide.

He has commanded, moreover, that the city shall not be put to the
sack, and that all the citizenry shall be permitted to continue to
reside in their own homes ... and that no proceedings shall be instituted against those who have in the past shown disloyalty to the
King.

All those regular soldiers presently abiding in the city shall remain
there at His Majesty's pleasure, as is laid down in the Articles of War.
Their lives shall be spared.

They shall all withdraw at dawn tomorrow, the 13th, to the
Ramblas and, as soon as they have done this, they shall straightways
send to the Marquis de Guerchy that he may post sentries at all the
entrances to the Ramblas in order to ensure that no soldiers attempt
to enter thither, and that he may likewise post guards on all the
Churches and Convents.

This evening, at six o'clock, Montjuich shall be surrendered. The
occupying troops shall post sentries wherever they are requested to
do so, in order to guard all the clothes and other personal effects left
therein.

Thereupon the harbour shall be handed over.

All fire-arms belonging to the regulars and to the other troops
presently in the city shall be deposited in the Palace, and General
Guerchy shall appoint an officer to guard them. They shall report on
the state of the granaries and the condition of the horses and the

cavalry and shall send instructions to the Officer Commanding to surrender the castle.

Given from our head-quarters before Barcelona, this day the 12th
of September, 1714.'

(Sampere y Miquel, *Fin de la nación catalana*, pp. 564–5.)

19
Creation of the Spanish Royal Academy

1715

'The Constitutions of the Academy were drawn up and published
on the 24th, and signed by the Marquis of Villena, in his capacity as
Director, and Don Vicencio Squarzasigo, Secretary to the new body.
They comprised five Articles, set out thus: The first explained the
reasons behind the foundation of the Academy; the second treated of
the Academicians, and the number which was envisaged, which was
twenty-four, including the Director and the Secretary; the third outlined the different duties of the officers of the Academy; the fourth
was devoted to the question of meetings; and the fifth was entirely
given over to the work which it was envisaged that the Academy
shall undertake. The principal purpose of the Academy was, and is,
to foster and to give rulings on the purity and elegance of the Spanish
language, and to expunge all errors which have crept into its lexicon,
its pronunciation, or its modes of syntax, as a result of ignorance,
affectation, carelessness, and, as it is expressed in the first Statute,
overmuch licence in matters of innovation. It was accordingly agreed
that, in order that these its rulings should be known to all, the
Academy should commit the fruit of its deliberations to paper, and
that this work should be known as the "Diccionario de la Lengua
Castellana". From this resolve have sprung six tomes in folio wherein
are set down all the words of the Spanish language in alphabetical
order, together with their true meanings, their proper usage and their
pronunciation, and also all proverbs and sayings of the Spanish
Language, together with other useful matters pertinent to it. In the
first volume is included by way of a prologue a discourse wherein is
told the history of the Spanish Language, and the curious will find in
this discourse many delights neatly garnered to save them the trouble

of poring through many and weighty works of erudition. There is in
this same volume, besides this discourse, a paper on etymologies and
another which treats of the orthography of the Spanish language.
And although more than thirty authors have written on this matter
of orthography in which carelessness and ignorance are so widespread,
it is noteworthy that the Academy has determined not to impugn nor
admit any word that has not established its orthography by virtue of
long and frequent use. Accordingly, it is most irksome that some
persons should have been driven by their curiosity and presumption
to ignore the useful application of this standard in printing, in school-
ing and in all other activity, and to invent, impugn and discourse
lengthily upon this matter of orthography, for, even though old
habits of speech and spelling may die hard, now that the Academy
has given us this standard, any deviation or departure from it is both
meddlesome and deleterious.'

(Belando, *Historia civil de España*..., Part Four, pp. 58, 59.)

20

The Sicilian Expedition

1718

'Letter to the Marquis of Villamayor:
... News will by now have reached Your Court of the destination
of our fleet and of the landing it has lately made in Sicily, taking the
city of Palermo of the 5th of this month. His Majesty the King
instructs and charges you, as soon as you receive this letter, to seek
an audience with His Majesty the King of Sicily and assure Him that
the despatch of our armies to Sicily does in no way originate in any
desire or any plan by His Majesty to break faith with Him and ignore
the Articles of the Treaty in which that island was ceded to Him, but
that it was occasioned by nothing other than the absolute conviction
and certain knowledge that plans were already afoot that did pay not
the least regard to reason, nor to the lawful rights of His Sicilian
Majesty, but were intended for the annexation of that same island
and to make a gift of it to the Archduke, that His territories might
be swelled by its acquisition, and His power, so injurious to all of
Europe, and so fatal both to the liberty of Italy and to the good of all,

might be thereby increased. His Majesty is in duty bound to resist such an extraordinary design and one so harmful to all of Europe, and to oppose the self-aggrandisement of His enemy. He is not unaware that His Sicilian Majesty was in no position to resist the Mediatising Powers who, together with the Archduke, wished to deprive Him of His Realm. All these reasons, which are both compelling and indisputable, forced His Majesty to send His armies to Sicily, and He hereby re-affirms that He entertained not the slightest intention of attacking His Sicilian Majesty.

His Majesty is confident that this expression of His motives will convince His Sicilian Majesty of the compelling reasons which forced Him to take such a decision, and He rests assured that this event will prove no obstacle to harmony and good relations between the two Thrones, and that His Sicilian Majesty will continue to embark upon enterprises that shall bring Him fame and glory. His Majesty does hereby reaffirm His resolve ever to use His every good office and the might of His arms to defend His Sicilian Majesty and to ensure His well-being, thereby strengthening the bonds of friendship, common interest and kinship which do join the two Governments and the two Nations and which shall never be severed.

May God keep Your Excellency and grant Him long life, as I do pray He shall.

San Lorenzo el Real, 25th July, 1718.

Don Miguel Fernández Durán. His Excellency the Marquis of Villamayor.'

(Belando, *Historia civil de España*..., Part Four, p. 171.)

21

The English have not declared war, but their Admiral, Byng,* attacks the Spanish fleet and takes it by surprise. The incident, narrated by an Italian of the Austrian persuasion

'August ... Admiral Byng's search for the Spanish fleet ended outside Messina harbour. The Admiral had under his command twenty-one ships of the line, every one of them well victualled and provisioned,

* i.e. the elder Byng, afterwards created Viscount Torrington.

and as soon as they hove into sight, the Spanish fleet turned tail and made for the open sea, splitting up as they did so into two squadrons, one of which headed for the east coast of Sicily. Admiral Byng, loath to let such a golden opportunity slip through his fingers, ordered seven of his vessels in pursuit of this last squadron. While yet the English had vouchsafed no indication of bellicose intent, one of the Spanish let loose a salvo at them and forthwith set at them with a will. The English took up the gauntlet and denied the Spanish the fruits of their enterprise. Admiral Byng was meantime engaged in the pursuit of the main body of the Spanish fleet, but the wind dropped, and while the English lay marooned and helpless the Spanish gained on them and made good their escape by using a number of galleys to tow their heavy ships out of danger. Admiral Byng ordered four of his speedier ships off in pursuit of the second squadron and they caught up with them near Syracuse where bitter battle was enjoined, the Spanish once again being the first to open fire. The outcome of this encounter was no more happy for the Spanish than had been that of the first. Eleven Spanish ships were taken, six sunk, and the remainder, which was as many as fifteen including the galleys, escaped to safety, some in Malta and others as far as Corfu.'

(*Diario di tutto quello successa*..., First Part, p. 52.)

22

Spanish Protest. Declaration of War

1718

Letter written to the Marquis of Monte-León in London.

'At just that time when I anticipated that your Excellency would have been in receipt of communiqués of Admiral Byng's vile action against the King's fleet, I did indeed receive a copy of your letter written on this matter to the Secretary of State, Mr Craig,* informing him that, after such an unexpected act of aggression, Your Excellency would be forced to cut short your embassy for peace, and in order that you might uphold the honour of the King's name and of his person, abstain from all forms of diplomatic intercourse. When this above-mentioned copy reached His Majesty's hands, he deemed your having written in such a vein right meet and proper, broadcasting the bad

---

* James Craggs, the younger (1686–1721).

faith of the English to the world. The premeditated action of Admiral Byng came at the time when mediation for peace was on everybody's lips – or at worst when we were all striving to find a way of guaranteeing the Italian states that are presently in the possession of the Archduke; at a time when Lord Stanhope was in Spain to make overtures to the court, and to sue for peace and for suspension of hostilities; and, moreover, at a time when our Lord the King had decreed that fresh proof of his Royal intent might be afforded by ensuring that the property of the Englishmen lately arrived in Cadiz with the last fleet to reach our shores from the Indies should remain unmolested and that all property confiscated from the English be returned to them.

In truth, no disinterested party could fail to marvel at the action of his Britannic Majesty's fleet under the command of Admiral Byng. Quite without cause or motive or pretext, and utterly careless of his King's self-appointed title of Peace-Maker and unmindful too of the interests of Great Britain, he attacked the Spanish fleet with the sole aim in view of stopping the Sicilian expedition. All this after having been in Naples conjoining this base action with Count Daun, after receiving large sums of money against the cost of his forces, and after having sent tried and trusty officials on approaching Messina to confer with the leaders of the Spanish Navy and to assure them that he would commit no act of aggression.

The greater part of Europe is impatient to discover how the British Embassy will be able to justify its action to the world after such a sudden breach of faith. If they resort to the frivolous pretext of claiming that Admiral Byng's orders were to safeguard the neutrality of Italy, then surely no one will believe them since it is common knowledge that that neutrality has long since ceased to pertain and that the heads of state who are signatories to the Treaty of Utrecht are de facto free from their obligations to safeguard it. Everyone knows that the Italian armistice is null and void, not only because of the scandalous contraventions of it by the Austrians in their ill-conceived retreat from Catalonia and Majorca and in other subsequent trespasses against it, but also because the letter of that Treaty does nothing more than oblige all the signatories to make peace with each other and with France.

Each and every individual can come to his own conclusions about the validity of these principles. And what will the world say on seeing that, four years after this neutrality had ceased to have effect for the reasons laid out above, the London ministry has chosen to breathe new life into it and act to uphold it, not any longer through friendly negotiation and mediation but with naked force and vile machiavellianism so as to take advantage of our trust and good faith? And all this is so beyond all manner of doubt that Admiral Byng has found himself caught up by remorse for his unwarrantable conduct. So much so, that in his account of this naval action, he recognises that he has no reasonable motive nor pretext for coming to grips with the Spanish and takes refuge in the falsehood that the Spanish King's ships were the first to draw up in battle formation and the first to open fire. What is even more astounding is that he should claim that he ordered his ships not to fire on the Spanish. If he had had no intention of attacking them, if he had wished to treat with them as friends, why should he pursue them from the straits of Faro to Syracuse? Why should he send with all despatch four of the swiftest ships in his fleet with orders to catch up with the Spanish? And why finally did he himself light his poop-lamps and follow them with the remainder of his fleet if not with the aim of keeping the Spanish navy in sight throughout the night? Did he undertake such an outlandish manoeuvre with the simple idea, in such a delicate and critical pass, of greeting our King's navy, especially since he had taken on board a large number of German troops from Rioxoles in Calabria?

The King our Lord considers that the English King, who is a wise, prudent and moderate ruler and is not blind to the fact that successes in war are but fleeting, must surely know that human happiness is subject to many and several acts of fortune and that God always protects the Just. Our King cannot be convinced that so base an action can have been carried out on His Orders, above all since to be so readily unmindful of true friendship is not compatible with a King's sense of indebtedness, and Our Lord the King has afforded Him so many proofs of friendship, even in the most troubled periods for His own Realm and even during the recent disturbances in England.

His Majesty could never be persuaded that such an unjust action, and one of which the whole world has shown its disapproval, could have been thought up by the British Nation which has always been a true friend to her allies and grateful to Spain for the many favours she has received of the generosity of His Catholic Majesty. His Majesty has every reason to believe that this event is the brainchild of some troubled and disquiet spirit, a sworn enemy of peace, of the honour of his King, of the interests and peace of mind of the British Nation, and of the common good, and that this person wishes to build his own fortune on the ruins of Europe and at the terrible price of world-wide holocaust.

For all the reasons stated above, His Majesty, who sees how ill is His generosity requited, and mindful of the hurt done to His honour by such an unforeseen offence, and persuaded that your embassy in this court can no longer be of any moment nor your person command any respect, has instructed me to inform Your Excellency that you are hereby granted leave to return to England and that it is his wish you do so. May God keep Your Excellency etc.'

(Belando, *Historia civil de España*..., Part Four, pp. 171–81.)

23
The British Declaration of War on Spain

1718

'...We find ourselves pledged by various treaties to maintain the neutrality of Italy and to defend the kingdoms, provinces and rights in Europe which are the possessions of Our good brother the Emperor of Germany. Ours is a burning desire to establish the peace and security of Christendom on the most just and lasting basis open to us. From time to time We have informed the King of Spain, through His Ministers, of Our thoughts and Our peaceful intentions and We had hoped that they would find His approval.

The King of Spain unjustly and aggressively invaded the island and Kingdom of Sicily, yet Our representations to him on this matter remained friendly. Notwithstanding this, We found ourselves obliged to reinforce and strengthen Our arguments with an armed fleet, and therefore last summer We sent our fleet into the Mediterranean, with the frank and sincere intention of only using the weight of its presence to keep up the peace negotiations and to reconcile the warring parties. In this way We had hoped to prevent any unfortunate developments in the situation.

The same desire to show Our most sincere object of maintaining peace led Us to send to Madrid Our most faithful and well-loved cousin and counsellor James, Earl Stanhope, one of Our principal Secretaries of State, with plenary power to offer all our sincere good offices to re-establish peace in Europe and to foment friendship with the King of Spain. However, in spite of the efforts We authorised him to make on Our behalf, and in spite of all the demonstrations of true friendship which We afforded on that occasion, Our ambassador-plenipotentiary returned without any glimmer of hope that the Spanish Court would entertain any peaceful notions. Similarly our

Admiral in the Mediterranean could find neither any inclination for peace nor any way of achieving it, and he was therefore instructed to stand by the states of the Emperor, and to protect them with force if necessary, for these were quite clearly imperilled by the invasion of Sicily and the large flotilla kept in that area by the King of Spain.

In spite of Our every effort, We found that the King of Spain would not listen to our entreaties for peace and agreement, and had not only thrown Our subjects resident in His territory into chains and confiscated their property, thus contravening the spirit and the letter of the solemn pacts existing between Our two countries, but had also ordered His own subjects to attack Ours and destroy their ships, their goods and their chattels whenever and wherever they came across them. Such despicable and unwarranted acts have forced Us to defend Our Kingdom and Our beloved subjects, exposed to the dangers of aggression and unable to defend themselves, and, against Our natural inclination, to bring all that has been perpetrated against Us and Our subjects from the very early days of Our reign out into the open once again, since it all runs contrary to the spirit of friendship and cannot be in Our eyes justified and is moreover inconsistent with the best interests of Our subjects.

The list of their complaints would be endless if We were to detail them all: broken treaties, well established and long standing privileges abrogated, the normal channels of trade tampered with in the most outrageous fashion. Our Ambassadors in Spain have from time to time petitioned the Court and made representations concerning these events, but in spite of the many and frequent complaints which they have entered on their behalf of late, they have scarce had even the most minor effect on the legislation emanating from that body, and in this way all the benefits which We had hoped to fashion for Our subjects by means of treaties and conventions have been rendered nugatory.

Besides all this, and, We judge, as a direct result of the pernicious influence of the counsels of the Prime Minister,† He has relegated the true interests of Spain to second place and His subjects have not only been dishonoured but tyrannised. The King of Spain, under the cover of His claim that He wishes to balance out the power of the Emperor and ensure the freedom of the Italian rulers, has raised a large army, put a number of men-o'-war at ready, and made quite extraordinary preparations for war both on land and sea; and all this He has undertaken in order to further His dangerous design of violating the Treaties of Utrecht and Baden,* which are the corner-stones of European peace, and of uniting, in one monarch, the crowns of France and

---

* Generally known as the Treaty of Rastatt (1714).   † Alberoni.

Spain. To prevent such an eventuality, much blood and much money has been expended. Every means which God has put at the disposal of the neighbouring sovereigns, who are all desirous of avoiding such an occurrence, must be used, for the benefit of present and future generations whose security should ever be our prime concern.

We shall leave untold the hostility which he has inspired in the Pretender to Our throne and his supporters, and the attempts made to subvert other monarchs from their allegiance to Our cause by means of threats of a kind most unseemly in a Christian prince. We would have erased all this from memory, this and many other outrages, had We but found in the court of Spain the slightest hint of a true and reasonable friendship. Since these proceedings only led in the end to an open declaration of hostilities, and not even the intervention of our good brother His Most Christian Majesty, nor any other means could obtain for Us, Our allies and Our subjects, any acceptable agreement or any satisfaction, We could no longer stand idly by, for Our honour had been impeached, our friends and allies unjustly invaded, Our subjects attacked and their property raped, their trade interrupted, and every conceivable hurt inflicted upon them, and duty provides but one course of action through which We can express Our great displeasure: the taking up of arms both in Our own defence, and to obtain justice for Ourselves, Our allies and Our subjects, who have been subjected to violent attack from the Spanish King.

We put Our trust in Almighty God, who well knows Our good and peaceful intentions, which have ever motivated Us, and, for all the reasons set out above, We have deemed it incumbent upon Us to declare war on the King of Spain. This We hereby do, and declare Our intention of waging this war with all diligence, together with Our allies and in the security of Our knowledge that Our beloved subjects will rally to Our standard in a cause in which the honour of Our crown, the faithful observance of solemn treaties and pledges, and the safeguarding of Our subjects' rights and interests, are at stake.

With this document, we enjoin the Commander-in-Chief of all Our forces, those of Our officers to whom the duties of Admirals of the Fleet shall fall, the Governors of Our various colonies and cities and strongholds, and all the officers and men who serve under them both on land and at sea, to commit themselves fully in battle and to oppose every undertaking of the Spanish King, His vassals and His subjects. And we forbid all our subjects from, and warn all men of all nations against, transporting men, munitions or any contraband material to any state, country or colony of the afore-mentioned King of Spain. Any person caught doing so will be condemned out of hand.

And we herein declare that it is Our intention to safeguard all the many subjects of the King of Spain who are in Our Kingdoms and their property if they act honourably towards Us, in spite of the ill-treatment that many of Our subjects have received in the Kingdom of Spain. Given in Our Court of St James, 27th December 1718, in the fifth year of Our reign.'

(Belando, *Historia civil de España*..., Part Four, pp. 191–3.)

24

The Coalition becomes threatening. Felipe V decides to dispense with his policies of aggression and with their prime advocate, Alberoni

1720

'We hereby Decree that

...Being ever disposed to obtain the benefits of international peace for Our subjects, and striving to this end to realise honourable and advantageous Treaties which shall be of lasting validity; and wishing, with this aim in view, to remove all obstacles which might cause the slightest delay to the realisation of an objective upon which the common weal depends to such a great extent, We have for this and other reasons of equal moment deemed it appropriate to remove Cardinal Alberoni from the control of the affairs of state which he has held hitherto, and at the same time to order him, as We herein do, by Our Royal Command, to absent himself from Madrid within eight days and from the Realm within three weeks, and to forbid him ever again to meddle in any affairs of state whatsoever, or to appear at Court or in any other place where We, our Queen or any other Prince of Our Household might be present.'

(Belando, *Historia civil de España*..., Part Four, p. 244.)

25

Articles of the Quadripartite Treaty of Alliance, pertaining to Spain

1720*

'... First: That to avoid disturbances, and to safeguard the Treaty drawn up in Baden† on the 7th of September of 1714, and the neutrality of Italy, in compliance with the agreement of the 14th March, 1713, His Catholic Majesty shall abdicate the Throne of Sardinia and renounce all His rights to the said Throne.

II. That, in order to ensure that the balance of power in Europe be maintained, the Crown of France and Spain shall never be united, as is agreed in the Act of Abdication of November 9th, 1712, and included in the Treaty of Utrecht, signed on April 11th, 1713; and that, to ensure greater security, the Emperor shall formally renounce, in His own name and in that of His successors, male and female, all claims to the Spanish Throne and to that of the Indies, and to all the States of which King Felipe was recognised as legitimate Sovereign in the Treaty of Utrecht, and that He does pledge Himself to make His Act of Abdication in the most solemn manner possible.

III. That, in conformity with this Act of Renunciation, the Emperor shall recognise King Felipe, and, likewise, His successors, male and female, as legitimate Sovereigns, granting each and every one of them the title befitting his or her station.

IV. That, in consequence of this, His Catholic Majesty shall renounce, in favour of the Emperor and His descendants, male and female; in His own Name, and in that of His successors, all rights and claims to the Low Countries and to the States He once possessed in Italy, including the Marquisate of Finale, sold to the Genoese in 1713, and shall likewise renounce the rights which He has hitherto claimed in the Realm of Sicily.

V. That it is established that, as the successors to the Duke of Parma and the Grand Duke of Tuscany could unleash a holocaust upon Italy, in the eventuality of there being no legitimate heir to the Throne, especially with the Spanish Queen claiming to be called to the Throne by Her birth, and the Emperor simultaneously insisting

* Although the main Treaty had been made in 1718.   † Ratstatt-in-Baden.

that in the absence of a male heir, the Empire be deemed arbiter of the succession, it is herewith established that, in the eventuality of this line producing no male issue, the son of the Queen be elevated to the Throne, and that, in default of the firstborn, the second and the others that follow, both male and female, in the order of those born in lawful wedlock, and that the Emperor shall be under an obligation to furnish conditional letters against future investiture. Likewise, that the Port of Leghorn shall be maintained as a free port as hitherto, and that, in default of a Grand Duke of Tuscany, His Catholic Majesty shall cede to the successor to the Throne the port of Longon on the island of Elba; it also being set down that no Ruler already sitting on the Throne of Spain shall be permitted to possess the said States, and that, to safeguard this more effectively, a body of Swiss troops shall be admitted to guard the following towns: Leghorn, Portoferrajo, Parma and Piacenza, and that these troops shall be in the pay of the Signatories to this League and shall undertake on solemn oath never to hand over the said towns to any person save the son of Her Majesty, the Queen of Spain.

VI. That, similarly, His Catholic Majesty shall, in the interests of peace, renounce all the rights reserved in his agreement with the Duke of Savoy made on the 11th June, 1713 and this document shall be annulled and the rights of Restoration to the Throne of Sardinia transferred, as agreed by the Emperor in the second article of the Convention with the Duke of Savoy.

VII. That the Emperor and His Catholic Majesty shall likewise pledge themselves to maintain and defend the agreements contained in this Treaty.

VIII. That the whole Treaty shall be implemented within two months of its having been drawn up and received ratification – which shall take place in London – and that they shall select a rendez-vous and appoint certain persons to treat for peace and that they shall restore to all individuals all property and privileges which these individuals enjoyed before the outbreak of the war.'

(Belando, *Historia civil de España...*, Part Four, pp. 253–5.)

26

The Two Great Rivals of The War of Succession mutually abdicate – The frontiers of Europe are established

1720

'Act of Abdication made in Vienna of the claims to the Spanish throne ... We, Charles the Sixth, by the grace of Divine Mercy, Emperor elect of the Romans &c. make it known now and for all posterity...

After the untimely death of His Most Serene Majesty, Prince Carlos the Second, King of Spain and of the Indies, on whose memory the sun shall never set, there ensued a bitter and prolonged war of succession which has for so long and so cruelly ravaged almost all of Europe, notwithstanding that the agreements signed at Utrecht and at Baden were sufficient and competent to settle the various differences, and thereby forestall a fresh outbreak of hostilities in Italy. God, of His goodness, was pleased to grant that, having entered into friendly discussions and given the predicament mature consideration, certain articles of non-aggression and alliance were reached this year 1718 between Ourselves and His Most Serene Majesty, Louis XV, King of France, under the guidance of His Most Serene Majesty, Prince Felipe, Duke of Orléans, who was at that time Prince Regent of that Realm, and His Most Serene Majesty Prince George, King of Great Britain, Duke of Brunswick and Lüneberg, Elector of the Holy Roman Empire. We had the sole aim in view that there should be a more widespread peace, that it should be stabilised among those Rulers who already enjoyed it and that it should be established and blossom forth once again among those who were still at war; all this in such a way that, their quarrels settled, all Europe might enjoy this great boon of peace.

There is no surer way to realise such a beneficial state of affairs than through these same treaties which are conceived according to the precepts and patterns of previous agreements and it is made irrevocable law (and the salvation of all Europe depends upon this) that the Crowns of Spain and France be decreed separate in perpetuity and the Crown of Spain and the Indies separate in perpetuity from that of the other European states which We now hold and are to retain under the Treaty. Given a balance of power and a equable apportion-ment of forces among the European rulers, it shall be decreed that the union in one person and in one lineage of the Crowns of many several states shall be decreed unlawful and We shall guarantee stipulations advantageous both to Ourselves and equally to the Rulers who are signatories to this non-aggression alliance and also to those who choose to agree to it under the widest interpretation of the said articles of this Convention.

The abdication which We are to make of any claim to the King-doms of Spain and the Indies forms a part of this Treaty, both because Our natural inclination to peace and Our concern for the common weal are much more powerful motives than any others and also because We wish to avoid any pretext for pernicious suspicions, and We shall therefore give up Our rights to the said Kingdoms of Spain and the Indies and have ordered Our ambassadors pleni-potentiary to sign the said Treaty in London. Similarly, moved to pity, (and lest we fall short of the wishes of the allied Rulers) by the deplorable state of Europe and by the desolation which threatened so many peoples and nations, and moved by the advantages con-tained in the said Treaty, We determined at last to make this concession and abdication of the Thrones of Spain and of the Indies chiefly in order that the abdication of His Most Serene Majesty, Prince Felipe V, King of Spain and of the Indies, of the Kingdom and Crown of France, proclaimed both in His Own Name and in that of his descendants on the 5th November 1712, in favour of His Most Serene Majesty the Duke of Orléans – which abdication was accepted as law in Spain and is a condition of Our own abdication – might also come into full force and effect, and also that through this Our abdication, those abdications made by His Most Serene Majesty the Duke of Berry in Marly on the 24th November 1712, and by the said Duke of Orléans in Paris on the 19th of the same month and year, and which were confirmed by the Treaties of Utrecht on the 11th April 1713, might be once again ratified and that the stipulation that it should at no time be lawful for the Crowns of France and Spain to be united in one person or in one lineage, should be established as a hard and fast rule for all time.

Moved therefore, by these matters of such great moment, and lest We delay for one hour more the peace of the whole of Europe, which We so greatly desire, and which We judge compassable by these two abdications, and having pondered deeply and given the matter mature consideration, We concede and abdicate for these reasons both in Our Own Name and in that of Our heirs and successors, male and female, all lawful rights, suits and claims which are made in Our Name to the Kingdoms of Spain and to the Indies, and to the Dominions of the Spanish Crown which under the Treaties of Utrecht and under this present agreement have been ratified as belonging to the aforementioned King of Spain and the Indies, and likewise, in complete possession of Our faculties, We, spontaneously and of Our own free will renounce, and abdicate, in virtue of the present Treaty, all Our rights in favour of His Most Serene Highness the said Prince Felipe, King of Spain and of the Indies, of His heirs, descendants and successors, be they male or female. If these are wanting, for whatever conceivable reason, We abdicate Our rights in favour of the House of Savoy, in accordance with the purport of the aforementioned Treaty, and in the order of accession laid down therein, viz, His Most Serene Majesty, the present King of Sardinia, Duke of Savoy, Prince of Piedmont, Victor Amadeo, His sons and male descendants begotten in lawful wedlock, and in default of male descendants in this line also, Prince Manuel of Savoy, His sons and male descendants begotten in lawful wedlock, and in default of heirs to this line, Prince Eugenio of Savoy, His sons and male descendants begotten in lawful wedlock with Princess Catalina, daughter of King Felipe the Second. In this We renounce in Our Own Name and in that of Our heirs and successors, all lawful rights which make Us claimants or in any conceivable manner endorse a claim on Our part to the said Kingdoms, be these rights of blood, or be they rights arising from past agreements and the laws of the Kingdom. We confirm and endorse Our abdication as King of Spain and of the Indies, which We have determined upon in the hope that it be recognised as de facto common law and Royal decree. We command that it be observed by all Our subjects of all Our Kingdoms and colonies, notwithstanding any laws, sanctions, treaties and practices which decree otherwise, and We do hereby expressly declare them null and void, and make good any de facto and de jure defects there might be in either the letter of the law or its execution, renouncing all benefits envisaged by the laws and in particular that of Restoration, all eventualities and even a gross breach of contract notwithstanding; and having pondered all this of Our own free will and in complete possession of Our faculties We do abdicate Our throne and make known Our will that all these caveat be null and void and repealed by Us, and We hereby give Our pledge that We shall in no wise oppose the peaceful and uninterrupted enjoyment of the aforesaid Kingdom by the said Ruler, the present King of Spain and the Indies, His descendants and successors, and that, consequent upon this Abdication, We shall

at no time cause them any disquiet, either by force of arms or by
any other means. Rather We do declare that henceforth any war
that We or Our successors undertake against them with the intention of recovering and taking possession of the said Kingdoms shall
be unlawful and, moreover, that any war that be waged against Us
in self-defence by His Most Serene Majesty, the King of Spain, or
His heirs, or by any person called to the thrones of the said Kingdoms in default of the aforesaid, shall be just and lawful; and that,
if any eventuality should have been overlooked in the letter of this
Our Deed of Abdication, it is Our will that it be supplied from the
provisions laid down in the said Treaty of London, which Act,
lately agreed upon, is and shall be in all matters the only body of
laws pertinent to this Our Act of Abdication. And We do hereby
give our pledge as King and Archduke that We and all Our heirs
and successors shall hold the letter of this Act of Concession, Abdication and Renunciation sacred and inviolate, and that We shall
endeavour to ensure that Our subjects do likewise. In this indomitable
and resolute faith, We have put Our name to this Our present Act
of Concession, Abdication and Renunciation and guaranteed it
with sacred oath sworn on the Holy Gospel in the presence of the
undersigned witnesses, from the which oath We shall never seek
release, and should any other person seek it in Our name, or should
it be offered Us without Our having sought it, We shall not admit
of it nor shall We turn it to Our advantage. We do hereby give
this Our present instrument of Abdication, duly signed with Our
name, and sealed with the Imperial Royal and Archducal seal, into
the safekeeping of His Most Serene Majesty, the King of Spain,
at the time and in the manner stipulated in the present Treaty.
Given at Vienna on the Sixteenth day of September in the year of
Our Lord, seventeen hundred and eighteen, in the seventh year of
Our reign as Roman Emperor, the sixteenth as King of Spain, and
the eighth as King of Hungary and Bohemia. Charles.'

'Abdication of His Catholic Majesty.
    ... We Felipe, by the Grace of God, King of Castille, etc. After
the untimely death of His Serene Majesty, Carlos the Second, King
of Spain and of the Indies, on whose memory the sun shall never
set, there ensued a bitter and prolonged war of succession which
has so cruelly ravaged almost all of Europe, notwithstanding that
the agreements signed at Utrecht and at Baden were sufficient and
competent to settle the various differences and thereby forestall a
fresh outbreak of hostilities in Italy. God, of His goodness, was
pleased to grant that, having entered into friendly discussions and

given the predicament mature consideration, certain articles of non-aggression and alliance were reached in London on the 2nd August in the year 1718 between His Most Serene Majesty, Louis XV, King of France, under the guidance of His Most Serene Majesty Prince Felipe, Duke of Orléans, who was at that time Prince Regent of that Realm, and His Most Serene Majesty Prince George, King of Great Britain, Duke of Brunswick and Lüneberg, Elector of the Holy Roman Empire. We have the sole aim in view that there should be a more widespread peace, that it should be stabilised among those Rulers who already enjoy it, and that it might be established and blossom forth once again among those who are still at war; all this in such a way that, their quarrels settled, all Europe might enjoy this great boon of peace. There is no surer way to realise such a beneficial state of affairs than through these same treaties which are conceived according to the precepts and patterns of previous agreements, and it is made irrevocable law (and the salvation of all Europe depends upon this), that the Crowns of France and Spain shall be decreed separate in perpetuity, and that, given a balance of power and an equable apportionment of forces among the European Rulers, the union in one person and in one lineage of the Crowns of many several states be decreed unlawful, and We shall guarantee stipulations advantageous both to Ourselves and equally to the Rulers who are signatories to this non-aggression alliance, and also to those who choose to agree to it under the widest interpretation of the said articles of this said Convention.

And as it is an integral part of these treaties that We abdicate and renounce Our claims to those kingdoms, countries and colonies which now form part of His Imperial Majesty's possessions in Italy and in Flanders, or which could be ascribed to Him as a result of the present Treaty, and of all the rights, kingdoms and colonies in Italy which in other times were part of the Spanish Crown, We, a born student of the arts of peace and of the common weal, – and this is the strongest of all those impulses which motivate Us – have determined, wishing also to avoid any pretext for pernicious suspicion, to give up Our rights to the said kingdoms, countries and colonies and to put Our signature to the said Treaty in Madrid on the 16th of January last, instructing our ambassador plenipotentiary at The Hague to sign it, which he duly did on the 17th of January last. Similarly, moved to pity (and lest we fall short of the wishes of the allied Rulers) by the deplorable state of Europe and by the desolation which threatened so many peoples and nations, and moved by the advantages contained in the said Treaty, We determined at last to make this concession and abdication of the kingdoms, countries and provinces and of Our rights to them, chiefly in order that, through the abdication of the Emperor from the thrones of Spain and of the Indies, Our Own abdication from the kingdom and Crown of France made on 15th November 1712, in Our Own name and in that of our descendants, in favour of His Most Serene Highness the Duke of Orléans – which abdication has become law in Spain and is a condition of the abdication of His Imperial Majesty – might come into full force and effect; and also, that through this Our abdication, those abdications made by His Most Serene Majesty the Duke of Berry in Marly on the 24th November 1712, and that of the said Duke of Orléans in Paris on the 19th of the same month and year, and which were confirmed by the Treaties of Utrecht on the 11th of April 1713, might once again be ratified, and that the stipulation that it should at no time be lawful for the Crowns of France and Spain to be united in one person or in one lineage, should be established as a hard and fast rule for all time.

Moved, therefore, by these matters of such moment, and lest We delay for one hour more the peace of the whole of Europe which We so greatly desire and which We judge compassable by these two abdications, and having pondered deeply and given the matter mature consideration, We concede and abdicate for these reasons, both in Our Own Name and in that of Our heirs and successors, male and female, all lawful rights, suits and claims which are made in Our Name to the said kingdoms, countries and colonies, both in Italy and Flanders, which, in virtue of the said Treaty, are presently in the possession of His Imperial Majesty – among which territories are to be held expressly included not only the Marquisate of Finale, ceded by His Imperial Majesty to the Genoese Republic in the year 1713, but also the realms of Sicily and of Sardinia according to the letter of the Treaty; it should also be understood that the Isle and Realm of Sicily shall be the possession of His Imperial Majesty, His heirs, successors and descendants in perpetuity, and that the right of reversion to the Crown of Spain be henceforth annulled; and that the Isle and Realm of Sardinia shall be returned and handed back by His Imperial Majesty, after he has taken possession of it, into the possession of the King of Sardinia, the Duke of Savoy, and that the right of reversion of that realm to the Crown of Spain be maintained against the eventuality of the line and issue of the said King of Sardinia being in default. And We do, in like fashion, and in full and complete possession of Our faculties, spontaneously and of Our Own free will, renounce and abdicate, in virtue of the present Treaty, all Our rights to the said realms, countries and colonies which previously formed part of the Spanish Crown and are now in the lawful and meet possession of His Imperial Majesty, in favour of His Imperial Majesty, His heirs, successors and descendants. We do make this Our abdication in Our Own Name and in that of Our heirs and successors, renouncing all lawful rights which make Us a claimant or in any conceivable way endorse a claim on Our part to the said Kingdoms, be these the rights of blood or be they rights arising from past agreements and laws of the kingdom.

We confirm and endorse Our abdication as King of the isles, countries and provinces of Italy and Flanders. We have determined upon this in the hope that it be recognised as de facto common law and Royal decree, and, as such, We command that it be observed by all Our subjects in all Our kingdoms and colonies, and especially by those State Councils which are commonly known as Parliament, notwithstanding any laws, sanctions, treaties and practices which decree otherwise, and We do hereby expressly declare them null and void, and make good any de facto and de jure defects there might be in either the letter of the law or its execution, renouncing all benefits envisaged under the law, and in particular that of Restoration, all conceivable eventualities and even a gross breach of contract notwithstanding; and having pondered all this of Our Own free will and in complete possession of Our faculties, We do abdicate and make known Our will that these caveat be null and void and repealed by Us, and We hereby give Our pledge that we shall allow His Imperial Majesty and His descendants, heirs and successors, be they male or female, to enjoy the peaceful and unopposed possession of the Kingdoms, Principates, countries and colonies which formerly belonged to the Crown of Spain and which are now in the safe-keeping of His Imperial Majesty, and of those territories which We have ceded to Him or are to cede to Him under the Treaty, and that, consequent upon this Abdication, We shall at no time cause them any disquiet, either by force of arms or by any other means. Rather We do declare that henceforth any war that We or Our successors undertake against them, with the intention of recovering and taking possession of the said Kingdoms, shall be unlawful, and, moreover, that any war that may be waged against us in self-defence by the Emperor or His descendants shall be just and lawful, and that if any eventuality should have been overlooked in the letter of this Our Act of Abdication, it is Our will that it be supplied from the provisions laid down in the said Treaty agreed upon in London, which is and shall be in all matters the only body of laws pertinent to this Our Act of Abdication, and We hereby give Our Royal pledge that We and all Our descendants

and successors shall hold the letter of this Act of Abdication sacred
and inviolate, and that We shall endeavour to ensure that Our
subjects do likewise. In this indomitable and resolute faith, We
order this Act of Concession and Abdication to be despatched, and
We have guaranteed it with sacred oath, sworn on the Holy Gospel
in the presence of the undersigned witnesses, from the which oath
We shall never seek release, and, should any other person seek it in
Our name, or should it be offered Us without Our having sought
it, We shall not admit of it nor shall We turn it to Our advantage.
We sign the present Act of Abdication in Our Own hand and
append to it Our Royal seal before the group of gentlemen listed
below, who were summoned by Royal Command to witness this
ceremony of signing and sealing: Don Carlos of Bourbon and
Centellas, Patriarch of the Indies and Our Chaplain and Chief
Almoner, Don Restaino Cantelmo, Duke of Populi, Knight of the
illustrious Order of the Golden Fleece and of the Saint-Esprit, Com-
mander-in-Chief of Our Armed Forces and Captain of the Italian
Bodyguard; Don Álvaro Bazán y Venavides, Marquis of Santa Cruz,
Gentleman of the Royal Bed-Chamber and Chief Steward to the
Queen; Don Alfonso Manrique, Duke of Arco, also Gentleman of
the Royal Bed-Chamber and Master of the Royal Hunt; Don Víctor
Amadeo Ferrero y Fiesco, Prince of Maserano, Knight of the illustrious Order of the Golden Fleece, Gentleman of Our Royal Bed-
Chamber and Lieutenant-General of Our Armed Forces. This Act
of Abdication is to be exchanged with another similar Act of
Abdication signed by His Imperial Majesty. Dated the 22nd of June
1720 in the Royal Monastery of San Lorenzo. Felipe.'

(Belando, *Historia civil de España*..., Part Four, pp. 256–61.)

27

Treaty of alliance agreed between Spain, France and Great Britain

1721

'This treaty was made up of seven articles which, in short,
stipulated:

I. That there should be a permanent union between the signatory Powers, in accordance with the stipulations of the Treaty of London of 2nd August, 1718.

II. That to preserve the union, the defence pact was agreed upon with the mutual guarantee of the States of each Sovereign; all three determining to attack whomsoever might contravene the treaties of Utrecht, Baden and London, as well as the one which was to be drawn up at Cambray.

III. That, as a consequence of Article II, the aim of this alliance was to smooth out the differences between the Court of Madrid and Vienna, and to place the international peace on a firmer footing.

IV. That if any one of the signatory Powers were attacked in direct contravention of the articles of the aforementioned treaties, His Britannic Majesty would come to their defence with 12,000 men – 8,000 foot and 4,000 horse – and that both His Catholic Majesty and His Most Christian Majesty would each supply the same number both of horse and of foot.

V. That in virtue of above stipulations, the three Sovereigns, parties to this alliance, would defend the rights, estates, and rank of the Duke of Parma.

VI. That for the greater satisfaction of both the other monarchs, His Most Catholic Majesty would afford that people of both nations could enjoy the same benefits and advantages as those enjoyed by Spanish nationals in trading.

VII. That this treaty would be ratified within six weeks.'

    (13th June)

(Belando, *Historia civil de España*..., Part Four, pp. 284, 285.)

28

An 'Auto de fe' in Spain in the eighteenth century

1724

'. . . THOSE HANDED OVER TO THE SECULAR ARM FOR PUNISHMENT IN EFFIGY.

1. Francisco Jerónimo López de la Cruz, native of the city of Sigüenza, resident in Madrid, married, physician by profession, being the most senior on the staff of the General Hospital, 64 years of age, died in the prisons of the Holy Office. He was condemned

to appear at the "Auto" in the form of an effigy, representing his person, wearing a "sanbenito"* and a crown of flames, and his bones were exhumed and turned over to the secular authorities together with his effigy, for his being a heretic and Judaiser. He was found guilty despite his pleas of innocence.

2. Beatriz de León y Contreras, native and inhabitant of Madrid, widow, 58 years of age, died in prison. She was condemned to appear at the "Auto" in the form of an effigy, representing her person, wearing a "sanbenito" and a crown of flames, and her bones were exhumed and turned over to the secular authorities together with her effigy, for her being a heretic and Judaiser. She was found guilty despite her pleas of innocence.

3. María Blanca Rodríguez, (alias) Blanca Nuñez, (alias) Correa, native of the town of Monforte in the Kingdom of Galicia, inhabitant of Madrid, by profession a schoolmistress, widow, 58 years of age, died in prison. She was condemned to appear at the "Auto" in the form of an effigy, representing her person, wearing a "sanbenito" and a crown of flames, and her bones were exhumed and turned over to the secular authorities together with her effigy, for her being a heretic and Judaiser. She was found guilty despite her pleas of innocence.

4. Jerónima Alvarado, native of the city of Seville, inhabitant of Madrid, twice widowed, of no fixed profession, 50 years of age, died in prison. She was condemned to appear at the "Auto" in the form of an effigy, representing her person, wearing a "sanbenito" and a crown of flames, and her bones were exhumed and turned over to the secular authorities together with her effigy, for her being a heretic and Judaiser. She was found guilty despite her pleas of innocence.

5. Francisco de Lara, deceased, formerly an inhabitant of Madrid, married, formerly cashier in the Tobaccos Department of the Royal Customs and Excise. He was condemned to appear at the "Auto" in the form of an effigy, representing his person, wearing a "sanbenito" and a crown of flames, and his bones were exhumed and turned over to the secular authorities together with his effigy, for his being a heretic and Judaiser. He was found guilty despite his pleas of innocence.

6. María Moliner, deceased, formerly an inhabitant of Madrid, married. She was condemned to appear at the "Auto" in the form of an effigy, representing her person, wearing a "sanbenito" and a crown of flames, and her bones were exhumed and turned over to the secular authorities together with her effigy, for her being a heretic

* A long white apron ranging from the shoulders and falling front and back.

and Judaiser. She was found guilty despite her pleas of innocence.

THOSE HANDED OVER IN PERSON.

7. Juan López, native of the city of Braganza in the Kingdom of Portugal, inhabitant of Madrid, widower, by occupation a silk-weaver and tobacconist, 80 years of age, at one time "reconciled" as a Judaiser by the Inquisition of Coimbra in the said Kingdom in the year 1667. He was now condemned to appear at the "Auto" wearing a "sanbenito" and a crown of flames for being a Judaising heretic and a relapsed penitent. He was handed over in person to the secular arm and, as he was penitent, he was garrotted before his body was committed to the flames.

8. Ana Nuñez Márquez, native and inhabitant of Madrid, by profession a schoolmistress, spinster, 55 years of age. She was condemned to appear at the "Auto" wearing a "sanbenito" and a crown of flames for being a Judaising heretic. She was found guilty despite her pleas of innocence. She was handed over in person to the secular arm and, as she was persuaded of her error on her way to the stake, she was garrotted before her body was committed to the flames.

9. Manuel Custodio de Soto y Herrera, (alias) Manuel de Guzmán Castro y Herrera, native of the city of Granada, stepson of Francisco de Robles and inhabitant of Madrid, bachelor of no fixed profession, 19 years of age. He was condemned to appear at the "Auto" wearing a "sanbenito" and a crown of flames, as a Judaising heretic. He was found guilty, despite his pleas of innocence. He was unrepentant and obdurately persisted in his errors and his blasphemous heresy. As he persevered in this vein, and was unheedful of the voice of duty and obedience, he was tied to a stake and committed to the flames while he was yet living.

10. Josefa de Vargas y Machuca, (alias) la Josefina, native and inhabitant of Madrid, married, 39 years of age, appeared at the "Auto" as a penitent, wearing a "sanbenito" with a cross painted on it and carrying a wax candle. She was reconciled by a formal abjuration for having been a Judaising heretic, and was sentenced to have her goods confiscated, to wear the garb of the penitent and to be committed to prison for one year.

11. Bartolomé Casado, native of the city of Valladolid, inhabitant of Madrid, by trade a cobbler, 54 years of age. He appeared at the "Auto" as a penitent wearing a "sanbenito" with a cross painted on it, carrying a wax candle and with a rope twice knotted round his neck. He was reconciled by a formal abjuration for having been a Judaising heretic, and was sentenced to have his goods confiscated,

to wear the garb of the penitent and to be committed to prison for life, with no chance of remission. The day after the "Auto" took place he was given 200 lashes through the usual public thoroughfares of the city, for being dilatory, consistently heretical and a backslider.

12. Juan Pacheco, native of the city of Cuenca, resident there, staying temporarily in Madrid, bachelor, of no fixed profession, 40 years of age. He appeared at the "Auto" as a penitent wearing a "sanbenito" with a cross painted on it, carrying a wax candle and with a rope twice knotted round his neck. He was formally reconciled and sentenced to have his goods confiscated, to wear the garb of the penitent and to be committed to prison for life, with no chance of remission. The day after the "Auto" took place he was given 200 lashes through the usual public thoroughfares of the city, having confessed to being dilatory in the Faith.

13. Francisco de Robles, (alias) Ramos, native of the city of Jaén, inhabitant of Madrid, widower, by trade a tailor, 36 years of age, stepfather of No. 9. He appeared at the "Auto" as a penitent wearing a "sanbenito" with a cross painted on it, carrying a wax candle and with a rope twice knotted round his neck. He was reconciled with a formal abjuration for having been a Judaising heretic, and was sentenced to have his goods confiscated, to wear the garb of the penitent and to be committed to prison for life, with no chance of remission. The day after the "Auto" took place he was given 200 lashes through the usual public thoroughfares of the city, having confessed to being dilatory in the Faith and a backslider. He was also sentenced to serve His Majesty in the galleys for the space of eight years at the oar without pay. He was ordered to be returned when the eight years were up to serve out his penance in prison.

14. Luisa Rodríguez, native of the town of Caracena in the Diocese of Sigüenza, inhabitant of Madrid, spinster, by occupation a servant-girl, 18 years of age. She appeared at the "Auto" wearing a "sanbenito" with a cross painted on it and carrying a wax candle in her hand, a twice-knotted rope around her neck. She was reconciled with a formal abjuration for having been a Judaising heretic and was sentenced to have her goods confiscated, to wear the garb of the penitent and to be committed to prison for life, but the lashes to which she had been sentenced were not administered on account of her sickliness ...

THOSE UPON WHOM PENITENCE WAS IMPOSED WITH ABJURATION OF JUDAISM.

21. Francisca Avendano, (alias) the Gypsy, native of the town

of Aranda de Duero, inhabitant of Madrid, spinster, by occupation a clothes-seller, 54 years of age. She appeared at the "Auto" as a penitent, wearing the insignia of a liar, a crown, carrying a wax candle and with a twice-knotted rope around her neck. She was convicted of being a liar, a sorceress and a heretic. She made a formal abjuration of her Judaism and was absolved "ad cautelam", and severely chastised and admonished. She was banished from Madrid and from the town of Aranda de Duero, and from an area 20 leagues around, for the space of 10 years, the first three of which were to be spent in the Royal Prison "la Galera" in Madrid, under the charge of a learned person who was to instruct her in the mysteries of our Holy Catholic Faith and to dissuade her from her superstitious deceits. The day after the "Auto" took place she was given 200 lashes through the usual public thoroughfares of the city.'

(*Relación del auto particular de fe ...*)

29

Felipe V abdicates in favour of his son, Luis

1724

'Decree of Abdication.

... Having pondered deeply these past four years and meditated long and thoughtfully on the miseries of this life, through all the illnesses, wars and tribulations which God has seen fit to visit upon Us during the twenty-three years of Our Reign, and not unmindful that Our eldest son, Don Luis, sworn heir to this Our Throne, is now come of age, married and endowed with judgement and talent enough to rule and govern this Kingdom wisely and with justice, We are resolved to renounce the cares of government and the running of the Realm and to Abdicate all Our Estates, Kingdoms and Domains in favour of the aforementioned Don Luis, our firstborn Son, and to go into retreat along with Our Queen, whom We have found well-disposed to this Our resolve and eager to come with Us into the sanctuary of this Our Palace of San Ildefonso, to serve God, and, with all these burdens of State taken from Our shoulders, to meditate on death and to care for Our bodily well-being. We hereby inform Our Council of this Our resolve that they may publish it in all those places they deem fit and that it may thereby come to the

notice of all Our subjects. Given in Our Palace of San Ildefonso
on the tenth day of January, 1724.'

(Belando, *Historia civil de España*..., Part Four, pp. 320–1.)

30

Luis I dies. The theologians give their considered judgement on whether Felipe V may return to the Throne

1724

'Sire: As Your Majesty has been pleased, through the note passed
to us by the Marquis of Grimaldi, to command this Assembly to
pronounce upon whether, in its judgement, Your Majesty's having
made a Deed of Abdication renouncing the Throne and stating
Your intention of never again ascending to it, nor taking up the
reins of government at any time, does constitute a moral impediment to Your wearing the Crown without any qualms of conscience,
and whether Your Majesty is under any obligation to honour Your
covenant, thereby paying no heed whatever to the demands of the
common weal, to the best interests of the Realm, to the fact that
the Peace-Treaties are as yet unconcluded and Their Majesties the
Princes still under age, as well to other considerations too many
and too obvious to mention, and has referred to the Council for
consideration of the Deed written in Your Own Hand in which
You abdicated in favour of the King, our Sovereign – may He be in
Heaven – this assembly, ever obedient to Your Royal commands
as it is meet and right it should be, does hereby declare, its heart
filled with respect and with humility, that: Having given this grave
problem and its momentous attendant circumstances profound and
searching consideration, this Assembly is of the opinion that, the
Deed of Abdication of both Crown and Government and the pledges
contained therein never again to assume these mantles of power
notwithstanding, Your Majesty is in duty bound, on pain of mortal
sin, to take up the reins of government or the Regency of the
Realm. The Assembly does not hold Your Majesty is subject to a
binding duty of this nature in respect of the Throne, for, whereas
the whole Nation will be placed in jeopardy if Your Majesty does
not return either to the task of government or to the role of Regent,

such grave risks are [not?] necessarily entailed in a refusal by Your Majesty to wear the Crown.

The right which this Assembly has to tell Your Majesty that the Deed of Abdication is not binding under these circumstances is that same right of which it availed itself when it informed Your Majesty of Your duty to govern the Kingdom or to assume the Regency, as, in the light of this latter duty, the substance of the Deed becomes untenable in law, and, this being so, not only theologians but also the precepts of right reason dictate that the vow in that Deed is not binding.'

(Belando, *Historia civil de España* ..., Part Four, pp. 363, 364.)

31

Felipe V announces the death of Luis I and His own return to the Throne

1724

'To Their Excellencies, the Venerable Rector, Director of Studies, and staff of the University of Salamanca.

We, the King:

To the Rector, Director of Studies and staff of the University of Salamanca. Your Excellencies: Between the hours of two and three on the morning of Thursday, the thirty-first day of August, God was pleased to release Our dearest and most beloved Son, King Luis, from this present life and welcome Him to the better one that lies hereafter, and, although His last moments were indeed most worthy of the life He led on earth, and in them He revealed once again His holy and pious zeal, receiving the Last Rites and Extreme Unction with the utmost devotion and humility, His death doth grieve Us mightily, as you will readily appreciate, and His departing is a loss both to Ourselves and to this Realm (the government of which, as you will understand, is a burden We now find Ourselves obliged to assume once again). It is Our wish to inform you of all this so that you, as good and loyal subjects, might help Us to express our grief by causing the public funeral-rites and obsequies to be performed which are traditional to such calamities, and We charge you to follow the letter of Our Royal Decree, and the legislation consequent upon that Decree, in the matter of mourning. In San Ildefonso on the 17th day of September, 1724. – We, the King. – By command of Our Lord, the King, Don Francisco de Castejón.'

(*Llantos, pompa funeral y exequias* ...)

32, 33, 34
Treaty of Vienna

(i)

1725

'Peace Treaty concluded between His Catholic Majesty, Felipe V, and Charles VI, Emperor of the Germanies.

... The Treaty comprises nineteen Articles, the substance of which is as follows:

I. The peace between the two Sovereigns and Their successors shall be all-embracing, Christian and permanent.

II. The Treaty of London, concluded on the 2nd of August shall be the basis of this peace, together with the Treaties of Baden,* drawn up on the 7th of September, 1714, and of Utrecht of the 14th of March, 1713, and which dealt with the neutrality of Italy; also His Catholic Majesty shall cede the Kingdom of Sicily to the Emperor and renounce all His own rights and claims thereunto, as, indeed, He has done in 1713.

III. In order to prevent the Crowns of France and Spain from ever being conjoined in a single Ruler, the rights inherent in the unbroken line of succession shall be formally renounced as was stipulated in the solemn Abdication of such rights contained in the Treaty of Utrecht.

IV. As a result of the aforesaid Abdications, the Emperor shall, in order to maintain the peace of Europe and the Balance of power therein, renounce in His own name and in that of His successors, all rights and claims to the Throne of Spain, and shall recognise Felipe the Fifth as lawful King of Spain and of the Indies, and shall never oppose His tenure of these Realms, either directly or indirectly.

V. His Catholic Majesty shall recognise the Archduke of Austria as Emperor of Germany and shall make over to Him the Low

* Rastatt.

Countries and those States of Italy which are now in His possession, including the Marquisate of Finale which has been sold to the Genoese, and renounce all rights thereunto.

VI. In consideration of this Peace Treaty, the Emperor shall once again recognise and ratify the stipulations of the Treaty of London with respect to the States of Tuscany, Parma and Piacenza, and, when Prince Don Carlos comes of age, He shall assume full possession of them in virtue of the Contingency Agreement, and neither His Catholic Majesty nor His successors shall be entitled to possess any one of these States nor be guardians to the Sovereigns that rule therein.

VII. His Catholic Majesty shall, in His own name and in that of His line, renounce the right of Reversion attaching heretofore to the Kingdom of Sicily, and this shall be transferred to the Kingdom of Sardinia as has been agreed.

VIII. Both Sovereigns shall undertake to guarantee to execute and defend this Treaty.

IX. The events of the war shall now pass into the annals of history, and there shall be a general amnesty for all persons involved therein, irrespective of rank and social status, both for clergy and for lay people, and all their goods, privileges and offices shall be restored to them and they shall be permitted to exercise these un-molested as they did before the war.

X. To avoid any possible founts of discord, the Emperor Charles VI and His Catholic Majesty, Felipe V, shall both continue to enjoy all titles to which They do at present lay claim, but Their successors shall enjoy only those titles deriving from States which actually do form part of their possessions.

XI. The Duke of Parma shall be confirmed and guaranteed in possession of His Duchy, as agreed in the Quadripartite Alliance.

XII. The Emperor offers to aid and defend the Spanish Royal line, and this He shall do by means of the Pragmatic Sanction, thereby binding all His heirs and all Estates of the House of Austria to observe this stipulation.

XIII. The towns and villages which do constitute the dowries of Their Most Serene Majesties, the Infants María Ana and Margarita Teresa, and which were mortgaged together with the income in rents deriving therefrom, shall be restored to Them.

XIV. In likewise as the Emperor has honoured the debts incurred by His Ministers in Catalonia, so similarly shall His Catholic Majesty honour debts so incurred in Milan, in Sicily and in Naples.

XV. There having arisen some disputes concerning the Palaces of Rome and The Hague, it is hereby agreed that the latter shall be the property of the Emperor and the former that of His Catholic Majesty, who shall give half the lands attaching thereunto as indemnity against its value.

XVI. All agreements made at a later date by common consent of the two interested Parties shall be included in the present Treaty.

XVII. The Treaty shall receive ratification within two months.

XVIII. Since the aforesaid cessions and abdications do form the core of this Treaty, the Acts of Abdication shall be inserted herein. The Abdications are here written out in full.

XIX. In order that this Treaty become Law, it shall be signed and sealed. This was duly done in Vienna on the 30th day of April, 1725.'

(Belando, *Historia civil de España*..., Part Four, pp. 282-3.)

(ii)
'Mutual Defence Pact, agreed between His Catholic Majesty and the Emperor of the Germanies.

... This second Treaty comprised six articles which may be summarised as follows:

I. There shall exist an unqualified state of sincere friendship between the two Sovereigns, Each undertaking to look to the Other's well-being, and Each undertaking to help repair any injury done the Other.

II. Since the King of Great Britain has given His word that the fortresses of Gibraltar and Mahón, together with a number of other ports, shall be restored to Spain, His Imperial Majesty, being an Ally, shall make it His business to see that this promise is fulfilled.

III. In order to afford even greater proof of this sincere friendship They both profess towards Each Other, His Imperial Majesty's shipping shall enjoy complete exemption from harbour dues throughout Spanish Dominions, as do now those ships of both the French and the English fleets.

IV. Should any ship of either One of the signatory Sovereigns be at any time attacked, the Other shall make common cause with the offended Party in seeking satisfaction.

V. In order to cement this union, it is hereby agreed that, whenever the hereditary States of His Imperial Majesty are attacked, either through individual acts of hostility or in a full-scale war, either on land or by sea, His Catholic Majesty shall send maritime assistance in the sum of fifteen ships of the line and shall contribute to the land forces by despatching twenty thousand men, fifteen thousand foot and five thousand horse, the expenses incurred in providing winter quarters for these troops being met by the

Emperor; and, similarly, whenever any of the colonies or European kingdoms of His Catholic Majesty are invaded, the Emperor will come to His assistance with all the means at His disposal and, in particular, thirty thousand men, twenty thousand of them foot and the remaining ten thousand horse, and the expenses incurred in providing winter quarters for these troops shall be met by His Catholic Majesty.

VI. This Treaty shall be ratified within three months.'

(iii)
'Peace Treaty between Spain and the Empire.
... The final Treaty contained five Articles which may be summarised as follows:

I. There shall exist a state of absolute peace and true friendship between, on the one hand, the Emperor His successors, all the Holy Roman Empire and each and every one of its Electors, Rulers, States and Orders, and, on the other, His Catholic Majesty & His successors, in such wise that no member whatever of either party shall be entitled to undertake any enterprise that is prejudicial to the interests of the other party, but rather shall each and every one endeavour to act in a way that redounds to the honour, advantage and benefit of the other, all other treaties which contain stipulations to the contrary notwithstanding.

II. Both parties shall forget for good all acts of enmity occasioned by the war, that this same boon shall be enjoyed by all parties and all subjects covered by the Treaty of Neutrality concluded at The Hague in 1703, and confirmed in Article XXX of the Peace Treaty of Baden.

III. Consequent upon this Treaty, trade shall be re-established between the subjects of both signatory Powers, as was the situation before the war.

IV. His Imperial Majesty, in His Own Name and in that of the Holy Roman Empire, agrees that, should the Duke of Tuscany or the Duke of Parma and Piacenza die without male issue, (in accordance with the provisions laid down in the Treaty of London in the year 1718, and agreed to by all the signatory parties, and in accord with feudal privileges within the Empire which spring from ancient laws and rights) the sons of Her Majesty the Princess of Parma and Her male heirs begotten in lawful wedlock shall inherit the aforementioned Duchies and States, as is set down in the Contingency Agreement, with the proviso that Leghorn shall remain a free port as it is at present. And likewise His Catholic Majesty shall in His turn cede Porto Longone on the island of Elba, and neither He nor any of His successors to the Crown of Spain shall ever become guardian to a Prince inheriting the said Duchies, nor shall such a Spanish Ruler retain any territory whatsoever in Italy, and, in compliance with Article V of the Treaty of London, no troops shall be ordered into the said Duchy and, should any of the aforementioned Dukes die without issue, Prince Carlos shall succeed to them, as laid down in the Contingency Agreement.

V. All agreements arrived at within six months of the ratification of this Treaty shall become part of this Treaty.'

(Belando, *Historia civil de España*..., Part Four, pp. 382–9.)

35

Preparations for the expedition to Oran

1732

'Declaration of His Catholic Majesty, King Felipe the Fifth.

... Our Royal will being such that We are determined not to allow any part of the Dominions which Divine Providence placed in Our safe-keeping when She exalted Us to the Throne of this Kingdom, and which the vast host of Our enemies later snatched with violent and cunning duplicity from out of Our hands, to remain cut off from union with the Church and with our Catholic Faith, We have meditated unceasingly on the possibility of gathering them back into the fold, but the endless problems facing Us have hitherto frustrated Our desire, and We have not as yet been free to turn the considerable forces which the Almighty has entrusted to Us to this momentous task: but now, although not entirely free from other cares, We are resolved not to delay for even one day more the recovery of the important fortress of Oran, which has often been a test of Our mettle and of the Christian piety of the Spanish Nation. We recognise that this town, in the hands of barbaric Africans, represents an insuperable impediment to the dissemination of Our Holy Faith and a source of strength to an Enemy who would fain enslave those who reside on the Spanish coasts across from Her shores, and We are apprehensive, and not without due reason, lest the position of this port afford a Nation, skilled in both maritime and land-warfare, formidable and even fatal advantages over the neighbouring provinces in Our Kingdom, should these be ever lulled into a sense of false security or should they ever find themselves ill-provided with military strength, with the which they are, at present, with God's help, so handsomely furnished. For the realisation of this important goal, We have ordered an army as many as thirty thousand strong, and comprising both foot and horse, to muster at Alicante where, supplied with the stores, artillery, munitions and equipment necessary to any such arduous undertaking, they shall be placed under the command of the Head of Our Armed Forces, the Count of Montemar, and other Commanders and gentlemen of quality, who have been appointed by Us and whose experience and courage will, We are confident, ensure that the enterprise will be crowned with glory and success. This force has been mustered in Alicante so that, once embarked in the considerable flotilla of vessels which have been made ready and which will be escorted by squadrons of ships of the line, galleys and galliots, all of which We have directed to be made ready for this purpose, they shall proceed forthwith to the recapture of Oran. And, as no human enterprise, however skilfully planned, can be assured of success without the aid of the Almighty, We hereby decree that public prayers be delivered up throughout Our Realms for the success of this vital expedition, which decree We do hereby promulgate in order that it may enjoy your obedience in similar wise to previous such declarations of Our wishes, and We live therefore in the certainty that your loyalty, love and devotion to Both Our Majesties shall incite you to proceed in this with all the zeal and fervour which are right and proper in a matter which so closely touches on the Faith. Seville, 6th June, 1732.'

(Belando, *Historia civil de España*..., Part Four, p. 540.)

36

The Capture of Oran and Mers-El-Kebir

1732

'His Majesty, doing honour to His title of Catholic King, did determine to recapture the important town of Oran together with its forts – that of Mers-El-Kebir, with its commanding position overlooking the Surjidero, and those of Santa Cruz, San Gregorio, San Felipe, San Andrés, Rosalcázar and Alcazava (which had all been held by the Moors ever since the third of April, 1708). With His troops stationed in defence of His states against any invasion of the Iberian peninsula, He entrusted an expeditionary force, thirty-two battalions strong, to His Excellency, the Count of Montemar, Commander-in-Chief of the Spanish Forces ... The army embarked in Alicante Bay on the fifteenth day of June of this present year, 1732, the whole force consisting of a considerable number of transport ships escorted by ten of His Majesty's men-o'-war, two armed frigates, two packets, seven galleys, and a number of light vessels from Ibiza, Valencia, and Mallorca, these last under the command of Rear-Admiral Don Miguel Regio, and the entire fleet under that of Rear-Admiral Don Francisco Cornejo who gave orders, at daybreak on the sixteenth, that the signal to weigh anchor be fired, whereupon the whole fleet set sail. Unable to make great progress on account of the continued calms and because the Mezzogiorno* and Levechet had blown up, he was obliged to put in twice at the Cape of Palos, the first time for three days and the second for a day and a night, but, the winds veering eventually to the north-east, he was able to proceed to within sight of the Barbary coast, east of Oran, and, with the wind dropping once again, he lay there a day and a half, until the east wind blew up and he was able to drop anchor at four o'clock in the afternoon of the twenty-eighth in the Gulf of Aguadas, which was the pre-arranged point for the landing. The Commander of the man-o'-war, San Felipe (with the aforesaid Commander-in-Chief, the Count of Montemar on board), veered to port, as soon as the Gulf of Oran hove into sight, and proceeded to spy out the lie of the land, conning the city and some of its fortresses and as far along the coast as the said Gulf de las Aguadas on Falcon Cape where he dropped anchor on the twenty-ninth of June, 1732.

The Count of Montemar, moved by an urge to expedite the commencement of army manoeuvres, having consulted with Rear-Admiral Cornejo, ordered the Commander to fire three signals on the cannon and to hoist a blue flag at the top of the mainmast as a signal that all transport ships should launch their long-boats and landing-craft, and one hour later he ran down the blue flag and hoisted a white one atop the foremast, letting off four rounds on the cannon: the signal for the first wave of Infantry to embark in the said long-boats and landing-craft. They took off to receive orders from the Commander-in-Chief, the Count of Montemar, from

* Mezzogiorno: a south wind.   † Leveche: an east wind.

the poop of the Command ship, where they were instructed to betake themselves at dead of night to the warship, "Castilla", on board which was Rear-Admiral the Marquis of Villadarias to whom it fell to lead the first landing-party. Under his command were Rear-Admirals the Count of Marsillac y Zueveghen and the Marquis of Santa Cruz, Field-Marshals Don Alejandro de la Motte, the Count of Marceda, the Marquis de la Mina and Brigadiers Brother Don Manuel de Sada, Don Luis Porter and Don Melchor Abarca, and he instructed them to hold themselves at the ready until first light on the 29th of June. At daybreak they took themselves off with more than six thousand infantry on board. They went astern of the Command ship to hear any last minute orders from the Count of Montemar, who instructed the Marquis of Villadarias to strike out for land forthwith and effect disembarkation as he had been previously commanded. These instructions he carried out, his own launch and those of the other Commanders in the van. They came to within a rifle shot of the shore where along a mile's length, the galleys and galliots were drawn up in battle formation. Making for the gaps between the larger vessels with the utmost discipline and in complete silence and painting a variegated and harmonious picture as they did so, they pursued their course to the shore. The first to leap out on to dry land was the Marquis de Villadarias followed by the other Commanders mentioned above and, in their turn, the soldiers. This they all effected without scarce getting wet. As the soldiers disembarked they fell into formation six deep on the sands, about a rifle shot from a small mountain. In the absence of any resistance by the Moors, the Marquis of Villadarias gave orders that the pickets (following previous instructions as to formation and to the importance of silence) should make their way uphill as soon as they disembarked and head for the Campo de las Aguadas where the Commanders and Brigade-Commanders ordered that, as the men came up, they should form into a continuous line with their backs to the sea and facing the mountain known as Carraza.

When the first disembarkation had been effected, the long-boats and landing-craft hurried back to the ships to take on a second wave of infantry, which was landed with the same ordered discipline as the first, the Count of Montemar leaping ashore with the other Generals, and, as had been arranged beforehand, certain picked sailors from each vessel disembarked the portable defences against cavalry,* the equipment for tunnelling, and the shovels, spades, picks and mattocks, and, carrying them up to where the troops

---

* 'Caballos de frisa': A large piece of wood with sharp pieces of metal – large nails, etc., used as a defence against cavalry-charges.

were drawn up in line formation, they were passed to the front of each regiment. The Commander-in-Chief also took steps to ensure that the single-decked vessels came in close to the shore and, once the gangplanks were fixed in position, the horses were taken off and, as soon as they were on dry land, fitted out and taken up to join the forces already in position. This the first two squadrons of the centre duly performed. It was now that some of the infidel horse appeared on Mount Carraza, with scarlet banners and drawn up (as is their wont) in squads, with a somewhat greater number of them over on the left. Doubtless this was because, once he had wind of the landing, their leader Hazen Buziraga (whose name means "Moustaches" in Arabic and so is generally known by that name) ordered men to come from Oran. As soon as they opened fire, the Count of Montemar issued an order that from each brigade a certain number of grenadiers be chosen, and that these, in their turn relieved the Jetares company of musketeers – a force of eighty stout men and true – should stay behind and and return the Moorish fire, thus preventing heavy casualties. It must have been about six in the evening this same day, the twenty-ninth of June, and all the foot and horse had been landed, when the Commander-in-Chief assigned two squadrons of horse from our right flank under the command of the Marquis de la Mina with four more squadrons under Brigadier-General Don Bernadino Maricón in support, to attack the infidels who had once again come down on to the plain to our left, but as soon as the Moors observed this precautionary manoeuvre on our part, they kept to the mountain, offering us no chance to attack.

... The Commander-in-Chief, spurred on by his desire to get a campaign that could drag on for many months over and done with in one single day, instructed his Major-General and his Adjutant to cross the line and give word to the Commander to set off in full battle formation and occupy the front of Mount Carraza, and, as soon as they had taken the summit, to wheel to the left and march in line-ahead formation, outflanking the enemy army, which was being hard pressed by the aforementioned Field-Marshal de la Motte into the said gully of the Old Hinterland and forced back up to the top of the Santo Mountain which runs right along until it overlooks Mers-el-Kebir.

No account can do justice to the discipline and morale which prevailed among the soldiers as they occupied the mountain and fought their way through thicket and scrub at an altitude, to whose cruelty the deaths of some of their number who could no longer breathe in that rarefied air, bears terrible witness.

This manoeuvre greatly contributed to our good fortune on this day, because, although the Moors retreated back up the valley, some of their number turned to face us as soon as they got to the top of Mount Santo; yet, seeing the rest of our army threading their way up the mountain to cut off their left, they once more turned tail and fled in great haste up the route known as Marcos Ortiz to another even higher mountain where it would be difficult for them to be followed, and nigh impossible for them to be attacked. Thereupon the Commander ordered the troops of the left to halt, and this afforded them an opportunity to take some refreshment. As soon as they had done so, they resumed their march until they came to the open ground known as the Galápagos where they waited for the remainder of the army to join them. The Commander-in-Chief instructed the Brigadiers Brother Don Manuel de Sada and the Marquis of Valdecañas to return to the old Campo de las Aguadas with the Irish Brigades and a detachment of horse, to guard the prisoners of war, and the guns and the medical supplies which had been landed. Field-Marshal de la Motte continued his march with the Grenadiers to cut communications to Oran through the Mers-El-Kebir hinterland, and the musketeers took the highest mountain in the area.

This same night the Commander-in-Chief despatched the cavalry-commander, Don Diego Yupulo, to convey to His Majesty the happy tidings...

...This night, there sounded throughout the camp a false alarm. No one knew who had raised it, and, since it was pitch-black, the soldiers were in a state of confusion and, spoiling for a fight, they fired a few rounds at random and there was no way of avoiding some casualties.

At about midday, there came from Oran a person of Greek nationality asking for the Commander-in-Chief. Field-Marshal de la Motte ordered a sergeant of the Flemish guard to bring him in, and, when he arrived in the presence of the Commander, (who they assured him was in overall charge of our forces) making signs that his business was of the utmost urgency, he took off his beret and took from it a letter which he handed over. His Excellency read the letter and straightways gave orders that the army should prepare for a march, and in the space of a quarter of one hour the General-Call-to-Arms, the signal for Parade and the order to set off were all given. The Commander-in-Chief set off with the army, as they came within sight of Oran, the French Consul (for it was he who had sent the letter) came out of the city and reaffirmed that the usurper Hazen Buziraga had, at midnight on the thirtieth, abandoned the city and its forts, taking all the Christian captives with him in chains, and that ninety-seven of his Turkish soldiers, who were garrisoning the fort at Mers-El-Kebir, had left after him, sacking the houses of many Moors as they went. He also confirmed that Hazen Buziraga had taken his troops to a place three days' ride off to the south.

In the said town of Oran were found three wretched old men and two old women who had been unable to make good their escape. The Commander-in-Chief straightways ordered the grenadier company to occupy the fortresses, and the Spanish troops the city gates, with strict instructions to allow nobody to enter the city. It was, none the less, impossible to prevent some soldiers seizing what booty they could find. High on the list of supplies they found were wheat, barley, oil, fat, honey and wool.

Before the Commander-in-Chief set off for Oran, he despatched the Royal Adjutant, the Count of Valdehermoso, with the Consul's letter to the King so that He might not tarry in hearing this piece of good news.

... First and second of July.

In the afternoon the same Commanding Officers were still in the city, and orders were given and arrangements made by His Honour the Count of Montemar for the most effective defence of the city and its forts.

The galleys stood off and dropped anchor in the Gulf of Oran.

... Second to third of July.

Commanding Officers Sueveghem, de Gage, Aramburu, Avellaneda Nazario.

Before midday, the ninety-seven Turks who were in Mers-El-Kebir put out a signal that they wished to parley about their surrender, and Field-Marshal Don Alejandro de la Motte despatched Monsieur Despeaux, a lieutenant in the Flemish grenadiers, to treat with the Turkish leader through an interpreter, a grenadier in the Flor regiment from Hainault. He took the precaution of sending four companies of grenadiers with this officer so that these might forthwith take possession of the outer fortifications, and, when the Turks pleaded for their liberty and for a safe conduct to Algeria, this was granted them by the said Field-Marshal. As soon as the Commander-in-Chief, the Count of Montemar, was informed of the capitulation of this fortress at Mers-El-Kebir, he moved his quarters there and sent a despatch to His Majesty through the Marquis de le Mina to the effect that the city and its forts had surrendered.

Log of the events in the campaign of His Majesty's army and

fleet (may God grant Him protection) – from sixteenth June of this present year 1732.'

(Belando, *Historia civil de España....*, Part Four, p. 540.)

37

Treaty of El Escorial, between Spain and France, sometimes known as the First Family Pact. 7 November

1733

'Article 1. There shall be between Their Majesties, Their heirs and successors, realms, domains, and subjects, in whatever part of the globe, union, friendship and universal alliance in perpetuity, and, in consequence of this, each and every one shall bring all his efforts to bear to contribute sincerely and effectively in all matters pertinent to the honour, glory, interests and safeguarding of the other...

Article 2. In virtue of the present Treaty, the said Monarchs do constitute Themselves as mutual guarantors of each other's realms, estates and dominions, both within and without Europe, as also of all the rights They each possess or may possess at any time in the future, and, should either of the said Monarchs be attacked, molested or insulted by any power whatever, and under any pretext whatever, the other does promise and bind Himself to obtain for His ally prompt and due satisfaction, be it through His good offices or be it by means of all His forces, even should this necessitate the declaration of war on the aggressor; and in this last eventuality, He does hereby promise not to lay down His arms nor to enter into any negotiation which is not commonly agreed to, and does not redound to the mutual satisfaction of the two Kings.

Article 3. His Most Christian Majesty does constitute Himself guarantor of the rights of Prince Carlos to the estates of Parma and Piacenza and to the Tuscan succession, in accordance with Article Five of the Quadripartite Treaty of Alliance, and promises to do His utmost to ensure its preservation and to afford whatever help prove necessary.

Article 4. If, in the defence of these rights, the question of hostilities with England should arise, His Most Christian Majesty shall make common cause with His Catholic Majesty.

Article 5. In the eventuality of the rights of the Spanish Queen, born Duchess of Parma, not having proper and sufficiently wide-spread effect, His Most Catholic Majesty does pledge Himself to uphold them.

Article 6. His Most Christian Majesty shall be active in bringing His every good office to bear to persuade the King of Great Britain to restore, at the earliest possible time, Gibraltar and its dependencies to His Catholic Majesty, and He shall not desist from this demand until His Catholic Majesty shall have received complete satisfaction on this point, be this by surrender of the said place to His arms, or be it by other means which He shall be persuaded will prove effective in obtaining this concession within a definite and predetermined period, promising also to use force to ensure its successful outcome should this prove necessary.

... Article 8. Recognising that the guarantees of the Austrian Pragmatic made without Their consent, are prejudicial to the House of Bourbon, and also that the election which is happening at this moment or is just about to happen as Emperor-Designate of a Duke of Lorraine* given in marriage to the eldest daughter of the Arch-duchesses, who are daughters of the Emperor, runs contrary to the security of the House of Bourbon and the Peace of all Europe, Their Majesties have determined to join forces and oppose this with every means open to them, declaring Their intention to go to war in order to put a stop to the designs ... of the Emperor, and that They shall continue to wage that war until such time as they shall have guaranteed the security of all the lands of Prince Carlos.

... Article 11. ... Their Majesties do declare that, having embarked upon a war against any power whatsoever, They shall not lay down Their arms unless it be by mutual consent and after having achieved the aims laid down in Article Three, and having obtained for Their respective royal families the greatest advantages possible, for these are to be the chief object of any peace settlement.

... Article 14. The present Treaty shall remain a closely guarded secret for as long as the signatories to it deem it to be in their interests, and shall be henceforth viewed as an irrevocable family pact, valid in perpetuity, and which shall be an everlasting safeguard of the closest friendship between His Catholic Majesty and His Most Christian Majesty.'

(Ferrater, Esteban de, *Código de Derecho internacional* ... , vol. i, pp. 154 ff.)

---

* This refers to the marriage of Francis of Lorraine to Maria Theresa, daughter and heiress of Charles VI.

38

Spain joins forces with France in the War of Polish Succession. Their object: Italy. Their fear: that Great Britain might enter the arena

1733

'London, 20th November, 1733.

On the 17th day of this month, our government was in receipt of a despatch from Mr Keene, His Majesty's Ambassador in Madrid, in which it was reported that His Catholic Majesty had resolved to join forces with France to wage war on the Emperor. That same day there came another by special messenger for the Count of Montijo, Spanish Ambassador at this Court, and, two days since, this Minister sought an audience with the King and laid before Him a detailed exposition of the factors which have lead His Sovereign to take up arms against the Emperor, at the same time expressing ... heart-felt gratitude for the pains and troubles His (Britannic) Majesty has taken in settling the differences with the Viennese Court with respect to the claims of His Majesty Prince Carlos,* sympathising with Him that the arrogance of that court should have proved an insuperable obstacle to their success, and assuring His Majesty that nothing is closer to the heart of his Master, the Catholic King, than that good understanding with His Majesty and all the British Nation should continue undiminished.'

(*Gaceta de Madrid,* 15 December 1733.)

---

* Carlos, son of Felipe V by his second marriage with Isabel Farnese.

39

The Kings' dream is realised, which demonstrates that their abilities are greater than is generally supposed: Carlos of Bourbon becomes King of Sicily and of Naples

1734

'On the 27th day of April there came with the mail-coach the Count of Val Hermoso, despatched by Prince Carlos to His Majesty, our King, and armed with the most welcome tidings that the Neapolitan Parliament had taken an oath of allegiance to His Royal Highness, and had presented Him with the keys to the city, giving expression to the love, loyalty and devotion they felt for His Royal Highness, Who in return received them with the utmost kindness and was pleased to confirm all their legal rights.'

(*Gaceta de Madrid*, 4 May 1734.)

40

The British attack on the Caribbean port of Cartagena

1741

'While the circumstances surrounding the tragic events resulting from the actions of the British army and fleet in the Caribbean port of Cartagena are so notorious that no disinterested judge could entertain any doubts about them, it is incumbent upon us to recount them in the words of Don Sebastián de Eslava, Viceroy of Santa Fe, writing on the 21st of May, and in those of his Adjutant-General, Don Pedro de Mur, who has come to Spain, bringing with him news of such vital consequence, for the accounts which are popularly held are distorted and defective. That they are so, is due not less to the meddlesome corruption of some wretched Gazeteers, than to the deliberate cunning with which the English Court, fearful of what

the British people might do in the heat of the moment, has contrived
to keep them in the dark as to the true facts of the case. We therefore thought it right and proper that the whole world be shown how
the King, who has comported Himself, ever since He opened
hostilities, in a most equable and a most justifiable manner, does not
now seek to turn truth on its head, but rather set down an unem-
broidered account of the facts so that it may be seen just how far
the Almighty has succoured His valiant army and abetted His rightful cause by the defeat and rout of His enemies...

... Against this town then, Admiral Vernon put out to sea from
Jamaica with the largest and most fearful fleet ever seen on those
seas, comprising eight three-deckers, 28 ships of the line, 12 frigates
and packets of from 20 to 50 cannon, two gun-boats, some fire-ships
and 130 transport vessels carrying more than 9,000 men as a landing party and 2,000 negroes with machetes to do the heavy work.

Against such a great army, the city could muster only the long
years of experience of the Viceroy of Santa Fe, Don Sebastián de
Eslava, 1,100 men from the battalions from Spain, from Aragón,
from Cartagena, and individual soldiers from pickets, 300 militia,
two companies of Negroes and freed Mulattoes, and 600 mountain-
Indians as labourers. And to defend the harbour, there were six
warships with 400 soldiers from their garrison and 600 seamen, two
ships to prevent the enemy launches from entering through Boca-
grande if they should attempt this, and try to land their troops there,
and the rest in Bocachica, to guard the entrance to the Bay. All of
these as well as the castles and batteries were under the able command of Rear-Admiral Don Blas de Lezo.

On the 13th of March, at nine in the morning, the first enemy
sails were sighted out by Punta de Canoa: a ship of 70 cannon, one
of 50, and a packet; but it was not until the 14th, when a sloop
succeeded in entering the harbour despite enemy chase with the
news that the English planned to mount an attack on Cartagena
come what may, that any credence was given to the notion that the
said ships could be part of the enemy fleet. The Viceroy hastened
the organisation of the defences, Don Blas de Lezo moved his quarters
on to the "Galicia" and the chain was thrown across Bocachica and,
with everything prepared, they awaited enemy movements...

... The fleet then anchored in the shelter of the creek and the three
ships veered around to join up with the four which were attacking
the castle, at which point the bombardment was intensified, as was
the reply of the gallant fortress, and that of the batteries on San
José and on Abanicos point, which were under the command of
Battalion Commander Don Francisco Garay and Naval-Lieutenant

Don José Polanco Campuzano, and likewise that of our ships; all this
to such effect that, when firing ceased at nightfall, four of the enemy
ships had to be towed off, dragging their masts and jettisoning
ballast as fast as they could – incontrovertible evidence of the crip-
pling defeat they had sustained...

Recognising, at that point, that they would not reduce the castle
by bombardment, and that their ships would not manage to make
the breach they now felt indispensable, the enemy busied themselves
making a clearing in the thick scrub of the hillside, and getting rid
of it so that they could there construct a battery of twenty cannon
of eighteen-bore, and it was with this that they eventually pounded
the castle. The Governor, discovering their plan, made a foray at
dawn on the 31st with the intention of either delaying them or
completely destroying what they had built, and this attack was so
sudden and so violent that it utterly succeeded in its intent, putting
them to flight and killing fifty of them, until some reinforcements
arrived on the scene and, being now outnumbered, he beat a retreat,
fighting all the way, and came off without losses either of men or of
the glory he had won.

On the first of April, the battery on Abanicos Point was set up
once again with nine cannon, and on the 2nd, at 7 in the morning,
the enemy battery commenced firing upon a corner tower of the
castle, using the additional fire-power of six pounding-cannon of
the Royal Artillery. Both this fire and that of the gun-boats on the
3rd of April was beyond belief, and this day the two squadrons, the
Blues and the Reds, all except the command vessels, also joined in
the bombardment of the afore-mentioned castle; these must doubtless have been considerably damaged by the battery on Abanicos
Point in particular, because, on the 4th, another attempt was made
to take this battery at all costs, and this the enemy duly achieved
after a very fierce struggle. The garrison there, spiking their guns,
withdrew without further loss. This same day, the 4th of April,
while the Viceroy and Don Blas de Lezo were sitting on the quarter-
deck of the "Galicia", a cannon-ball blew off the legs of the Viceroy's
stool, and albeit the splinters cut his feet and injured Don Blas de
Lezo in the arm, their wounds were so superficial that neither of
them allowed this to prevent him from continuing to give the necessary commands, or made him move one inch from the danger.

That day the two squadrons, the gun-boats, the batteries of cannon
and mortars did not cease their fierce bombardment of the castle, and
they opened a sizeable breach, large enough for an assault, destroyed
the best of the defenders' artillery, and pressed them to the utmost
limits of their endurance. The position was so grave that on the 5th

when, two hours before nightfall, the Governor saw the enemy
advancing in three columns with fifty launches bearing down upon
the castle, he despaired of being able to defend that heap of ruins
against such enormous odds, and resolved to hoist the white flag
and give the signal of capitulation, but, as the only response he
received was the full broadside of the batteries and the advance of
the infantry, as if the signal had gone unnoticed, he decided to
retreat in order to save his courageous soldiers and to go with them
to the main defences of the city.

... The fleet was already in the bay, lying at anchor off Perico
Point, and they had attempted a landing at Manzanillo, but had
been resolutely repulsed by our pickets. On the twelfth, one of their
three-deckers approached the "Conquistador" from the rear as she
lay a little light in the water, and, spreading her sails as soon as the
breeze sprang up, veered down upon her and towed her off. By this
manoeuvre the enemy managed to clear the entrance to the port
which they straightway exploited by putting in their gun-boats, a
frigate of fifty cannon and several packets with which they began
to bombard the city, and this they continued to do unflaggingly
until the 27th, making a landing possible by forcing our pickets to
withdraw under fire from their frigates and their packets.

This landing they finally achieved at dawn on the 16th, with
their vessels giving covering fire from three sides, and they did put
their men ashore at Manzanillo, at the Gracia Brickfields and at
those in Alsidia. Each body of troops formed up in columns which
marched, despite fierce opposition from our forces, to the Gavala
Brickfields where they halted and set up defence positions, extending their right flank up to the foot of the hill of Our Lady of La
Popa, and their left as far as the coast.

On the 17th, they managed to take the convent of Our Lady of
La Popa and also the Lozano Brickfield, sustaining some losses in
the action.

On the 19th, they attacked the important post of Cruz Grande
on the road to La Boquilla which was guarded by militia, but, when
these had given way to the force of the enemy attack and abandoned
their post, the Viceroy sent in reinforcements consisting of four
pickets of veteran troops who not only managed to catch up with
the enemy but attacked them with such force that they routed them
utterly, killing seventeen of their number who were left lying out
in the field.

The enemy had resolved to storm the castle of San Felipe de
Barajas sometimes known as San Lázaro, which stands on a mountain away to the east overlooking the city, parallel to the edge of

the outlying township of Jijimaní, at a distance of seven hundred paces from the city...

A little before three in the morning, the enemy began to advance through the Hornaveque, coming under heavy grape-shot from our batteries on the castle and being subjected to rifle-fire from our earthworks, both of these greatly abetted and heartened by the efforts of Don Blas de Lezo at the Media Luna battery. The King's Lieutenant, Don Melchor de Navarrete, who was in charge of the outlying earthworks, brought up some pickets from the reserve to strengthen them, and, having reported to the Viceroy, returned right speedily with fresh reinforcements under the command of Don Pedro Casellas, and it was these that carried on the fighting, wreaking the by now famous havoc among the enemy. Our troops could by now no longer bear the role of passive defenders of the patched ruins and they sallied forth at six in the morning and hurled themselves at the enemy, bayonets fixed, forcing them to retreat in total disorder, and to abandon on the field of battle their ladders and testudos and the tools they had brought to make earthworks for the attack, and also eight hundred dead and a further two hundred wounded, among them a number of officers. Although the officers were carried to first-aid posts and their wounds tended most solicitously, most of them died within a few days; among their number figured a captain in the Grenadiers and four noble subalterns, one of them the son of Lord Forbes, another the nephew of the Colonel, and also Brigadier Grant who had commanded the attack. Moreover, it had been learnt prior to this that one of those fatally wounded by cannon fire in the action at Bocachica had been a Commander in the Engineers. In all our army no more than twenty men were either killed or wounded.

The same day, the 27th, at ten in the morning, the gunboats stood off and joined up with the squadron and, two hours before dawn on the 28th, the land batteries also fell silent.

As the firing ceased, the enemy trumpets were heard more loudly and more incessantly than before, and, at daybreak, a sailor from Biscay who had been held captive in the enemy camp managed to effect his escape and reported that the enemy had completely abandoned their positions and gone on board ship, taking their equipment and provisions with them. Thereupon the Viceroy ordered five pickets in pursuit to harass their rearguard as much as possible, but when they arrived on the scene they found the whole army embarked and all that remained was a few tents, some kegs of powder, some resin, some cannon-balls, a number of rifles, some drums and some earth-shifting tools. They took nine British soldiers

and a Captain of Negroes prisoner, occupying all the enemy positions except the Manzanillo which was still in enemy hands, its
small garrison protected by the guns of the whole fleet.

At ten that morning, a small boat came with a letter from Admiral
Vernon proposing an exchange of prisoners, and this was duly
carried out on the 30th in the manner agreed to by the Viceroy.

The Viceroy was quite unable to compute enemy losses with any
accuracy and so was obliged to rely upon the accounts of the
prisoners exchanged. They reported that more than fifteen hundred,
including the cream of the officers, had been killed or wounded during the morning action of the 20th, and that at least that number,
or even more, had perished during the seventeen days of fighting
over at San Luis de Bocachica; but the greatest number of all had
died on account of the ravages of scurvy and dysentery which were
now claiming more victims than ever.

They also informed the Viceroy that, of the vessels which carried
out the bombardment of the castle itself, seventeen were so badly
battered that they were out of commission, – eleven could not pursue
their role in the campaign without major repairs and the other six
were not able to put to sea.

Determined to leave the harbour defenceless and to ensure free
access to it, the enemy busied themselves from the first until the
fifth of May in the demolition of the harbour ports. They moved all
their vessels to Bocachica on the fifth, sixth and seventh, and, on
the eighth, more than twenty of them, together with a number of
men-o'-war, set sail for Jamaica. This process was repeated by the
remaining vessels, and, on the twentieth, Admiral Vernon set sail,
covering his rearguard with fourteen ships of the line and several
packets and sloops.

These are the most important details of what has been the greatest
expedition the oceans of the Americas have seen ever since they were
discovered. Without exaggerating the might or the size of the
English forces, the courage, constancy and success of the King's
Commanders and their men have earned pride of place in the annals
of history, for, had they been lacking in any one of these virtues,
they must surely have broken under the immense labours which it fell
to them to perform and under the ceaseless ravages of the bombardment, and the successive assaults of an insolent and overweening army.

But, nevertheless, evidence has been presented to show that the
victory was complete, for, piecing together the several accounts of
deserters, and prisoners, and previous details of the effects of the
attacks and skirmishes it may quite confidently be concluded that at
least six ships were fired, for on the 2nd, 4th and 6th great columns

of smoke were sighted out at sea and these could not but have been occasioned by such firings. It is equally certain that the deaths o'ertopped the nine hundred mark, for, besides the many lost at Bocachica, in the actions in the harbour and the siege, when the Viceroy despatched a detail to man the positions abandoned by the English when they went back on board ship, they found the whole road, for the distance of three leagues, littered with corpses and with traces of recently dug graves. Further confirmation of these considerable losses was afforded for those on land by the sight of the enemy fleet evidently short of men to perform the vital task of manning the ships. On the other hand, God has been so liberal of His Divine Mercy in His dealing with our own force that we have lost but two hundred men during the long two months of our defence, despite having been ceaselessly battered by cannon and mortars and been but rarely free from a shower of red-hot fire-balls, incendiary grenades, flaming arrows, all of them making our present trials and tribulations scarcely tolerable. We must even pay due homage to the part played by the winds: the fresh breezes, which have kept up all the time, have carried the evil stench of rotting bodies away from the city.'

(*Diario de todo lo ocurrido en la expugnación* ...)

41

Treaty of alliance between Spain and France signed at Fontainebleau and known as The Second Family Treaty (25 October)

1743

Article 1. There shall be sincere friendship ... (as in the First Treaty) ... so that both the allies, and those who declared themselves enemies, of one of Their Majesties shall be held to be in like relation to the other.

Article 2. Their Majesties declare themselves mutual guarantors of all Their estates and rights, and, should one of them be attacked or insulted, the Other shall pledge Himself to obtain prompt satisfaction on behalf of His ally, be this through His good offices, or be it through the declaration of war; This with the guarantee that they shall not enter into negotiations unless it be by prior mutual assent. And, in the eventuality of differences arising between their Majesties, Their ministers and military commanders, pledge that they shall not act or enter into any agreement independently of the other, or perform any act prejudicial to Their alliance, but rather that They shall each offer a detailed exposition of the causes of their differences in such a way that the party which provoked them may offer reasonable justification for its actions, maintaining the trust that shall always be the foundation of this friendship, giving this good faith priority over self interest, expansion and conquest.

Article 3. As His Catholic Majesty finds Himself constrained to employ His forces in the fight to make good his rightful claims to the throne vacated by the late Emperor Charles 6th, and His Most Christian Majesty is resolute in actively repulsing the advances of the Court of Vienna and its allies, They do both pledge Themselves not to lay down their arms, nor to allow Their interests to become separate, until They shall have achieved Their respective ends, so that even when one of Them has accomplished His aim before the other, He shall continue to help the other, and to consider Himself bounden to the other, unless by mutual agreement He be freed of his obligation.

Article 4. Consequent upon the King of Sardinia's having put His name to a treaty with the Court of Vienna, after already and separately having pacted one with the Sovereigns signatories to this agreement, His Most Christian Majesty enters into an obligation to declare war on Him and to persist in that war with the utmost rigour maintaining the stipulated strength in the field.

Article 5. His Catholic Majesty pledges Himself to maintain in the field the forces which were under the command of His Majesty Don Felipe and the Duke of Modena.

Article 6. His Catholic Majesty whose chief purpose in pursuing His own rights in the matter of the succession of the Emperor and in the claims of His wife the Queen, is none other than to secure for His son, His Majesty Don Felipe, an inheritance befitting His noble birth, proclaims that He cedes to Him all the said rights and consents that the said Prince enter into the possession of the state of Milan and be recognised as Sovereign of all estates and dependencies pertaining thereunto, within the same frontiers that applied when the Emperor held it together with the Duchies of Parma and Piacenza, with the proviso that the Queen shall enjoy the said Duchies for as long as She lives.

Article 7. Their Majesties, deeming it in Their best interests to have the Emperor as an ally, have agreed to draw up a public treaty of alliance to which that Monarch may be a signatory, and this desire has motivated Them to agreement that no means, not even military action, shall be overlooked in Their efforts to restore to Him all His estates, and in seeking reparation for all the hurts done to Him and to His claims, in order that He may be enabled to maintain Himself in a manner befitting His dignity as Emperor, and also that mutual contributions shall be made such that He be in a position to equal the Austrian forces with His own.

Article 8. With respect to England's declaration of war on Spain and to the excesses and hostilities to which His Christian Majesty has been subjected, Their Majesties have agreed to get together to decide upon the timing of His Most Christian Majesty's reciprocal declaration of war on England, and, in the interim, They shall concert Their efforts to produce sufficient sea-power to ensure that as many people offer the wherewithal to equip fighting ships as possible. (This is the same allusion to Gibraltar as is contained in the First Family Pact.)

Article 9. The Island of Minorca and the port of Mahón being of no less importance to Their cause, His Most Christian Majesty pledges Himself to work for the recovery of the said island and harbour, with all the forces and all the means at His disposal.

Article 10. Their Majesties shall work together to force the English to give up their new colony of Georgia, and also every other stronghold set up in territory belonging to His Catholic Majesty in the Americas, and to restore to Spain all lands already occupied and any they shall occupy during the course of the war.

Article 11. His Catholic Majesty hereby declares that He shall rescind the licence granted the English to trade in Negroes, and that He shall only permit His own subjects to participate in this traffic.

Article 12. His Most Christian Majesty shall continue to lend His voice in the representation made by His Catholic Majesty to the Holy See in His suit to obtain some concession in lieu of the Duchies of Castro and Ronciglione to which the Queen enters a claim as Princess of Parma.

Article 13. [Omitted]

Article 14. His Most Christian Majesty hereby also enters into an obligation to be guarantor that the kingdoms of Naples and Sicily shall be in the keeping of Don Carlos and His heirs, in like manner as that prescribed in article Six in the case of Don Felipe.

Article 15. His Catholic Majesty enters into an obligation, either for the duration of the present war or for the period of pacification, to obtain and safeguard for His Most Catholic Majesty the restoration of those lands ceded by France to Sardinia under article Four of the Treaty of Utrecht, in particular the forts at Exiles and Fenestrellas.

Article 16. The present Treaty, to which Their Majesties append their signatures, believing it in Their mutual interests and of great succour to the House of Bourbon, shall be kept private and secret for as long as They deem advantageous and shall be henceforth viewed as an irrevocable family pact of union and friendship.'

(Ferrater, Esteban de, *Código de Derecho internacional*..., vol. i, pp. 156 ff.)

42

Peace. The Treaty of Aix-la-Chapelle

1748

'In the name of the Holy Trinity.

His Most Christian Majesty, His Majesty the King of Great Britain and Their Lordships of the Estates-General of the Low Countries, each fired with a sincere desire for reconciliation with the other two, and for making a contribution to an immediate re-establishment of peace throughout Europe, and persuaded that those other Powers who have been hitherto enemies will readily concur in any plan which has as its end a healthy buffer to national disasters and will not put any obstacle in the path of ready acquiescence to policies the aim of which is the happiness of Their peoples, have invested plenary power, with this end in view, in ... (there follow their names), who have after mature deliberation agreed to the following Preliminary Articles.

I. The Treaties of Westphalia, and Breda, of 1667, that of Madrid in 1670 between the Thrones of Spain and England, of Nijmwegen, Ryswick, Utrecht and Baden of 1713, and the Quadripartite Alliance signed in London on the 2nd of August, 1718, shall serve as a basis for the following Preliminary Articles, and are hereby renewed with full effect, with the exception of those Articles which have been, or shall be, annulled by these Preliminary Articles.

II. All territory conquered since the outbreak of this present war, both in Europe and in the East and West Indies, shall be restored to its rightful Sovereign and in its present state.

III. Dunkirk shall remain fortified to landward, as it is now, and, to seaward, the provisions of previous treaties shall be observed.

IV. The Duchies of Parma, Piacenza and Guastalla shall be handed over to His Most Serene Majesty Don Felipe as part of His dominions, with the proviso that they revert to their present Lord, should His Majesty the King of Naples and Sicily succeed to the Spanish Throne, or should the said Most Serene Majesty die without issue.

V. The Most Serene Duke of Modena shall be confirmed in the possession of His states, goods, rents, privileges and status in the same wise as He possessed them before the present war, or shall be indemnified for that which cannot be restored to Him.

VI. All territory which, before the outbreak of this present war, formed part of the Most Serene Republic of Genoa shall be returned to it, together with all the rights, privileges and prerogatives which it enjoyed in 1740.

VII. His Majesty, the King of Sardinia, shall be confirmed in the possession of all the territories which He enjoyed both of yore and of late, and, in particular, of the acquisitions He made in 1743, of the Vigevano and a part of the lands of Pavia and the County of Angera, in the same state as when that Ruler came into them as a result of the Act of Cession made in His favour.

VIII. His Britannic Majesty shall be included in the present Preliminary Articles in virtue of His being Elector of Hanover, as also shall be the Electorate of Hanover.

IX. It being the case that His Majesty the King of Great Britain has, as Elector of Hanover, entered certain monetary claims against the Spanish Crown, His Most Christian Majesty and Their Lordships of the Estates-General of the Low Countries do hereby enter into an obligation to use Their good offices with His Catholic Majesty to obtain for His Majesty the King of Great Britain the honouring and payment of these claims.

X. The Trade Agreement concerning traffick in Negroes, signed at Madrid on the 26th March 1713, and the annual Naval Agreement are especially endorsed until such time as they shall have expired.

XI. Article Five of the Treaty concluded in London on the 2nd August 1718, which guarantees succession to the British Throne in the House of His Majesty, the present incumbent, and where all matters which could conceivably be pertinent to the person who has taken the Title of King of Great Britain and to His descendants, male or female, is set down, is hereby expressly endorsed and renewed as though it were here inserted in its entirety.*

* His Holy and Imperial Majesty, His Holy and Most Christian Majesty and the Estates-General of the Low Countries hereby enter into an obligation, in Their own name and in that of Their heirs and successors, to uphold and guarantee succession to the British Throne, in accordance with the law of the Realm, in the House of

XII. The claims of the Elector Palatine to the Fiefdom of Plesting shall be remitted to the General Congress so that it might pass judgement on them.

XIII. His Most Christian Majesty, His Britannic Majesty and Their Lordships of the Estates-General of the Low Countries enter into an obligation to use Their good offices, and take pains to settle through the General Congress and give a ruling upon the dispute over the Grand-Mastership of the Order of the Golden Fleece.

XIV. The Head of State raised to the dignity of Emperor shall be recognised as such by all those powers that have not hitherto done so.

XV. The disputes over the territories of Hainault, the office of Abbot of Saint Hubert, the Frontier Posts lately set up, and other matters of this ilk shall be remitted to the forthcoming Congress and shall be decided there.

XVI. All hostilities on land, between those Powers who are at present at war with each other, shall cease within six weaks from the date on which this present treaty is signed and sealed, and at sea they shall cease in accordance with the terms and periods stipulated in the Cease-Fire Agreement signed by England and France in Paris on the 19th of August, 1712.†

His Majesty the King of Great Britain, the present incumbent, and also to vouch for all the states and countries which His Majesty the King of Great Britain has in His possession, and not to afford nor grant asylum in any corner of Their estates to that person who during the lifetime of James II took the title of Prince of Wales, and after His Death, of King of Great Britain, nor to any of the descendants of the said person, should he ever produce any issue; and They do hereby undertake, in Their own name and in that of Their heirs and successors, never to come to the assistance of the said person nor to that of his descendants, either directly or indirectly, on sea or on land, nor to afford him counsel nor succour nor assistance of any kind, neither in money nor in arms nor in supplies nor in ships, nor in troops nor in seamen nor in any other guise, and to observe these same provisions in the case of any other person acting under the instructions, or on the commission, of the said person or his descendants, who might work to undermine His Majesty's Government or the peace of His realm either by openly waging war or by conspiring in secret or by fomenting sedition or rebellion or by indulging in piracy against His Britannic Majesty's subjects, etc.

† Article III states: To remove any ground for possible disputes arising from the situation of any vessels, merchandise or other effects captured on the high seas during the cease-fire, it has been mutually agreed that any ships, merchandise and effects captured in the Channel or in the North Sea (that is, that sea which lies between Norway and Great Britain and includes the British waters) after twelve days shall have elapsed from the date of the signing of the said cease-fire, shall be returned by each party to the other.

This period shall be of six weeks for any prizes taken on the seas that lie between the Channel, the British waters and the North Sea, on the one hand, and Cape St Vincent on the other.

Also of six weeks for those taken beyond that Cape as far as La Línea both on the Atlantic and in the Mediterranean.

And lastly of six months beyond La Línea and throughout the world, and to this there shall be no exception, nor shall any other distinction be made with respect to either time or place.

XVII. The restoration of lands, etc., set out in Article II above, shall not come into effect until such time as all the interested Powers shall have agreed to the present Preliminary Articles.

XVIII. The said Concessions, restitutions and establishment of the possessions, etc., of His Most Christian Majesty shall all be made at the same time and proceed with the same speed.

XIX. All those Powers concerned in the present Preliminary Articles shall endorse, as strongly as possible, the guarantees laid down in the Royal Decree of the 19th of April, 1713, with respect to the succession to the late Emperor, Carlos VI, made in favour of the daughter of the present incumbent and of her descendants in perpetuity, in the order established in the said decree, but nevertheless with the exception of the concessions already made by the said Princess and of those included in the stipulations of the present Articles.

XX. The Duchy of Silesia and the county of Glatz shall be guaranteed, by all these powers and parties signatories to these present Preliminary Articles, in the possession of His Majesty within the same frontiers as when they formed part of the lands of His Majesty the King of Prussia.

XXI. Every act committed during this present war shall now pass into the annals of history and, on the day on which all parties sign the agreement, each and every one of them shall have all those possessions which He enjoyed or should have enjoyed at the outbreak of the war restored to Him, and He shall be confirmed in full possession of them, all despoilment, seizure and confiscation occasioned by the present war notwithstanding.

XXII. All the Powers participating in the dispositions laid down in the present Preliminaries shall be invited to agree to them at the earliest opportunity.

XXIII. All the interested Powers who are signatories to the present Preliminary Articles shall afford each other reciprocal guarantee that they shall be put into effect.

XXIV. Signed and sealed copies of the present Preliminaries, ratified by the signatories, shall be exchanged not later than three weeks from the date of the agreement.

We, the undersigned Ambassadors Plenipotentiary of His Most Christian Majesty, His Majesty the King of Great Britain, and Their Lordships the Estates-General of the Low Countries, in virtue of the powers invested in us, have agreed to the above conventions and do hereby testify to this by appending our signatures to the present Preliminary Articles and impressing our seals upon them. In Aix-la-Chapelle, 30th April, 1748.

Count San Severino de Aragón.
Lord Sandwich.
F. H. van Wassenaar.
G. A. Hasselaar.'
(*Mercurio Histórico y Político*, Madrid, June 1748, pp. 39–47.)

43
The Concordat between Spain and Benedict XIV

1753

'By special messenger from Rome, the King* received on the 2nd of this month, His Holiness' copy, duly signed and sealed, of the Concordat lately drawn up and concerted between the two Courts to their mutual satisfaction, the purport of which is as follows:

POPE BENEDICT XIV
AD PERPETUAM REI MEMORIAM

It being the case that a Treaty comprising eight Articles has been lately drawn up and duly signed by Our Beloved son, Silvio, Cardinal-Presbyter of the Holy Roman Church, by name Valenti, Our Ambassador Plenipotentiary, and a member of the Holy Apostolic See, and by Our beloved son Doctor Manuel Ventura Figueroa, Our Chaplain and Judge Advocate at the Papal Palace, and Ambassador Plenipotentiary of Our Most Beloved son in Christ, Fernando, Catholic King of the Spanish Empire, – viz. on the 11th day of January last, – with the aim of reaching due settlement of several important issues, principally on matters pertaining to jurisdiction, the right of Royal patronage, and other matters which had been left unsettled by the Treaty, drawn up, agreed to and signed in October of 1737 between this said Holy Apostolic See and Felipe V, in this life Catholic King of the said Spanish Empire, of lasting fame, and approved and confirmed by both parties, the purport of which is as follows:

His Holiness, Our Most Blessed Father, Pope Benedict XIV, who rules the Church with such happy issue, having ever been fired by a keen desire to preserve sincere and cordial relations between the

* Fernando VI of Spain.

Holy See and the Catholic Nations, Monarchs and Kings, has never ceased to give unequivocal and specific indications of this His passionate concern for the illustrious, devout and pious Spanish Nation and for the rulers of the Spanish Empire, known as the Catholic Kings, who have ever been sturdy in Their Faith and in Their affection for the Apostolic See and for Christ's Vicar on earth. Therefore, not unmindful that in the stipulations of the last concordat, signed and sealed on the 18th of October 1737, between His Holiness Pope Clement XII, of holy memory, and King Felipe V, whose fame shall be endless, it was agreed that the Pope and the King should appoint certain persons to argue Their respective points of view, while yet sympathising with the views of the Other, and that these persons should settle the long-standing controversy over the claims to worldwide Royal Patronage, which matter had hitherto been left undecided, His Holiness did not overlook the necessity, right from the earliest days of His Pontificate, of exhorting the two Cardinals Belluga and Acquaviva, lately deceased, to persuade the Spanish Court to appoint an embassy with whom the matter in question could be debated; nor did He thereafter omit to set down all those matters which He deemed conducive to the intentions and rights of the Holy See in one Epistle, penned in His own hand, which He gave to both the said Cardinals that the matter might more easily be examined. Having recognised that in practice this was no way to realise His desires, and that these Epistles and the replies they provoked were so far from smoothing over the points of contention, that rather these last were on the increase because of them, and that controversies which had been thought long forgotten were being raised once again, and that this was happening to such an extent that a woeful schism, which would be dangerous and even fatal for both parties, now loomed on the horizon; and having been afforded tangible proof of a pious propensity in the mind of King Fernando VI, upon whose head the crown sits most happily, for an equable and just settlement of the differences which have arisen, and which were now on the increase, and, His own heart filled with this same desire, His Holiness felt that such a golden opportunity to draw up an Agreement should not be allowed to slip by, and this agreement is expressed in the following chapters and shall be set out in proper and legal format at a later date and signed by the Proxies and Ambassadors Plenipotentiary of both parties in the manner which is customary with such conventions. His Majesty, King Fernando VI, having expounded to His Holiness, Our Blessed Father, the need that exists for certain reforms in the internal discipline of the secular and regular clergy, on Spanish Soil, His Holiness hereby gives an undertaking that, once the Articles which call out for emendation shall have been set down in detail, He shall not fail to act upon them in accordance with the precepts laid down in Canon Law, in the Constitutions of the Church and at the Holy Council of Trent, and, should all this come to pass during His Pontificate, as He fervently desires it shall, He gives a solemn undertaking that, even though He be overburdened with work and bowed down with years, He shall do everything within His power to ensure a happy issue in this matter and shall exercise all that same zest and energy which, many years ago, during the reigns of His predecessors, when He was still in minor orders, He threw behind the issue resolved in the Bull "Apostolicii Ministerii", behind the founding of the University at Cervera, and behind that of the Illustrious Collegiate Church of San Ildefonso, and in other matters of great moment for the Spanish Empire. There being no controversy about the legitimacy of the Spanish Kings' Royal Patronage, that is to say about Their right to nominate to Archbishoprics, Bishoprics, Abbacies, and Benefices attaching to Ecclesiastical Courts, viz. those set down in the Chapter Books, when these fall vacant in the territories of the Spanish Crown – which right is endorsed by Bulls, Apostolic Privileges and other deeds produced by them, and there being no controversy about the rights of the Spanish Kings to nominate to Archbishoprics, Bishoprics and Benefices which fall vacant in the Kingdoms of Granada and the Indies, nor about Their right to nominate to a number of other specific benefices, it is hereby declared that the Royal Throne be permitted to continue without interference to nominate when such vacancies occur, as it has been hitherto; and it is agreed that those persons nominated to Archbishoprics, Bishoprics, Abbacies and Benefices attaching to Ecclesiastical Courts shall in future continue to expedite their respective bulls in Rome in the same manner as hitherto and without any innovation whatsoever. But, there having been grave controversy about the right to nominate to Benefices in Religious Houses on Spanish soil, with the stated exception of those in the Kingdoms of Granada and the Indies, Their Catholic Majesties, having laid claim to such a right in virtue of Their Universal Patronage, and the Holy See having continued to put forward the arguments It believed to militate for these benefices being unfettered and included in the giving of the Holy See, and their collation in the Apostolic months, and, in some cases, of the Diocesan Bishop in whose see they fell, They have, after a long dispute, mutually agreed to settle Their differences in the following way. His Holiness, Our Most Blessed Father, Pope Benedict XIV, reserves for Himself, His successors and the Holy See the right in perpetuity freely to appoint

to fifty-two benefices, which shall be listed below, in such a way
that His Holiness and His successors after Him shall be able to
reward and provide for Spanish clerics who shall earn this favour by
their probity and saintly way of life, by writings of great moment,
or by services rendered the Holy See, and these fifty-two benefices
shall ever remain in the giving of the Holy See, whenever and however they fall vacant, even should the Crown occasion their doing
so, and even should it be found that any of them fall within the
terms of Royal Patronage, and albeit they are in a diocese where a
cardinal has important favours to bestow. Such petitions shall never
be listened to in preference to the Holy See, and the Bulls for these
fifty-two benefices shall be issued always from Rome, and the usual
emoluments paid to the Datary and the Papal Treasury as now; all
this without imposition of any imposts nor any fiscal letters-patent,
as shall be stated hereinafter.

... To ensure the future good government of Appointments, Pre-
sentations, Nominations and Institutions to benefices falling vacant
in the said territory of the Spanish Crown, it is agreed: First: that
Archbishops, Bishops and Collators of lesser standing shall continue
in the future to present to the same benefices as they have in the
past, always providing these fall vacant in the Diocesan months of
March, June, September and December, even should these fall vacant
when nobody sits on St Peter's Throne; also that, in these same
months and in the same way, the Ecclesiastical Patrons shall continue
to present to the benefices in their giving, as hitherto, with the proviso
that the alternative months hitherto admitted shall henceforth never
be countenanced; Secondly: that the present practice of filling the
offices of Prebend by public examination and competition shall continue and the incumbents be selected in the same way and in the
same circumstances as hitherto, without the slightest innovation of
any kind, and that the status quo shall be preserved absolutely with
respect to those benefices which are in the appointment of individuals
among the laity; Thirdly: that, not only shall parishes and livings
as priests be conferred in the future by public examination and competition, as hitherto, when they fall vacant in the Diocesan months,
but also when they fall vacant in the months set aside for them to
revert to the Holy See, even when the presentation to them forms
part of the Royal Prerogative, and in all these cases the patron shall
present to the Diocesan Bishop that person he shall deem most fit
from the three approved as suitable by the Synodal Examiners "ad
Curam animarum"; Fourthly: that, having already stated above
that the rights of ecclesiastical patrons to present to the benefices
within their patronage during the four Diocesan months shall remain

inviolate, and it having been the practice to date that some Chapters, Rectors, Abbots and Brotherhoods established with the authority of the Church do have recourse to the Holy See that a Papal Bull confirm the elections they make, there shall be no change at all in this matter but rather everything shall remain as it has been hitherto; Fifthly: that, always with the exception of the fifty-two benefices freely to be disposed of by the Holy See, and always with the exception of the stipulations set out above, His Holiness, motivated by His desire for a friendly conclusion to all the outstanding points of contention with reference to Universal Patronage, does cede to His Catholic Majesty and to the Kings who shall succeed Him, in perpetuity, the universal right to nominate and present to all the Metropolitan Churches, Cathedrals, Collegiate Churches and Dioceses in the Spanish Kingdoms, and, as now, to all posts of high office post Pontificalem and to the remaining cathedral offices, to the high posts and all others in the collegiate churches, to canonries, prebendaries, abbacies, priorships, benefices, parishes, sinecures, patrimony and all forms of ecclesiastical offices and benefices both in the secular and the regular arm, both with and without duties, of whatever kind, either existing now or to be instituted at some time in the future, provided that those responsible for their foundation do not reserve for themselves or their successors the right to present to those benefices within the domains and realm of Spain as now defined under the Catholic King; and this shall have universal application, and shall include even those benefices that fall vacant during the Papal months and all other exceptions both general and specific, as well as all instances of benefices falling vacant during the Diocesan months when Archbishoprics and Bishoprics are untenanted, and all other cases. Moreover, the Holy See makes over the rights in Its possession of preferring to office within Spanish territory, either in Its own name or through the Datary, the Papal Treasury, The Spanish Nuncio or the Papal Commissioners, to His Majesty the Catholic King and to His Royal Successors, investing in them the universal Prerogative of presenting to the said benefices within the frontiers of Spain as defined at present, and grants to Them the use of this right in like manner as the rest of the Patronage attached to the Royal Throne, and concedes that It shall not, at any time in the future, grant to any Papal Nuncio in Spain, nor to any Spanish Cardinal or Bishop, permission to confer benefices during the Papal months, without express permission from His Majesty or His Successors; Sixthly: in order that all this system operate smoothly in the future, and as far as possible the authority of the Bishops remain undiminished, it is agreed that all those nominated for, and presented to, the benefices stated above by His Catholic Majesty and His Successors, even should these fall vacant as a result of Royal provision, must without exception apply to their respective Diocesan Bishops for induction and initiation, without this necessitating any Papal Bull unless it be for confirmation of the elections, as set out above, or for granting of a dispensation in the case of the nominee or candidate presented to the benefice being under age, or in any way subject to impediment under Canon Law, or unless it be for a Papal Blessing or any other matter beyond the Ordinary jurisdiction of the Bishop, and, in these and similar cases, recourse shall always be had to the Holy See as has hitherto been the case, to sue for that blessing or that dispensation, and payment shall always be made to the Datary or Papal Treasury in the time-honoured sum, without imposition of any imposts nor fiscal letters-patent, as shall be stated hereinafter. Seventhly: that, with this same end in view of ensuring that the authority of the Diocesan Bishops shall remain undiminished, it is agreed and hereby made plain that it is not to be understood that the concession and transfer of the said rights of Nomination, Presentation and Patronage in any way implies the granting of any ecclesiastical jurisdiction to his Catholic Majesty and His successors over the Churches contained in the said articles, nor over the persons He nominate or present to the said Churches or benefices, and that these must always remain subject to the authority of their respective Diocesan Bishops in the same way as must those preferred by the Holy See to the fifty-two benefices reserved for Its own patrimony, and these may never claim any exemption from their jurisdiction, always with the exception of the supreme authority which the Bishop of Rome has, as Shepherd of the Universal Church, over all Churches and all persons in Holy Orders, and with the exception of the Royal privileges which adhere to the Crown in virtue of the Royal Protection, above all over the Churches which fall within Royal Patronage. Eighthly: His Catholic Majesty, recognising that as a result of the patronage and the rights conceded to Him and to His successors, the Datary and Papal Treasury shall lack the moneys normally received in annates and from the expedition of Bulls, and that this will result in grave deficiencies in the Papal Exchequer, does hereby enter into an obligation to remit to Rome, as compensation, and in one lump sum, the amount of three hundred and ten thousand Roman scuti for the use of His Holiness, which sum shall yield at three per cent an annual increment of nine thousand and three hundred scuti in the same coin, which is that sum calculated as the income from all the rights stated above. There having sprung up in the past some

controversy around some of the provisions made by the Holy See
in the Cathedrals of Palencia and Mondoñedo, His Majesty, the
Catholic King, does hereby agree that the nominees shall enter into
possession once the present Concordat has been ratified. And the
long-standing dispute over the imposition of imposts and fiscal
letters-patent having once again reared its head on account of the
claims made for Universal Royal Patronage, and His Holiness, Our
Most Blessed Father, in order to put a stop once and for all to these
arguments which come to the fore from time to time, and having
shown Himself eager in His resolve to abolish the practice of such
imposts and fiscal letters-patent, motivated by nothing more than
the knowledge that, should they be abolished, He would find Himself
against His will forced to place fresh burdens on the Papal Exchequer,
since the moneys which were raised by these fiscal letters-patent
were used, in their greater part, to pay the stipends and gratuities
of the Ministers who work for the Holy See and deal with all the
business of the government of the Church throughout the world, His
Majesty the Catholic King, motivated not only by His inherited
devotion to the Holy See, but also by the individual love and affection He bears the Blessed Person of His Holiness, has agreed to
come to His assistance by granting Rome a lump sum which, if not
completely, will at least in some part lighten the burden on the
Papal Exchequer in its efforts to pay for the upkeep of the said
Ministers, and that this sum shall be of six hundred thousand Roman
scuti which at three per cent will produce an annual increment of
eighteen thousand scuti in the same coin, which sum will facilitate
the abolition of the said imposts and fiscal letters-patent not only
in the case of appointments to the fifty-two benefices reserved in the
Patrimony of the Holy See, in that of the confirmation stated above
of a number of elections, and of recourse had to the Holy See to obtain
dispensations concerning appointment to benefices, but also of every
other single instance, to such effect that the practice of exacting
imposts and imposing fiscal letters-patent shall be abolished for ever,
although this abolition shall not prejudice those already imposed.
There was one other point of contention, not in this case to do with
the rights of the Holy See and its Nunciature in Spain to the fruits
and income of the Episcopal Churches lying untenanted in the
Spanish Realms, but to do with the usages, practices and effects of
the said rights, and it has proved necessary to come to some agreement and compact about these. To smooth over these issues, which
are continually giving rise to dispute, His Holiness, Our Most
Blessed Father, rescinding, abrogating and declaring null and void
all previous Papal constitutions and all agreements and pacts made

hitherto between the Holy Roman Curia, its Bishops, Chapters and
Dioceses and every other opposing body, undertakes, from the date
of the ratification of this concordat, to ensure that the fruits and
income of the untenanted churches, both those given freely and
those exacted, shall be turned to pious uses, as is laid down in
Canon Law, and hereby promises that He shall grant to no person
in Holy Orders, even though he be exceptionally meritorious, and
no matter what the cause, the right to make use of the income and
fruits of His Episcopal Churches, even for pious ends, with the
exceptions already outlined, which shall come into effect, conceding
to His Majesty, the Catholic King, and His successors the right to
choose in future the gatherers and administrators of the funds, always
with the proviso that they be persons in Holy Orders and aptly
suitable, so that the said funds may be properly administered under
Royal Protection and honestly used to the ends set out above. And
His Majesty, as homage to the Holy See, undertakes to deposit in
Rome, at the disposal of His Holiness, a lump sum of two hundred
and thirty-three thousand, three hundred and thirty-three Roman
scuti, which at three per cent will produce an annual increment of
seven thousand scuti in the same coin, and, in addition to this, His
Majesty promises to afford His Holiness an annual subscription of
five hundred scuti from the income of the Crusades, for the maintenance and expenses of the Papal Nuncios; and He does this in
consideration of the income and fruits of the untenanted Churches
and the obligation never more to grant permission for this income
to be expropriated. His Holiness, as Vicar of Rome, and His Majesty,
as Catholic King, do hereby witness Their mutual undertaking, in
Their own names and those of Their successors, and Their resolve
that every several one of the preceding Articles shall be observed
in perpetuity, and do hereby declare Their resolve that neither the
Holy See nor the Catholic Kings shall ever lay claim to any more
than is set down and contained in the said Articles, and that any
action which shall at any time in the future run contrary to all or
any one of these same articles shall be held to be unlawful, invalid
and worthless. To ensure the validity and the observance of all
those articles laid down in it, this Concordat shall be signed in the
traditional way and shall come into effect in its entirety as soon as
the sums of compensation stipulated in it shall have been paid and
the Treaty ratified. We, the undersigned, in virtue of the powers
invested in us by His Holiness and His Most Catholic Majesty, do
witness this present Treaty with our signatures and do append to it
our own seals. In the Papal Palace of the Quirinal, today, the 11th
day of January in the year 1753.

S. Cardinal Valenti – Place of seal.
Manuel Ventura Figueroa – Place of seal.'
(*Mercurio Histórico y Político*, Madrid, March 1753, pp. 63–68,
70–79.)

44

The Campaign against the Jesuits reaches Spain. The Pope throws the weight of His authority against it, thereby contradicting the claims of the enemies of the Society

1759

'News has reached the ears of His Holiness from, among other sources, letters addressed to Him by several Spanish Bishops, to the effect that, in Madrid and in several other parts of the Realm, not only are evil spirits going abroad and spreading malicious rumours and those same inflammatory libels against the Company of Jesus with which they are attacked by envious and blasphemous persons in other countries, but in addition they are vaunting the Approval of other libels and even their publication in Rome: libels in which glimpses are afforded of a plot to suppress the Society and to foment disapproval of leave granted by the Bishops to the Jesuits to administer the Holy Sacraments and to act as confessors.

His Holiness (not without grave personal affliction) has pondered these lying falsehoods and is deeply perturbed by the thought of the pernicious effects which the discrediting of such a responsible body of religious people and one so well deserving of the Church and whose Order continually gives rise to all sorts of exercises conducive to the advancement of the Faith and to the well-being of many souls, might have. It is therefore the wish of His Holiness that any person who has been led to believe such falsehoods should now be undeceived, and should know that such an attitude is utterly foreign to the spirit of the Catholic Church and that it is His mind to countenance no attack nor any persecution of a body of religious so utterly dedicated (by their very Statutes) to the greater glory of God, to the Christian education of the young, to a Godly way of life and to the spiritual well-being of the faithful.'

(MS Bibl. Nac. Madrid, No. 10893 – 'Trasumpto de la carte que escribió al Nuncio ...'.)

45

Prelude to the war with Great Britain. Preparation of Public Opinion

1761

'... Lord Bristol, Ambassador of His Britannic Majesty in Madrid, put in a formal request in the name of his Sovereign, demanding to be informed whether the King intended to join forces with France against England, and insisted upon an unequivocal answer to his question, stating that, should this be refused him, he would interpret it as a formal breaking off of diplomatic relations and a declaration of war, and should straightway depart these shores. His Majesty the King, our Lord, instructed he be given his answer to the effect that he was at liberty to quit our country whenever and howsoever he chose, for it was the person who posed such a question who was making the first break in diplomatic relations and heralding the outbreak of war. And so it is that diplomatic relations between our court and the English have been broken off, and His Majesty's Ambassador in London, His Excellency the Count of Fuentes, has been instructed to return to Spain forthwith. The King's resolve has been greatly facilitated by the haphazard conduct towards us of the British Ambassador over many years. His Majesty was also not unheedful of the danger which His American colonies have run ever since the English, disgruntled by their most advantageous terms offered by the French during the treaties for peace, were seen to covet so unashamedly the few possessions which still remain of His Most Christian Majesty's empire in the Indies. And who can doubt that they would not be long in turning their attention against Our own colonies and attempting to annex that New World with its shipping and its trade for themselves?'

(Mercurio, *Histórico y Político*, Madrid, vol. CLXVII, pp. 448–9.)

46

Cleaning of the City of Madrid and New Legislation concerning its upkeep: sidewalks, gutters, cess-pits, cobbles and the banning of pigs

1761

'... The King, Our Lord, having entertained many several ideas for laying down new cobbles and cleaning up the streets of Madrid, was especially taken by a plan drawn up by an engineer, Don Francisco Sabatini, and His Majesty gave this plan His royal seal of approval in Aranjuez on the 14th of May this year, at the same time issuing instructions that another project for the same purpose devised by His Excellency, Don Diego de Rojas y Contreras, Bishop of Cartagena, Governor of the Council, should also be put into effect, and appointed His Excellency as overseer of the works and empowered him to take any steps he might deem necessary to ensure its successful completion. This royal edict was published and contains thirteen articles which may be summarised as follows:

I. Householders shall repair their property or rebuild it, and, should it be very old, they shall shore up the front and side walls with three-foot square granite tiles to prevent their crumbling into the streets, and these tiles shall have a hole through the middle so that they can be levered back into position should this prove necessary.

II. The same shall be done by all religious communities, parish churches and hermitages throughout their houses and places of worship, out of the rent and from the income they earn by the work of their hands. The same shall be done by the communities of Observantine Friars, the Discalced Carmelites and the Capuchins, out of the alms they collect. With the exception of the Fathers of San Cayetano, all nunneries, and their churches, and public hospitals and homes for abandoned children, – for in these cases the work will be paid for out of public funds, unless the said hospitals or nunneries are in the vicinity of the houses of their patrons or of other lay persons of quality – all communities shall make these repairs out of their own pocket, especially when they own houses which they can rent out. Any queries should be referred to the Governor of the Council or to the Ministers especially appointed by the Council to deal with these matters. All these works shall be completed within two years. And if any person fails to comply with this order, the works shall be undertaken out of the public purse and the money stopped out of rents, or the community involved mulcted to cover the costs. In order to set an example, His Majesty undertakes to make repairs, as stipulated above, to the fronts of the houses in the Calle del Tesoro and to the Royal Library.

III. Householders and heads of communities shall erect guttering of lead or tin-plate to stop roofing tiles from falling into the streets.

IV. The said householders and heads of communities shall install glazed earthenware piping for the dirty water from the kitchens and all liquid waste, and this piping (which shall conform to official design) shall take all the waste from all rooms to a drain, or wherever else is thought fit.

V. The said householders and heads of communities shall install piping throughout all their property to convey all solid waste to a sewage-pit of sufficient depth, and this shall be covered with a flagstone from a yard to four foot square. These pipes shall have air-ducts coming through the roof in the form of a chimney and shall be made of glazed earthenware piping and lead to the pit, until such time as it be possible to construct the underground sewage system invented by Don José Alonso de Arce, one time architect and engineer to this Court.

VI. The said householders and heads of communities may appoint persons of their own choosing to carry out this work and are hereby authorised to raise their rents by five per cent to cover the cost of the work.

VII. Sweepings, rubbish, dirty matting, &c., shall be put out in the doorways and courtyards and stables whence it shall be removed at public expense and taken outside the city limits.

VIII. The same shall be done in the Main Square. All the rubbish from building sites and roof repairs shall be taken outside the city on Saturdays and charged to the householders involved.

IX. With the exception of the strip of pavement running along outside the houses, the cobbles for the streets shall be paid for out of public funds and shall be hewn from blocks of granite and shall be one foot square, fashioned to a point underneath, and decorated with a criss-cross pattern like those in the courtyard, portico and entrance of the New Palace.

X. Tiles of the said granite one foot wide shall be placed over the open channels that carry the waste which is disposed of by the houses, and that coming down from other streets, without these tiles being permitted to make the surface of the roads in any way uneven, and these channels shall go direct to the channel in the main street.

XII. In order to gain some idea of the cost of repaving the streets, the Carrera de San Jerónimo, from the corner by the Italian church as far as the Church of Buen Suceso, shall be split up into two parts as an experiment, the one to be paved with flint and the other with granite, so that the costs of the two different methods of paving may be compared.

XIII. It shall be strictly prohibited for pigs to be allowed to wander the streets of Madrid, notwithstanding any claims to privilege made by the religious of San Antonio Abad; and these religious shall be compensated from the public purse for any expenses they may incur in having the said pigs taken out into the country.'

(*Mercurio Histórico y Político*, Madrid, May 1761, pp. 291–5.)

47

Communiqués from Fuentes in London. Great Britain, having defeated France in the Americas, now entertains even grander aspirations and makes illegal acquisitions. The Spanish Ambassador thinks war inevitable

1761

'The state of affairs at present over here has come to a critical pass, and now is the time that we must strike while we still can, to call a halt to Her unbounded ambition for, if She be allowed to continue unimpeded in Her victorious march, this could well prove fatal for the Crowned Heads of Europe and could one day serve as a springboard for Her to realise Her unbridled aspirations.' (26 October 1760)

'I can now confirm to Your Excellency that my previous surmises were correct: there is no hope of our gaining anything by negotiation. The English want to keep us at the conference-table solely to gain time and to extricate themselves from the difficult position in

which they find themselves by playing false to us. They fear, and
rightly so, that we could destroy them at this time. They are driven
on blindly by overweening pride; the situation is critical and we
must recognise, now that their designs are out in the open, that we
could have no more dangerous an enemy.' (11 November 1760)

'In the last resort, we shall be forced either to take up arms or to
submit to any conditions the English care to impose upon us, and
we shall be faced with the frightening results of not having taken
proper precautions against the kind of dire situation in which we
now find ourselves placed, and not the least of our worries will be
that the English might succeed, with their superior forces, in seizing
the whole of the Americas, and in that case it would scarce be
possible for us, entering the arena unaided, to contain them within
proper limits, as we could so easily do today.' (9 January 1761)

(Palacio Atard, *El tercer Pacto de Familia*, p. 106.)

48

Text of the Third Family Pact (4 February)

1762

'All Europe must by now be aware of the risks to which the balance
of international sea-power is now exposed. They have only to consider the ambitious designs of the British court and the despotic
manner in which it is attempting to make the high seas its own
private preserve. The English nation has afforded ample proof
through all Her machinations, in particular in these past ten years,
of Her design to make Herself absolute Mistress of the high seas,
and not to permit any other nation more than a modicum of trade
under special licence from Her. It is to this end that She declared
the war against France which She is still now waging, and that She
has turned a deaf ear to every attempt to put an end to it, no matter
how advantageous the terms offered were to Her; and it is to this
end that Her Government has obstinately refused to return any
of the Spanish possessions in America, which the English have
expropriated, and it is to this end that She has arrogated to Herself
exclusive cod-fishing rights and other privileges, established solely
on a temporary basis.

His Catholic Majesty,* opposing such blatantly obvious machinations on the part of the English, occasioned as they were by greed and covetousness, and finding Himself sorely provoked by the equally indecent and offensive conduct of His Britannic Majesty's Government in the arrogant way in which Her ambassador threatened to declare war on His Catholic Majesty should the terms of the treaty which it was rumoured His Catholic Majesty had compacted with His Most Christian Majesty† not be revealed to him; and finding Himself already the victim of a formal declaration of war made against Spain on the 4th day of January last, he has resolved to join forces with the French for the duration of this present war.

To this effect, and in order to ensure that the two Monarchs' political outlooks continue with firm resolve to work in harmony, both when They come to treat for peace, – whenever the English shall be prepared to listen to Them and cease to be prey to that arrogant and stubborn attitude which has hitherto proven an insuperable barrier to the peace feelers put out by His Catholic Majesty and His Most Christian Majesty, – and when it comes to making arrangements for the most suitable way of combining Their two forces, Their Majesties have deemed it advisable to draw up a specific treaty against these eventualities, and one which shall be uniquely concerned with the present situation and shall be consequent upon the permanent alliance set down in the Family Pact, signed on the 15th day of August last, thereby guaranteeing, both for the duration of the war and forever after, God willing, glory and good fortune to all Their descendants and all those peoples which Providence places in Their care throughout the centuries.

This conforms to the intentions of both Sovereigns and to the spirit of Article sixteen of the said Family Pact, which states: "The stipulations for mutual defence set out in the preceding articles, in the time and in the manner which have been therein laid down, shall be held to be a binding obligation, in virtue of their being a family tie and of their springing from the friendship and brotherly union which the two Monarchs, signatories to the present agreement, desire shall be observed by all Their descendants; and the stipulations regarding mutual defence shall be regarded as the minimum that either one of the powers be permitted to provide when the other is in need. However, since it is the intention of both Rulers that, once war has been declared by or against one of Their two Realms, that war shall become the personal enterprise of the other, it is decreed that, once the two Powers are engaged in open conflict against the same enemy or enemies, all obligations to furnish

* Carlos III of Spain.   † Louis XV of France.

assistance as set out above shall cease to have effect, and in their place there shall be an undertaking to wage the war side by side, with all Their might, and that the two major Powers who are signatories to this agreement shall henceforth establish working agreements especially tailored to the particular demands of the war in which they are involved, and shall at that time decide as to Their respective tasks and as to the apportionment of Their mutual benefits, as also to the strategy of all Their mutual undertakings, both political, and military, and that, once these plans are adopted, the two Kings shall pursue them together without any disagreement." And to draw up the present agreement, Their Majesties have in the present instance invested plenary power in the following: His Catholic Majesty in Don Jerónimo Grimaldi, Marquis of Grimaldi, His Gentleman of the Bed-chamber with Portfolio, and His Ambassador Extraordinary to the French King; and His Most Christian Majesty in the Duc de Choiseul, Peer of the French Realm, Knight of the Illustrious Order of the Golden Fleece and of the Orders of His Most Christian Majesty, Second-in-Command of the Armed Forces, Governor of Touraine, Postmaster-General, Minister and Secretary of State with special responsibility for the War Department and the Admiralty. And these two persons, in virtue of the said plenary powers, and having conferred together, have agreed to the following articles:

Article 1.

His Catholic Majesty promises His Most Christian Majesty, and enters into an obligation, to wage war on England with all the means at His disposal, until such time as She be forced to come to Her senses and sue for peace in a reasonable fashion.

Article 2.

His Most Christian Majesty, for His part, promises His Catholic Majesty, and enters into an obligation, that, upholding the same principles that, even before these obligations were formalised, His Ambassador in London, Bussy, set out in one of the Notes he delivered when he was engaged in attempts to safeguard the peace and to make it more stable, He shall, in any future peace negotiations with the English, be mindful of those Spanish interests discussed in London; and that He shall do this with the aim of persuading the English to restore all those Spanish possessions they have seized during the course of this war against the neutrality of His Catholic Majesty, and to admit of the rights of the Spanish to fish unmolested for cod off Newfoundland, and also to withdraw from all those strongholds on the Spanish owned coast of New Granada in the Americas, which they have occupied; and He enters into this obligation so that the stances of France and Spain in any negotiations may be seen to be identical and to develop along identical lines; and His Most Christian Majesty hereby gives His word that He will admit of no settlement nor lay down His arms in the fight against England until such time as His Catholic Majesty shall declare Himself satisfied with the terms of any agreement, and the provisions made therein for His own particular interests.

Article 3.

Consequent upon the undertakings contained in the two articles above, the two signatory Monarchs do hereby pledge Themselves to wage war on the English and keep faith with one another; to discuss and agree upon all tactics before putting them into operation, and to behave with like fidelity and constancy One with the Other, in such wise that, from the date of the signing of this convention, all losses and all conquests shall be held to be mutual, and, at the end of the war, shall be shared among Themselves as though They were one and the same power and all losses had been sustained and all conquests achieved by one and the same Realm.

Article 4.

The two signatory Monarchs shall therefore enter into an obligation, and do hereby pledge Themselves, not to make peace nor truce with England unless it be at one and the same time and by mutual consent, and to communicate to each Other promptly and faithfully all direct and indirect propositions for peace that may be made to either one of Them.

Article 5.

His Catholic Majesty confirms the generous concession of His rights to the Islands of Dominica, Saint Vincent, Saint Lucia and Tobago, which He made in favour of His Most Christian Majesty when He was making peace with England, and gives leave that His Most Christian Majesty use this right as if it were His own, should the need arise for Him to employ it as compensation against war losses.

Article 6.

Thereupon, His Most Christian Majesty undertakes to surrender to His Catholic Majesty the island of Minorca and the port of Mahón, conquered from the English, and agrees that Spanish troops shall occupy that island and fortress and that the French garrison shall withdraw. His Catholic Majesty shall hold the said island and stronghold as surety, for the duration of the war, and His Most Christian Majesty consents that, at the end of the war, they shall revert to the Spanish Crown to which they originally belonged, should God bless the combined enterprise of the two Monarchs in such a way that They do not find Themselves obliged to restore this possession, and that it is not absolutely vital to France as compensation during the settlement with England.

Article 7.

The first act which the two signatory Powers undertake to perform during this war against England is to communicate Their union to His Most Faithful Majesty*, and to attempt to persuade him to join forces with Them in this cause, as indeed He owes it to Himself and His subjects to do, for there is no people more oppressed by the yoke which the English attempt to impose on all those Nations who enjoy some sea-power and overseas possessions. In truth, it would not be just that Spain and France sacrifice themselves to achieve an object they share with Portugal, while She not only tenders Them no support, but, indeed, continues to trade with Their enemy and grant Her safe harbour on Her shores. His Catholic Majesty and His Most Christian Majesty have compacted to make representations to the King of Portugal, stressing that He cannot remain neutral in this war. It is to be hoped that no threats will be necessary, and that His Most Faithful Majesty will be persuaded by these representations from the two Monarchs, especially by those of His Catholic Majesty, considering that They are so closely related and are bound also by the closest ties of friendship.

Article 8.

There are other maritime Powers which are no less interested in bringing low the English colours for the same reasons outlined above, but the two major signatory Powers would not regard in such a bad light their continued neutrality as they do of that of Portugal. Therefore, should any of the said Powers wish to join in the fray and take part in the war against the English, it is agreed that they shall be welcomed, but no force shall be used to persuade them to do so.

Article 9.

In this war, and in any other in which France and Spain shall be Brothers-in-arms against the English, the two Sovereigns have resolved that neither of Them shall permit any foreign Nation to export to His States cloth, silk, material, nor any other kind of woollen stuffs nor any class of hardware. Throughout the war, France alone shall be entitled to import this merchandise into Spain, and Spain alone shall enjoy similar rights in France, always with the proviso that none of this material originates from England, the common enemy. The two signatories shall introduce rigorous provisions in Their respective states to ensure against any breaches of this undertaking by Their subjects.

* José I, King of Portugal (1750–77).

Article 10.

It being consistent with the dignity and security of Prince Felipe, Duke of Parma, brother of His Catholic Majesty, son-in-law and cousin of His Most Christian Majesty, that those lands belonging to the Duchy of Piacenza which the King of Sardinia claims as his own under the provisos of the Treaty of Aix-la-Chapelle revert to Him, the two Royal Signatories undertake, as a token of the affection and friendship They bear the said Prince-Duke, to take pains to obtain for the King of Sardinia compensation in direct proportion to His losses occasioned by this reversion, and this undertaking is made by His Most Christian Majesty in recognition of the promise made by Him to the said King, while His Catholic Majesty is content for His part to aid and abet His Most Christian Majesty in fulfilling His promise.

Article 11.

The two signatory Powers are in agreement that, should it prove advisable to communicate this convention to a third Power, either in full or in part, such a communication shall only be made by common consent of the two signatories.

Article 12.

This Agreement shall be ratified by the two signatory Powers, and an exchange of copies made within one month of the date of signing, or earlier should this prove possible.

We, the undersigned, Ambassadors Plenipotentiary of His Catholic Majesty and His Most Christian Majesty, in virtue of the powers invested in us do order our credentials to be faithfully transcribed and appended to this document, and do witness this present Treaty with our signatures and append to it our own seals. Versailles, 4th February, 1762. – Marquis Grimaldi. Duc de Choiseul.'

(Palacio Atard, *El tercer Pacto de Familia*, pp. 348 ff.)

49

*Peace reigns. The Conquests in Portugal and the capture
of Sacramento compensate in part for the loss of Habana
and Manila. Permanent treaty agreed between Our Lord
the King and His Most Christian Majesty, on the one hand,
and his Britannic Majesty on the other, Paris, 10th of
February 1763; to which treaty His Most Faithful Majesty
acquiesced that same day*

1763

'In the name of the Blessed and Indissoluble Trinity; Father, Son
and Holy Ghost, Amen.

Be it known to all those whom it may in any way concern. The
Almighty has been pleased to sow a spirit of friendship and brother-
hood in the hearts of those Rulers whose quarrels have caused
upheaval in all four quarters of the globe, and to inspire them with
the design of spreading the sweet fruits of peace where there has been
hitherto a long drawn out and bloody war which had its beginning
in the disputes between France and England during the reign of ...
King George II ... and has continued during the reign of George
III, His heir and successor, and has drawn Spain and Portugal into
its embrace.

... Article XII: The Island of Minorca shall be restored to His
Britannic Majesty, as shall also the fortress of San Felipe, in the
same condition which pertained when it was taken by the armies
of His Most Christian Majesty, together with the artillery with
which the said island and said fortress were furnished at the time
of their capture.

... Article XVI: The Question of the prizes captured by subjects
of the British Crown from the Spanish during peace time shall be
referred to the tribunals of the British Admiralty, as is laid down in
international law, and the legality of the said prizes, vis-à-vis the
Spanish and British nations, shall be decided, and compensation paid,
according to international law and in accordance with the laws
of the country which moved the peace.

... Article XVII: His Britannic Majesty shall see that all fortifications erected by His subjects in Honduras and elsewhere in the

Americas on Spanish soil shall be demolished ... and His Catholic
Majesty shall not permit the subjects of His Britannic Majesty or
those working for them in the said places to be in any way disturbed
or interrupted as they go about their business of felling Log-wood
or Campeachy-wood trees, loading them up and carrying them off;
and He hereby grants permission for them to erect the necessary
dwelling-places and work-sheds for themselves, their families and
their belongings, and vouches for their safety therein ...

Article XVIII: His Catholic Majesty, in His Own Name and that
of His successors, hereby relinquishes any claim He may have
entered in the name of the Basques or of any others of His subjects
to enjoy rights to fish in the waters off Newfoundland.

Article XIX: His Highness, the King of Great Britain, shall restore to the Spanish Crown all lands conquered on the Island of
Cuba, together with the city of Habana; and this city and all other
forts on the said island shall be restored in the same condition as
they were in when they were taken by the armies of His Britannic
Majesty ...

Article XX: As a consequence of the restoration set down in
the preceding article, His Catholic Majesty makes over to His
Britannic Majesty all rights to Florida, together with the stronghold of St Augustine and the Bay of Pensacola, and also all those
territories occupied by Spain in North America to the east and to
the south-east of the river Mississippi, and does constitute Himself
as guarantor of them ... His Britannic Majesty undertakes for His
part to permit the inhabitants of those countries, ceded to Him as
above, the right freely to practise the Catholic Faith, and shall to
this end issue express instructions and take effective measures to
ensure that His new Roman Catholic subjects shall be able to practise
their faith in accordance with the Roman rights, in so far as that is
countenanced by British Law.

... His Catholic Majesty ... shall be permitted to remove all those
possessions belonging to Him, both artillery and other effects ...

Article XXI: The Spanish and the French armies shall, without
any exception, withdraw from all those territories, encampments,
lands, cities, towns and castles belonging to His Most Faithful
Majesty on the continent of Europe, which have been conquered by
the arms of Spain and France, and shall return them in the same
condition in which they were when they were taken together with
the artillery and munitions with which they were supplied.

We, the undersigned, Ambassadors Extraordinary, and Ministers
Plenipotentiary, in virture of the plenary powers invested in us,
have witnessed this present treaty with our signatures, and do

append to it our own seals. Dated at Paris, 10th February, 1763.
    Marquis Grimaldi – Choiseul.   Duke of Praslin – Bedford.'
    (*Colección de los tratados de paz* . . . , Vol. III, pp. 235 ff.)

50

The Order to reduce the size of capes and hats worn at Court which was to lead to the 'Esquilache revolt'

1766

'Prohibition on the wearing of full length capes, wide soft-brim hats, round hats, caps pulled down hard on the head, and masks in the Royal Palaces and at Court.

    The Royal Decrees and proclamations of 1716, 1719, 1723, 1729, 1737 and 1740 prohibiting the use of masks, of full-length capes, wide-brimmed hats, caps pulled down hard on the head, bonnets and hair-nets, and in particular the Royal Decree ... renewed in 1745, having proved ineffective in banishing from the Court the unsightly and perilous custom of wearing disguise, We do hereby make the provision that no person of whatever quality, rank or condition may, in any part of Our Court or anywhere in the vicinity of Our Royal Person or in the walks and countryside round about, use the said dress of full-length cape and round hat as a means of disguise; for it is Our will, and We hereby make an order to this effect, that all civilian persons of whatever class – and hereinunder are included all persons that do live on rents or on their properties or receive salaries in virtue of their employ, or in virtue of honorary posts which they hold, and all others, together with those of their household staff and servants who do not wear livery as is sometimes the practice – shall use the short cape (that shall be at least one quarter of its own length from the ground), redingote, or short cloak, and shall wear only powdered wigs or else their own hair, and a three-cornered hat such that they shall at no time be disguised or their face be hidden from view, and, as for the artisans and the rest of the populace (that is, those not entitled to wear military dress), although these may use the cape, it shall be only with a three-cornered hat or a cap of the style permitted the common people and the poorest and most beggarly among them; failure to comply with this being punishable by a fine of six ducats or twelve days in prison for the first offence ... and as for persons of quality, distinguished as such by their income or their holding of high office, the Courts shall inform Us of the first contravention of this edict, together with the penalty which they deem fit and proper; it is, however, Our wish that the said penalties shall not be applied to muleteers, carters and others who bring goods to the Court and do but pass through, provided that they are dressed in their own clothes and are not in disguise; but, should such persons tarry at Court for longer than three days to effect some business, even though this be in inns and taverns, they shall use the three-cornered hat and not the round one, and only these caps We have permitted, and shall keep their faces uncovered, under penalty as set out above.'

(Novísima recopilación de las leyes de España, Book III, Section XIX, Law XIII.)

51

Shocked by the disturbances in Madrid occasioned by Esquilache's law about the cape and hat, Carlos III bows to the popular will

1766

'Royal Despatch given in the Pardo Palace on the 25th of March 1766 (addressed to Bishop Diego de Rojas y Contreras, Governor of the Council).

The King has hearkened with His customary mercy to Your Lordship's message, and gives His royal word that He will fulfil and ensure the execution of all those promises made yesterday, of His own great mercy and love, to the people of Madrid; and that He would have granted the same favours whenever and wherever their cries had reached Him. However, His Majesty expects from the same people of Madrid that, in keeping with the loyalty and gratitude which they owe Him in return for the benefits and favours with which He has graced them, and especially in return for the great kindness which he has just bestowed upon them, they shall maintain that unruffled, peaceful and undisturbed atmosphere which should pertain throughout the Realm, and shall abstain from forming rebellious gatherings and mobs either to protest about their grievances, or to indulge in wild demonstrations of acclamation. And all the while there is no positive proof of the said calm, the measures herein proposed by His Majesty shall not be put into effect.'

(Sáinz de Robles, Federico, *Historia de Madrid*, vol. II, p. 284.)

52

The rebellion at Zaragoza, which was provoked by economic causes, is calmed down by labourers with the almost complete lack of involvement on the part of the authorities, who were taken by surprise

1766

'... Zaragoza awoke on the morning of the first of April of this present year, 1766, to find posters, lampoons, and threats, from the People, affixed in her public places, demanding the immediate expulsion of the Mayor of Zaragoza, the Marquis of Avilés, and his son, and threatening that, if, before the week was out, the price of wheat, oil, and beans was not reduced, the house of the Mayor and (those of other important persons) would be razed to the ground ... and also that the Mayor, his son and Domesain would be killed ... On the fourth, in order to goad the common people into hatred of those mentioned above, the rioters, who had hitherto lain low, gave vent to their anger in the following terms.

Copy of the Proclamation of the rebellious mob in Zaragoza:

"We, the watchdogs of the common weal in this city, do hereby call upon all persons desirous of upholding the Rights, Prerogatives and Privileges which are envisaged under Civil and Public Law and countenanced by International Law to support us in our struggle against our cruel enemies who hoard up for themselves the rightful possessions of the poor in Christ, and do inform them that, having affixed in public places three posters containing friendly warnings to the Mayor and to his entourage, and having experienced no alleviation of our lot, but rather being forced to watch these individuals continuing to wallow in their corruption, we do hereby order the people that, should there be, between the date of the publication of our first declaration and the eighth of this present month, no moves made to improve the common lot, as we so fervently desire there should be, they shall furnish themselves with whatever they need and that they shall, at a prearranged signal, muster at the given place to put into effect those acts of violence and hostility permitted us in such cases, and, in order that it be made common knowledge and that no man be able to claim ignorance of it, we do order this our declaration to be affixed in the usual public places and do append to it our signature, and it is hereby witnessed by the undersigned, our secretary. Zaragoza, 4th April, seventeen hundred and sixty-six. We, the watchdogs of the common weal, By order of the aforesaid, Justice ..."

The Marquis of Castelar, Captain-General in Zaragoza, issued an authority to the citizens to bake their own bread. The people stoned the agents of the law and demonstrated to shouts of "To Castelar's! Long Live the King!" Castelar pleaded with them to remain calm, but was unsuccessful in his attempts to stop them taking off and sacking the house of the Mayor. The Mayor took to his heels. The Archbishop of Zaragoza and Canon, now Saint, Pignatelli also intervened but to no effect. The sacking and looting went on for several days until Domingo Tomás was granted leave by Castelar to restore order with a group of labourers. As a result, the Captain-General was able to issue the following edict:

"I, the Marquis of Castelar, Captain-General and Governor of the Realm of Aragón, President of the Royal Council of Aragón, which body has authorised this declaration, do hereby decree: That for the greater peace and safety of the city it shall be publicly decreed that from the moment of the divulgation of this order, it shall be prohibited for citizens, both men and women, to band together or to go abroad in groups of four or more, and that this decree shall be obeyed on pain of death, and that this decision shall be broadcast to the people and that they shall be warned that the only persons permitted to band together, or to carry offensive weapons, or be armed in self-defence, shall be those labourers and honourable citizens of those parishes who have, as a token of the love they bear His Majesty Our King, offered themselves for the defence of the nation and the orderliness of this city. And it is hereby decreed that all inhabitants of Zaragoza shall kindle torches and light their houses so that this same end of establishing a reign of law and order in this city shall be served by banishing from the streets those who are the source of the present disturbances, and by facilitating the task of distinguishing between the friends of the State and Her enemies. This order shall be obeyed until further notice. Zaragoza, seventh day of April, seventeen hundred and sixty-six. The Marquis of Castelar." '

(Relación verdadera y circumstanciada, de todo lo acaecido en la ciudad de Zaragoza ...)

53

After the enforced downfall of Esquilache, a call for an energetic politician: The Count of Aranda

1766

'Since We are so greatly pleased by your person and the zeal with which you serve Us, We have appointed you President of the Council. You will take up office from tomorrow, and We trust that you will fulfil the duties of this office in a manner compatible both with Our conscience and with your own.

Aranjuez, Eleventh of April, seventeen sixty-six.

We, the King – to the Count of Aranda.'

(Dánvila y Collado, Manuel, Historia del Reinado de Carlos III, vol. ii, p. 358.)

54

Expulsion of the Society of Jesus

1766

'Carlos, by the Grace of God, King of Castille etc. To his Most Serene Majesty, Prince Carlos, Our dearly beloved son, to Our royal family, and to all the Prelates, Dukes, Marquises, Counts, Persons of quality, and all means of religious Orders, Knights-Commander of the Military Orders, and their Deputies, Governors of Our castles, strongholds and palaces, to the Members of Our Royal Council, the President and other Members of Our tribunals, Officers and Administrators of Our Palaces, Court and Chancery, and to all Our Royal Magistrates and Intendants, Petty Magistrates, Governors, Lord Mayors and Mayors, and all other Judges and Justices in these Our realms; both of untied lands and of those tied to landed estates, abbeys, and orders, of whatever state, condition, quality and importance, both now and at any time in the future; to each and every one of you may it be known that in accordance with the conclusions reached, on the twenty-ninth day of January last, by the members of Our Royal Council in extraordinary session convened on account of the recent troubles, and, bearing in mind opinions of other persons of exemplary character, renowned for their experience in these matters, who have reached the same conclusions and reported their feelings to Us, and not unmindful of the grave responsibility which We bear as King to preserve justice, law and order throughout Our realm, and directed by other considerations of great moment, We have, in virtue of the supreme temporal authority invested in Us by the Almighty to safeguard Our subjects and encourage them in their respect for the Crown, taken the resolve to banish from all the lands attaching to Our Crown, in Spain, in the Indies, in the Philippines and elsewhere, the regular clergy of the Society of Jesus, both Jesuit priests and their coadjutors and the lay brothers who have but taken their first vows, and also the novices who have chosen to follow them; and to order that all their properties on Our soil be confiscated; and, to ensure that this Our decree be observed in all Our lands, We have, by means of Our Royal Decree, issued on the twenty-seventh day of February, invested exclusive plenary powers in the President of Our Council, the Count of Aranda and granted him authority to proceed forthwith to put this Our royal resolve into practice.

And We are therefore resolved and hereby do issue instructions to Our Council to this effect, that this Our royal decision be published throughout Our Realm, making known Our faith in all the other religious orders, and Our satisfaction with them and with the way they earn Our appreciation by their humility and unimpeachable doctrine, their obedience to the monastic rule, their exemplary service to the Church, their praiseworthy work as teachers, their uninterrupted provision of men to help the Bishops and parish priests in their task of offering pastoral guidance to the people, and their abstention from the affairs of state as foreign to the asceticism expected of the monk.

Also it is hereby made known to the Diocesan Bishops, Town

Councils, Ecclesiastical Chapters, and other bodies established in authority throughout Our Realm, that the just and momentous reasons, which Our Royal Person has recognised, have forced Us to take these necessary measures against Our will, having recourse only to the temporal powers invested in Us, and We are in this matter following Our own benign instincts as Father and Protector of all our peoples.

We do hereby declare that by confiscation of the properties of the Society, it shall be understood that reference is made to their goods and effects, both chattels and real estate, as well as all rents on ecclesiastical property to which they have lawful entitlement within Our territories, without any prejudice to any *responsibilities vouchsafed them by their founders,* or to their individual sustenance which shall be of one hundred pesos for each full priest for the remainder of his natural life, and of ninety pesos for each lay-brother, which sums shall be paid out of the fund established from the sale of the goods belonging to the Society.

From these provisions for the granting of sustenance, all those Jesuits of foreign extraction who, without proper cause, reside in Our lands, either in Colleges or in private houses not part of Jesuit establishments, and who wear the cloth or perform the duties of an abbot, or whatever the office in which they are employed, shall be excluded and they shall all, without any exception, be obliged to leave Our Realm.

Nor shall these novices, who of their own free will follow in the footsteps of their superiors, be included within these provisions, since they have not yet taken solemn vows and are still at liberty to leave the Order.

We do declare that, should any Jesuit renounce the cloth (for they are all to continue as clerics), or should any of them give just cause for resentment on the part of the Court, either through his actions or by his pen, the pension assigned him shall cease forthwith. And although We are far from entertaining the notion that the Body of the Society should depart from the strict path of duty and encourage or permit any of its number to write against the respect and obedience due to this Our resolution, under cover of penning Apologies or Deferences calculated to disturb the goodly order of Our Realm, or should, through secret emissaries, conspire so to disrupt Our Realm, We do hereby declare that, in such an unlikely event, the pension assigned the whole Society shall cease.

Every six months a sum of money equal to half the annual allowance paid to the Jesuits shall be made over to them at the Banco

* * There seems to be some error in the Spanish at this point.

del Giro* through the good offices of Our Ambassador in Rome
who shall take particular note of those who have died or who have
ceased to be entitled to their pension as a result of their own mis-
demeanours, in order that the allowances for such persons may be
cancelled.

As for the provision and administration of sums equal to those
now paid by the Society to good works, such as grants to poor
parishes, conciliar seminaries, and charitable institutions, and to
other pious ends, We shall consult with the Diocesan Bishops as to
what is required and shall make separate arrangements to ensure
that no money is denied any truly pious cause, nor any public
undertaking placed in jeopardy, nor the rights of a third party
ignored.

We hereby do declare that it shall be law and general practice
never to permit any individual of the Society nor any body or
community of that Order to darken our shores again, no matter
what pretext they might allege for doing so, and that neither Our
Council nor any other Court of the Realm shall listen to any plea
to the contrary, but rather that they shall impose the heaviest
sentences on any person disobeying this Our Royal edict, and on
any persons aiding and abetting any such attempt, and that they
shall be charged with inciting to riot.

No Jesuit, though he abandon the Order and have Papal dispensation to do so, whether he renounce the cloth or remain a cleric,
or become a member of another order, shall be welcome in these
Our Realms unless it be with special permission from Us.

If he should succeed in obtaining such permission, which shall
only be granted after all the circumstances have been taken into
consideration, he shall be obliged to take an oath of loyalty to the
Crown before the President of Our Council, and to enter into an
undertaking that he will have no dealings, either in public or in
private, with individual members of the Society or with its General,
nor take any steps nor make any overtures to others, nor insinuate
either directly or indirectly on behalf of the Society, on pain of
being held a traitor to the State, at which time evidence in camera
may be entered against him.

Nor shall he be permitted to teach, preach or hear confessions in
these Realms, even should he have renounced the order and shaken
off his oath of obedience to the General, though he may enjoy
benefices which do not entail any such duties.

No subject of Our Crown, be he in holy orders or be he a lay
person or a member of a religious order, shall be permitted to apply

* International Banking House.

to the General of the Society for a Licence of Affiliation, on pain of being held a traitor to the State at which time evidence in camera may be entered against him.

All those who do at present have such licences shall hand them in to the President of Our Council or to the Magistrates and Justices of the Realm that they may make no further use of them and that the licences themselves be filed away; while yet it shall prove no impediment to them to have had them in the past, provided that they comply readily with this provision and hand them in forthwith. The justices shall keep secret the lists of those who have handed them in, so that the reputation of such persons shall not be affected.

Because this ban on the Jesuits is so absolute and admits of no exception, any person keeping up contact with them shall be punished in proportion to the enormity of his offence.

We hereby do outlaw all writings, speeches, and incitements either for or against these provisions but rather impose absolute silence in this matter on all Our subjects, and do hereby order that all those who break this rule shall be punished as guilty of "lèse majesté".

In order to forestall any altercations and misunderstandings between private individuals who have no right to pass judgement on or interpret the orders of their Sovereign, We do hereby expressly forbid all persons to write, print or distribute broadsheets or pamphlets which treat of the expulsion of the Jesuits from Our lands, unless it be by special permission of the Government, and We do hereby prohibit the Chief Censor and his assistants and all the Justices of Our Realm from granting permission for licences so to do, since this whole matter should be under the direct jurisdiction of the President and members of Our Council and be dealt with in the full knowledge of Our Attorney-General.

We most emphatically charge Their Excellencies the Diocesan Bishops and the Superiors of the religious orders not to grant leave to those under their authority to write, print or speak in public on this issue, for We shall hold them responsible for any unlooked for transgression of this by any one of their number, as We judge provided for under the Law of King Juan the First and the Royal Decree of the 18th of September last, which is conducive to its prompt execution, for which all men should strive, since it is in the public interest, and it behoves them to do so as individuals lest they incur Our royal displeasure.

We do hereby instruct Our Council to formulate and broadcast to the people a Royal Decree which contains the provisions set out above, to be couched in the strictest possible terms and to ensure that it reaches the ears of all Our subjects and is observed to the letter, and that the Justices and courts exact those penalties laid down to ensure its prompt and strict observation, and to make all the necessary orders and to give this matter priority over all other business because of its importance for Our Royal Person. We have been pleased to order that copies of this Royal Decree be sent to the Holy Office and to the Council of the Indies, to the body responsible for the religious orders, and also to the Treasury, so that they might know of this Our resolve and act upon it.

And that it may be promptly and strictly adhered to in all Our domains – Our royal decree of the 27th of March which contains the aforegoing resolution which shall be observed and fulfilled exactly as it is set out therein having been published in full session of Our Council – it was agreed that this present declaration shall be published as Law and Pragmatic Sanction, as though it had originated in Parliament and been authorised by that body, as indeed it is Our will it shall be, and that it should there suffer no alteration whatever, to which end, should this prove necessary, We do hereby declare null and void and of no effect whatever, any thing which might run contrary to it. We do therefore charge Their Excellencies the Archbishops, Bishops, Superiors of all religious orders, both mendicant and monastic, Visitors, Provisors, Curates and all other Clerics and Ecclesiastical Judges in these Our realms, to observe the Pragmatic set out above to the letter, and not to countenance any contravention whatsoever of its stipulations, and We do hereby order the Members of Our Council, the presiding Magistrates, the Members and Officials of Our Court, Our Palace, Our Tribunals and Chancery, the Petty Magistrates, Governors, Lord Mayors and Mayors and all other Judges and Justices in these Our realms to keep, obey and observe the said law and Pragmatic Sanction, and to observe it in its entirety and to make any arrangements necessary to ensure compliance with it, without it proving necessary for any other decree to be issued besides this one, which shall take effect from the moment of its publication in the usual manner in Madrid and in the cities, townships and villages in these Our realms, for it is thus that service to Our royal person and the good and well-being of all Our subjects is best served. That is Our will and We desire also that the printed version of this Our Epistle, bearing the signature of Don Ignacio Estéban de Higareda, that person who has served longer than any other as clerk to Our royal despatch and to Our Council of State, shall be afforded the same attention and obedience as the original. Given in Our palace of El Pardo on the second day of April in the year seventeen hundred and sixty-seven.

We, the King. I, Don José Ignacio de Goyeneche, Secretary to

Our Lord the King, set this down at His Command. The Count of
Aranda. Don Francisco Cepeda. Don Jacinto Tudó. Don Francisco
de Salazar y Aguero. Don José Manuel Domínguez. Recorded by
Don Nicolás Berdugo, Vice-Chancellor. Don Nicolás Berdugo.

PROMULGATION

In the City of Madrid on the second day of the month of April in
the year seventeen hundred and sixty-seven, before the gates of the
Royal Palace, opposite the main balcony to the King's appartments
and at the Gate of Guadalajara, which is where all the dealings and
trade of the merchants and officers take place, and in the presence
of Don Juan Esteban de Salaverrí, Don Juan Antonio de Peñarre-
donda, Don Benito Antonio de Barreda and Don Pedro Jímenez de
Mesa, Officers of the Royal Household and Court, the aforegoing
Royal Pragmatic was promulgated to the sound of drums and
trumpets by a town-crier in the presence of many several members
of the said Royal Household and Court and a host of others, to
which fact I, Don Francisco López Navamuel, Clerk to the Royal
Despatch and the Members of the Council, do hereby attest, Don
Francisco López Navamuel.

This is a copy of the original Royal Pragmatic Sanction together
with its promulgation, which I hereby witness.'

(*Pragmática sanción de su Majestad en fuerza de ley...*)

55

Peace-treaty with Morocco

1767

'Preliminary Articles which shall serve as the basis of a peace
settlement between His Catholic Majesty and His Imperial Majesty
the Ruler of Morocco, as communicated to Sidi Ahamet Elgacel on
the 20th of May, 1767.

1. The peace settlement shall be binding and shall be adhered to
in perpetuity by both Sovereigns, and Each shall show towards the
Other true friendship. To facilitate this, it is hereby agreed that
They shall deal with each Other as equals and whenever possible
strive to procure the well-being of the Other, in such wise that, not

only shall They display no hostility towards each Other on the high seas, but rather shall Each protect the Other and come to His aid whenever He be in need; and this obligation They undertake to fulfil not only on the high seas but also along the length of Their coasts and in Their harbours, coming to each Other's aid and furnishing each Other's needs; and all aid thus supplied shall be charged at a proper and just rate.

2. That They may henceforth avoid all those troubles arising from a mutual inability to understand the passports carried by the Other's shipping, it is hereby agreed that all such passports shall be issued in a format such that no ability on the part of those that examine them to read the language of the other shall be required. It is agreed that all ships caught not carrying such passports shall be escorted back to their country of origin by those corsairs or war-ships who apprehend them, and that the small ships used by fisher-men to fish in their native waters shall not be required to carry passports.

3. No warship of either nation may require a warship of the other to do more than produce these same passports for inspection. Not only may no demand be made for a search of the other's cargo, or any other inspection whatever, but neither may a demand be made that the other launch its boats; the vessel issuing the demand that passports be produced shall be the one to launch such a boat, and from it only one man shall be permitted to board the other's vessel, and this shall be the person who shall carry out the said verification of documents. Any enemy who shall be found on board one of these vessels shall be unharmed and none of his goods and belongings tampered with.

4. All those of one party wrecked on the shores of the Other shall be treated with the utmost hospitality, and every effort shall be made to salvage their vessels and no demand be made for pay-ment for such operations, or, at worst, no more be charged than proper and fitting.

5. There shall be free trade between the two Nations and any vessel of the one shall be entitled to remain in the harbours of the other for as long as she requires, and every citizen of the one shall be empowered to buy and sell, and to load and unload goods of whatever class, wherever and whenever he choose and with whom-soever he desire, on the soil of the other, even inland, unless the said goods be contraband.

6. All landing and sailing dues payable by the one in the country of the other shall be adjusted as far as is possible against those dues exacted from the shipping of other Nations, so that the two Realms

may share a mutual advantage. All men-o'-war, shall, however, be exempted from payment of any such dues and shall, moreover, not be required to pay anchorage nor any other tariff normally imposed.

7. In order to facilitate and foster trade between the two Nations, Each shall set up a Consulate in that harbour She deem most suitable, together with Vice-Consuls in all other ports where they are required, and these shall protect the interests of their nationals, take legal proceedings against them whenever the occasion arises, and issue the necessary passports.

8. Fishing will be permitted only in the immediate vicinity of the harbours and only under licence, and the Harbour-masters shall prescribe the limits within which this shall be permitted.

9. Any person from one nation found on the shores of the other, either as a result of his having anchored off them out of necessity or out of ignorance, or with more sinister purpose in mind, shall be handed over, together with the vessel concerned and all its cargo, to the nearest Consul or Vice-Consul of his Nation, that this official investigate the offence and that the punishment attaching thereunto be fixed by a member of his own Nation.

10. In order to safeguard this mutual trade, His Imperial Majesty shall inform the Algerians and the other Berber peoples, and any other Christian nation who is at war with Spain, that they shall not be permitted to attack the Spanish within thirty miles of His Imperial Majesty's shores, nor in any part of those waters that lie between the Spanish coast and the continent of Africa and that fall between two lines, one drawn from Cape Spartel to Trafalgar and the other from the Zaffarin Islands to Cape Sacratif. And, should His Imperial Majesty not succeed in persuading them to comply with this request, He shall take whatever steps He choose to safeguard the said trade.

11. Any vessel sailing under the flag of His Imperial Majesty and putting in at a Spanish port shall be subject to the quarantine regulations issued by the Consul.

12. His Imperial Majesty shall grant leave for the fishing-barges from the Canaries to anchor in the Estuary of the River Noun, which lies to the south of Cape Noun, or in some other harbour on His soil yet further off to the south of the said river, so that the Canary fishermen may salt their catch there.

13. In the ports of Ceuta, Al-Hoceima, Peñon* and Melilla, grazing-land shall be set aside for the herds belonging to the garrisons stationed there, and the boundaries of these pastures shall be fixed by Commissioners appointed by both Nations, and these

* Peñon Island, off Algiers.

shall be given wide powers and their decision shall be final and binding on both signatories.

14. Any Spaniards deserting from the said Garrisons, and all Moors seeking asylum therein, shall straightway and with no delay be returned to their respective camps by the first Officers or Governors to apprehend them, unless it be that the desertion of such persons is motivated by a change of Faith.

15. All citizens of either Nation who seek refuge or sell their wares in the territory of the other, shall be granted asylum, for all such persons shall be guaranteed their freedom, whatever the cause of their emigration.

16. All Christians seeking refuge in the garrisons or on board the warships of His Catholic Majesty lying at anchor in His Imperial Majesty's ports, shall also be guaranteed their right of asylum, as shall any Mohammedan seeking refuge on board the warships of His Imperial Majesty.

17. All internal differences between citizens of the Spanish Nation, both of a criminal and of a civil nature, shall be settled exclusively by the Consul, and, should he be absent at the time, the culprit shall be detained at the Consul's pleasure.

18. The property of all Spanish citizens who die on His Imperial Majesty's soil shall be at the disposition of the Consul, and, should such persons perish in some place where there is no Consul, the property shall be placed in the safekeeping of the Justices, and the said consul shall be informed of their death, until the Consul decides how it is to be disposed of. In the same manner, the Justices of the Spanish Realm shall lay hold of all property belonging to any Moor who dies on Spanish soil until such time as His Imperial Majesty receives communication from them as to the death and determines how the property shall be disposed of. All this unless it chance to pass that the lawful heir to the said property be on hand, in the which case all the said property shall straightways be made over to him, should the deceased not have made a will naming some other party as beneficiary.

19. If it should happen that anything occur which run contrary to the Articles stipulated above or be inconsistent with the spirit of true friendship which the two Nations shall profess towards one another, this should not be held a sufficient cause for the peace-treaty to be broken off. In such an eventuality, the injured party shall communicate its grievance to the other and demand satisfaction. Should such satisfaction not be forthcoming within a period of six months from that date, then the peace shall be deemed to have been violated.

20. If such a lamentable violation of the peace ever come to pass, then a six-month moratorium on hostilities shall come into force, during which time any individual of either Nation shall be permitted to leave the country of the other, taking with him all his goods and effects, and all such persons shall be free to enter the garrisons occupied by their forces and to go on board any vessel of their own choosing, without any harassment whatever, and without their journey being imperilled in any way whatsoever.

Individual Articles

The succour of the garrisons being so vital in times of need, it is expected of His Imperial Majesty that He allow all necessary supplies to get through to the said garrisons.

It is also expected that His Imperial Majesty follow the example set by His Catholic Majesty and entreat the Algerians to set free all slaves of Spanish nationality who, by reason of age or infirmity, are no longer in a fit state to serve any purpose.'

(Rodriguez Casado, *Política marroquí de Carlos III*, pp. 409 ff.)

56

An attempt to solve the African question. An abortive assault on Algiers

1775

'Madrid, 18th July.

On Sunday, the 16th last, the whole Court put on its finery to celebrate a most happy event: the birthday of Princess María Josefa.

The King of Morocco having declared war on Spain this last year, while yet this Realm had not afforded him the least cause for complaint, nor in any manner failed to comply with the letter of the Treaty which at that time bound the two Realms in friendship, His Majesty the King found himself obliged to take very stiff precautions to protect those of his strongholds bordering on lands under the sway of that Moorish Ruler from attack. The moves He made were extremely effective as the successes of the Melilla siege readily attest, but yet His Majesty was not contented with this alone, and, accordingly, He mounted an expedition consisting of a considerable strength of both land forces and sea-going ships, with the aim of teaching the Africans a severe lesson and of safeguarding as far as possible His subjects' freedom to journey the high seas in safety.

This force mustered in Cartagena harbour and was due to put out to sea on the first of July last, bound for Algiers, where it was planned to mount a surprise attack in reprisal for the grave hurts done our shipping by subjects of that Protectorate, but contrary winds kept up for a considerable length of time and the squadron could not put out of harbour nor succeed in getting away from our shores until the end of the said month.

The fleet finally arrived off Algiers and the two commanders – His Excellency Count O'Reilly, Commander-in-Chief of the land-based forces, and His Excellency Don Pedro Castejón, Commander-in-Chief of the Marine strength – gave orders forthwith to stand at anchor in the bay itself until such time as circumstances were favourable for an attack. They observed that the enemy were well provided to mount a resolute defence, doubtless because the un-expected delay of the convoy in Cartagena had given them due warning and made them suspect its true destination, and the Commanders therefore decided to distract the enemy's attention from the spot they had selected as the most likely site for a landing, and accordingly ordered the "San José" and the "Orient" to stage an attack on two fortresses and a number of other redoubts in enemy hands. This they did with notable vigour and considerable success, despite the great dangers run by the first-mentioned of them which, with her masts and rigging hit, a hole blasted through her hull and her mainstays split in twain by a ball, drifted in the current to well within range of the enemy cannon.

The two Commanders, having agreed on a site for landing the army, and judging the circumstances propitious, issued orders to their respective forces that the landing was to be effected at dawn on the eighth. So it was that the small landing-craft formed up in seven columns and, with support from an escort of the necessary number of men-o'-war, made for the shore where, at four in the morning, and in complete silence, the first landing-party, eighty strong, was put off with the greatest discipline and despatch, a league and a half to the east side of the city. The remainder of the force followed suit over the next few hours, the whole operation being effected with unbelievable speed. Although by now the number of enemy oppos-ing our advance was considerably swollen, our forces would have had little trouble in securing a valuable position on a nearby hill, had it not been for the reckless bravery of the advance-guard which,

heedless of the repeated orders and ceaseless arguments of its Commanders, threw itself into the fray at once to try to take this hill.
Those who were put ashore in the second wave had no alternative
but to support the attack of the advance-party, and either to emulate
its foolhardiness or join with it and thereby ensure that their combined retreat would be as orderly as possible. Thus, general battle
was enjoined and the fighting continued undiminished the whole
day long.

Seeing that the men were exhausted by the heat of the sun and
the ruggedness of the terrain, as well as by the suddenness with
which they had found themselves involved in full-scale operations,
and realising, moreover, that the original plan was not now practic-
able, Count O'Reilly, supported in his resolve by the other Commanders, decided to re-embark the whole force, which he duly did
during the following night, taking off all the guns, munitions and
other equipment which had been landed the previous day.

It is singular how warm both Commanders are in their praises of
the morale, bravery and tenacity shown by all the officers and men
of both services, under such trying circumstances, and in the face
of such a welter of complicated and sudden manoeuvres, and they
are united in their conviction that the whole operation would have
met with unqualified success had not the advance-guard been over-
zealous to get to grips with the enemy and had they not thrown
themselves into the fray in such an ill considered fashion.

The losses of the Moors during this action must have been considerable. We have ourselves lost 600 dead among whose number
figure Field-Marshal Marquis de la Romana, and Lieutenant-Colonel
Don Jerónimo Capmani.'

(Supplement to *Gaceta de Madrid*, 18 July 1775.)

57

First moves towards assisting the rebels in North America in their struggle against Great Britain

1776

'Your Excellency: I have informed His Majesty of the report you
made in your despatch of the 7th of June, on your highly secret
discussions with the Comte de Vergennes on the subject of the aid

which His Crown proposes to make available to the rebels in the British colonies and the other assistance they plan to afford them in secret. The wisdom of His Government in the way in which it is working at one and the same time to weaken the English and thus work for their downfall, and to make the colonials see sense right from the very outset of their independence, is plain for all to see.

His Majesty applauds the actions of the French Court and deems them well suited to the common interests of Spain and of France, and is resolved that, since they both share this common desire to keep the rebellion alive, it is only right and proper that they should both share the cost of supporting it. His Majesty has accordingly instructed me to send Your Excellency the enclosed credit of one million "livres tournois" to be used in this enterprise. We do not ourselves have the means at our disposal to send this aid directly to the rebels with the necessary secrecy and privacy, but Your Excellency is hereby granted leave to discuss with the Comte de Vergennes the best method of utilising this sum of money and how best to ensure that it reaches the rebel forces, and to decide whether it is better that it be sent openly in the manner now adopted by the French, or whether there is some other and more expeditious method of sending it. His Majesty hereby authorises you to send this sum of money by whatever method Your Excellency and the Comte de Vergennes believe most effective.

So as to avoid arousing any suspicions or giving rise to any rumours, I have told the Treasury that this money is to be used for a purchase which His Majesty has instructed Your Excellency to make on His behalf, and I have written this in my own hand to keep it from the eyes of others.

May God preserve Your Excellency and grant you a long life. Madrid, 27th June, 1776. – Marquis Grimaldi. – His Excellency the Count of Aranda.'

(Yela Utrilla, Juan Francisco, *España ante la independencia de los Estados Unidos*, vol. ii, pp. 9–10.)

58

Letter of Introduction from the North-American Delegation to Aranda

1776

'Sir,

We have pleasure in informing Your Excellency that we have been sent by the United States of America to foster good relations between our own States and the Crowns of Spain and France. It is with this purpose in our hearts, as well as because we wish to present to Your Excellency our personal respects, that we declare our intention of paying Your Excellency a visit tomorrow, at whatever hour Your Excellency deems suitable, or on some other day should tomorrow not prove convenient for Your Excellency.

We have, Sir, the honour of being Your Excellency's obedient and humble servants. – B. Franklin. – Silas Deane. – Arthur Lee. Ambassadors Plenipotentiary of the Congress of the United States of America. – To His Excellency, the Count de Aranda, Spanish Ambassador to the French Court. – Paris, 28th December 1776.'

(Yela Utrilla, Juan Francisco, *España ante la independencia...*, vol. ii, pp. 26 ff.)

59

Representations of Arthur Lee to the Spanish Court, setting out the reasons for the American Revolution

1777

'It would appear that the present struggle between Great Britain and America has not been thoroughly understood, and it would, therefore, seem not amiss to give a clear explanation of it.

America has made a declaration of independence and has repulsed two successive attempts on the part of Great Britain to bring Her to heel. On both occasions, America has fought alone and has had only Her zeal, Her sense of outrage and Her enthusiasm to atone for Her lack of experience and of preparation.

But now Great Britain is redoubling Her efforts in Her determination that this coming campaign shall decide the fate of America. It is in such a situation that America now stretches out Her hand in friendship to Spain and France and offers them the trade She has now denied the English. The value of this offer is two-fold since it promises to deprive that arrogant enemy of the trade She would otherwise enjoy. For this reason it must surely be a matter of supreme importance to the two Crowns concerned and not one to be taken lightly by either of them. It is surely reasonable to suppose that neither France nor Spain wishes for Great Britain to come off victor in the present struggle and to gain back America, either by defeating Her in battle or by forcing Her to come to terms. It therefore follows that the only question still left open is the following:

Is it wiser for the two Sovereigns to grasp the hand of friendship proffered Them, and declare Themselves for America right away, or is it more prudent for Them to await the outcome of the present conflict?

To decide which is the wiser course of action, we must first gain some idea of what the outcome of this present conflict is likely to be. Since Great Britain is determined to throw all Her forces behind this latest attempt, we must conclude that the most likely outcome is either the defeat of America, or some compromise based on a mutually held conviction that their respective forces are so equally balanced that no absolute victory would be possible for either, in which circumstances America, despairing of any substantial aid from Europe, would press for just such an agreement. It is patent that the insistence of both Spain and France on maintaining a neutral posture in this conflict leaves the field wide open for Great Britain to pour all Her forces into the American arena and thereby makes just such an outcome all the more likely. Either of the aforesaid solutions of the present conflict would be perilous indeed for both Crowns and would greatly strengthen the British position. If Great Britain is successful and defeats America, She will have acquired a powerful weapon in Her arsenal when She turns to face the said nations, and one which She will not hesitate to use and to go on using for a very long time to come, as anyone who recognises that the British Crown is not unaware that, at the very least, certain people have not looked unkindly on what She called that most dangerous of rebellions, and who is familiar with the Head that wears that Crown – which is one that never allows anything to be forgotten and is an utter stranger to forgiveness, – will readily appreciate. If the war ends in compromise, and Great Britain and America are once again harnessed together, then France and Spain will stand to lose the same advantages and be forced to go in fear of the same course of events as if America had been defeated, and one can conceive therefore, of no more propitious time for Them to show Their hand and to decide the outcome of the war than the present.

For in truth, what hour could be more propitious than this, when Great Britain is still sore pressed by those that were Her colonies, when the issue of the conflict hangs in the balance, and when the entry of Spain or France, not to speak of them both together, would beyond any shadow of a doubt ensure the laurels of victory to America, and make certain that Her independence from England is lasting and permanent? What could be more tempting than to deprive Britain of this huge source of mercantile wealth, this field of operations for Her Navy, and this part of Her Empire? The British Government is so unanimously persuaded that a war in Europe would inevitably mean the loss of America, that there is nothing it fears more. There is not a single Englishman who is unaware of this, and this is the reason that every time He addresses Parliament, the King finds Himself obliged to assure that Body of the continued peace of Europe before they will pay any attention to His exhortations to persist in the war with America, and it is for this same reason that the King has bent over backwards to prevent a split between Spain and Portugal and has lately abandoned the latter. It is reasonable to assume that Great Britain will turn a blind eye to anything short of a gross act of aggression in order to avoid being caught up in a war in Europe while She is still involved in the American conflict. During the last war, America furnished Britain with twelve thousand marines and twenty thousand soldiers, which would now be denied Her, and She would now find three times their number in arms against Her. Her trade with America which (according to Mr Pitt, who was at that time in charge of Her war effort) was a decisive factor in Her victory during the last war, would now be a potent force against Her. It was from America that all the British expeditions against the Isles possessed by Spain and of France were supplied, and it is from there that an invasion of Her own islands can so easily be launched, and, in short, all those advantages which Great Britain enjoyed in the last war can now be turned against Her. For, what could possibly prevent Her from being forced to taste the bitterness of defeat where She once enjoyed the sweets of victory? What policy could ever prevent those two Sovereigns, whose prosperity is so incompatible with Her own, from taking advantage of a golden opportunity like this to humiliate Her; an opportunity which, should it be permitted to pass by, may never come again? For, should Great Britain succeed in strengthening Her position by the annexation of America, either by force of arms or by treaty, all threats of war against Her in the future will be empty, for, as America has been seen up to now as a giant still in its infancy, Great Britain, reunited with such a growing force, shall hold sway over those She hates, and shall be the unquestioned arbiter of the fate of Europe. Now, therefore, is the moment to clip Her wings, once and for all. One of the most respected bodies in English public life reported with lively foresight something like two years ago to the British King, that His government was placing the Nation "in such a position that, by merely tolerating the existence of her rivals, She might succeed in saving Her own skin". Events have most assuredly proved the accuracy of this prediction, and it only remains for Spain and France to take action. – Arthur Lee – Commissioner Plenipotentiary from the Congress of the United States of America. – Burgos, 4th March 1777.'

(Yela Utrilla, Juan Francisco, *España ante la independencia*..., vol. ii, pp. 72 ff.)

60

Letter from Franklin to Aranda, proposing an alliance against Great Britain

1777

Passy, April 7th, 1777.

'I hereby entrust to Your Excellency's safe-keeping a copy of my credentials as Ambassador Plenipotentiary to the Spanish Court, such that, should Your Excellency deem it expedient, You may present them to His Majesty. I am, however, given to understand that the present moment is not propitious for such an Ambassador to present himself at Court and, knowing full well that Congress would have me do nothing which would occasion the least displeasure in a Realm to which it is so heavily indebted, I fear I must postpone my arrival until a more auspicious occasion. Meanwhile, I beg Your Excellency to do me the service of personally conveying to His Majesty this letter in which are set out the proposals contained in the resolution of Congress of the 30th December, 1776. To wit:

"To His Excellency the Count of Aranda.

"Should His Catholic Majesty wish to make an alliance with the United States and wage war on Great Britain, the United States shall undertake to support any attack He may make on the port and city of Pensacola, always provided that the United States shall continue to be permitted to sail freely up and down the Mississippi and to make use of the port of Pensacola. The United States shall declare war on the King of Portugal (assuming that it prove true that the said King of Portugal has indeed provoked the United States by banning all her shipping from His ports and confiscating some of Her vessels), always with the proviso that such an enterprise does not incur the displeasure of the French and Spanish Courts and that they are in a position to support it."

On the assumption that the two Nations be closely united in this common enterprise, and that they both deem it tactically sound to mount an attack on the British Isles in the Carribbean, Congress, in addition to what is set out above, proposes to provide supplies to the value of two million dollars and to furnish six frigates, each of at least twenty-four guns, fully equipped and ready to go into service in the joint Fleet, and also to take all other measures at its disposal, as befits a true ally, to ensure the success of the said attack, and to do all this without being motivated by any desire whatever to occupy the said isles in Her own name.

All these proposals are open to debate and may be altered to suit the circumstances.

With the greatest respect, I have the honour etc.'

(Yela Utrilla, Juan Francisco, *España ante la independencia...*, vol. ii, p. 94.)

61

Preliminary Treaty between His Catholic Majesty and Her Most Faithful Majesty* concerning the boundaries of their respective possessions in South America. The Treaty ratified by His Majesty in San Lorenzo el Real on 11th October 1777

1777

'... His Catholic Majesty and Her Most Faithful Majesty, having been imbued by Divine Providence with a sincere desire to heal the breach which has separated Them and Their respective Nations for nigh on three centuries with respect to the boundaries of Their domains in America and in Asia, have, that They might achieve this and restore henceforth that harmony, friendship and good understanding that become Their close family ties, the mutual love they do profess, the interests of the Nations They so fitly govern, and the sublime qualities inherent in such great Monarchs, resolved upon agreement, drawn up and agreed to the present preliminary treaty:
... Art III. Since one of the chief causes of the differences between the two Crowns has been the setting up of the colony of Sacramento by the Portuguese, and Her having laid claim to the island of San Gabriel and other posts and territories along the north bank of the River Plate, together with Her demands that both Nations shall have shipping rights in the Plate, and even up the River Uruguay, it is hereby agreed, for the mutual benefit of the signatories and to ensure a permanent peace between them, that the said shipping rights in the Plate and the Uruguay and all those territories running along both north and south banks of the said rivers shall be the exclusive property of the Spanish Crown and its subjects, Spanish territorial rights extending along the north bank of the rivers, from where the waters of the Periquí or Pepín-Guazú flow into the said Uruguay on its western bank, to a dividing line which shall be drawn, starting at the sea and taking in the stream known as the Chuy and Fort San Miguel and running along the shores of Lake Mirim and thence across to take in the head waters and springs of the Negro, which river, along with all the others which flow into the

* The King of Spain and the Queen of Portugal.

aforesaid Plate and Uruguay up to and including the said Pepín-Guazú, shall belong exclusively to the Spanish Crown, together with all the land encompassed by these boundaries, and including the said colony of Sacramento and all its territories, the island of San Gabriel, and all other posts lying within it which have hitherto been in the possession of the Crown of Portugal or to which She has entered a claim ... to this end Her Most faithful Majesty, in Her own name and in that of all Her descendants and successors, does herewith abdicate in favour of His Catholic Majesty and His descendants and successors all rights and claims to the said territories which have pertained hitherto or which now pertain to Her Crown either in virtue of Articles V and VI of the Treaty of Utrecht, or from any other cause.

   ... Art. XXI. In order to place this said friendship and union of the two Kingdoms, and the peace which shall spring from it on a secure footing, and to obviate any possibility of discord between the two signatories even over their possessions in Asia, Her Most Faithful Majesty, in Her own name and in that of all Her descendants and successors, does herewith abdicate in favour of His Catholic Majesty and all His descendants and successors, all conceivable rights and claims to the Philippines, to the Ladrone Islands or to any other Spanish possessions in those seas, and She does herewith renounce any entitlements which She might enjoy under the Treaty of Torde-sillas of the seventh of June 1494 and under the agreement concluded in Zaragoza on the 22nd of April 1524, including that of the sum paid in the sale contained in the said agreement, or any other such entitlement which runs contrary to the stipulations contained in this present Article.

   Art. XXII. . . . His Catholic Majesty undertakes to restore to Her Most Faithful Majesty the island of Sta. Catalina and to evacuate all His troops by a date that shall be no more than four months from that of the ratification of this Treaty, both from the said island and from part of the mainland which lies immediately opposite it, and undertakes to leave behind artillery, munitions and other effects, to the same amount and in the same condition as those found there by His men when they occupied the island.

   Dated at San Ildefonso on the First day of October in the year seventeen hundred and seventy-seven. The Count of Floridablanca. – Don Francisco Inocéncio de Souza Countinho.'

   (*Colección de tratados de paz . . .*, vol. III, pp. 236 ff.)

62

The town of Pensacola, Florida, surrenders to the Spanish under Don Bernardo de Gálvez

1781

'Articles of surrender negotiated and agreed by Don Bernardo de Gálvez ... Field-Marshal of His Catholic Majesty's Armed Forces, Comptroller, Superintendent and Governor-General of the Province of Louisiana and Commander-in-Chief of the Expedition, and ... Mr Peter Chester ... Captain-General, Governor and Commander-in-Chief ... Chancellor and Vice-Admiral, in the name of His Britannic Majesty, of the Province of West Florida, and Mr John Campbell, Field-Marshal and Commander of the British Forces in the said locale.

Article I.	Article I.
All strongholds and positions occupied at present by the forces of His Britannic Majesty shall be handed over (within the stipulated time-limit) to His Catholic Majesty's forces. The English troops and Marines shall pull out with full military honours: arms shouldered, drums beating and banners unfurled ... At a distance of five hundred yards from their various positions, they will surrender their arms (their officers keeping their swords) and straightway be taken aboard suitable vessels which shall convey them to a British port of Commander Campbell's choosing. All the troops and Marines shall continue under the direct authority of their respective officers and undertake not to take up arms	Agreed but for the Jamaican ports and St Augustine in Florida. As for the exchange of prisoners, the Spanish shall be given priority over their allies. His Britannic Majesty shall meet the cost of transporting those whom He plans to set free in the exchange, to Spanish ports.

against Spain or any of Her allies
until such time as the English
shall have set at liberty a similar
number of Spanish or allied
prisoners ... as is dictated by
established precedent...

Article VIII.
A ship shall be provided and
equipped by His Catholic Majesty,
to transport the Governor to...
Great Britain ... and, for the
duration of his stay here, he shall
be permitted to reside in
Government House, Pensacola...

Article XVI.
No restriction will be placed on
the freedom of the inhabitants to
continue in the practice of the
religion of their choice.

... Fort George, 9th May 1781.
Peter Chester, John Campbell,
Commander-in-Chief.'

Article VIII.
Agreed, save that he shall
reside elsewhere and not, as he
requests, in Government
House.

Article XVI.
Agreed for one year until my
Sovereign gives a firm
decision.

Pensacola camp, 9th May
1781. Bernardo de Gálvez.'

(Diario de la Expedición contra la plaza de Panzacola...)

63

An eye-witness account of the capture of Minorca and of the taking of the castle at Mahón

1781

'... On the far side of the arsenal lie the two encampments, one
French, the other German,* separated one from the other by about
half a league. In each, there are things well worth seeing, but especially in the French camp, where there is not a single officer's tent but

* A mistake? Surely, the Spanish.

that it has a little garden attached, and some of these are pretty in the extreme.

... Alongside the Dragoon quarters lie the artillery stores ... and, not far from there, the Spanish camp. Here there are none of the gardens and niceties that adorn the French lines, but in their place, solid evidence of the toughness and discipline of the Spanish fighting-man: a huddle of tents, ravaged by the rigours of winter, and a number of miserable huts, which the men built for themselves, are the only protection they have known all winter long, and none of them have beds or blankets or greatcoats to keep them warm. But this same soldier who has paid so little attention to his own well-being in camp has not lain idle and, with great steadfastness of purpose and not a little skill, has succeeded in erecting some quite excellent installations; this is where the real comparison lies: redoubts and batteries con-structed so accurately and with such precision that the English com-manders themselves were struck dumb with amazement when they discovered that they scarcely had a single day free...

The thick hail of shells to which the English subjected our men... did not prove sufficient to stop these works going on apace, and so far were they from fear of the enemy cannon and of these shells that, when they were offered a quarter for every pound of unex-ploded shell, they got into the habit of trying to blow the fuse off the shells or to snuff it out by firing at them, until the commander found himself obliged to rescind the order.

They (the English) staged a spirited defence until the night of the third of February and the morning of the fourth, when they decided to throw everything they had into one last concerted effort to beat off the attack. The hail of fire fell thick and fast – Our lines must have been treated to 400 shells alone – but when the English saw that this in no way intimidated their attackers, they determined on the morn-ing of the fourth to surrender.

At about nine in the morning a white flag was seen to flutter ... on the battlements of San Felipe castle ... and a short time later an English officer appeared and came over to our lines ... by nightfall the terms of the surrender had been agreed: the garrison would be taken prisoner and would be conveyed under the aegis of the King of Spain back to an English port, on the understanding that they would none of them take any further part in this war against the Spanish and the French, and in return they would be permitted to march out of their position with full military honours.

The exodus of the English garrison began. It was a sight to be seen: the soldiers came out in formation, drums beating, banners unfurled and making quite delightful music. Both officers and men wore brand-new scarlet uniforms, the Hanoverians with lapels and cuffs in either white or black and silver buttons and braid ... the light-infantry were the very essence of good taste and perfect symmetry in their elegant, graceful uniforms. The Artillery were in blue with lapels and cuffs of blood-red and buttons of gold. The whole force marched right through the middle of the French lines with all the traditional arrogant military bearing of the English until they came to the rear where the Burgos regiment stood. There they halted and the standard-bearers turned once more towards the city, dipped their flags in salute and handed them over to us. At this signal, all the troops handed over their arms to the men of the Burgos regiment. As they lay down their arms and unbuttoned their cartridge belts there was no one present but felt a lump in his throat... The officers were granted leave to keep their swords and they were escorted, still in formation, by a company of dragoons, to El Locio, a small town some two leagues distant. The last to emerge were the Commanders, Murray and Draper, and they were greatly interested in our men, our trenches and our batteries, and were openly amazed that so few could have been responsible for so much, for the French had scarce had time even to become wearied, and when the French General asked the British commander what he thought of his men, he replied that they seemed fine but that he knew whom he had really to contend with. They were close to Crillon's quarters ... when an argument blew up over the proper meaning of one of the clauses in the treaty of capitulation, and Murray said that he knew full well how pointless it was for him to dispute the question now that he had been taken prisoner-of-war, and that he would perforce be obliged to accept Crillon's interpretation. His Excellency, however, replied that this showed how little Murray knew him if he thought him capable of doing anything unbecoming to a magnanimous victor, and that, should any of the clauses in the treaty not be to his liking, or should he repent of having put his signature to them, then he would be perfectly willing to permit him to take his men and go back once more into the castle, and that he was himself quite prepared to mount another attack and take it once again.'

(*Relación de la toma del Castillo de San Felipe en Mahón* ...)

64

Diary of Aranda: discussions with the recently independent colonies on the question of borders

1782

'1st Session. 3rd August 1782.

On Saturday the 3rd of August, at ten in the morning, I received a visit from Sir* John Jay. As he came into my office, I handed him a large map, on which was written:

Amérique septentrionale avec les routes, distances en milles, villages et établissements = les 8 feuilles françois et anglois = par le Dr Mitchel traduit de l'anglois par le Rouge Ingenieur Geographe du Roy rue des grands Augustins 1753....

He asked to see local and area maps. I told him I would show him these later, but that the important thing was first to get a general idea of what we were talking about, and to agree in principle to draw a demarcation line between the colonies that were to remain Spanish and those that were to fall to the thirteen states of the Union, and that we should be guided solely by consideration of what was permanent and of great moment, and that we should not stop to quibble over a hundred leagues here or there, and that whatever happened, the line would run through lands belonging to uncultured barbarians and that each party would then have the task of civilising them so that they might serve as a peaceful barrier between the two Empires.

Once we had agreed in principle on this, I asked Jay where he would draw his dividing line and, saying that we should adopt some clear-cut frontier like the Mississippi, he put his finger on the headwaters of that river and followed it down nearly as far as New Orleans. I then asked him if he had it in mind to steal Western Florida from us, which was not only ours of old, but which we had just won back from the English.

His answer was that since the States were assuming all the rights that had hitherto pertained to England, and that this was the recognised frontier of English domains in the Americas, it followed that the Spanish could not deny them the right to draw the frontier from

* He had no such title.

the source of the Mississippi down as far as the rightful border of West Florida. I turned his own weapon against him, stating that, since Spain has now reconquered Florida, and it was because of Florida that the Treaty of Paris had fixed the frontier along the course of the Mississippi, it therefore followed that Spain should be entitled to assume those rights pertaining to Florida in virtue of Her conquest of it.

He countered this with a statement to the effect that, in their charters and constitutions, the States of the Union had had, while part of the British Crown, no fixed frontiers to the rear, and that, accordingly, that part of the Mississippi which had not done service in the past as a boundary to Florida was not now part of the territory reconquered by Spain, but rather formed part of British dominions and should therefore be considered the rightful territory of the States of the Union.

I told him that this imaginary extension of their own territories by the British Crown away into no man's land accorded equal rights to any other Ruler in these untenanted wastes of Her imagination, and that Spain could just as reasonably draw a couple of parallel lines, one from Louisiana and the other from the coast of Florida, and lay claim to all the undiscovered lands that lay between them, as far as the frozen north where the lines would presumably eventually meet up, and that such a method would chop the world up into little squares which everybody might quite justifiably claim as their own. It was surely much more logical that whoever owned the Mississippi delta and the lower reaches of the river should have a right to call the whole length of the river Her own, and that he would do better to forget these imaginary lines with which the English were pleased to amuse themselves, because even the map which I had handed him had them in on it, and I, personally, had never dreamt of paying them the slightest attention. The lands in the keeping of the States of the Union were firmly delineated on that same map and the other local and area maps which we would come to study in due course; all those lands lying outside the frontiers dictated by that map were inhabited by uncivilised barbarians and our two parties were therefore equally justified in claiming them as their own, just as they were surely equally idiotic to do so. We thereupon concurred in this, and agreed to start by claiming only those lands which were not under contention, and thereafter each to dress his own naked carcass as best he might.

I then put to him my own ideas for mutual participation, always with the understanding that, below a certain point at least, the river should remain the private preserve of one of the parties. He begged me to show him on the map just what I had in mind, which I offered to do, and we agreed that I would let him have a map with all the details clearly marked out on it, and that he would study it carefully and raise any difficulties that he could foresee so that I could then try to solve them.'

(Yela Utrilla, *España ante la independencia*..., vol. II, pp. 355 ff.)

65

Articles of Peace and Trade Agreement between His Catholic Majesty and the Ottoman Porte, ratified by His Majesty on 24th December

1782

'... Article I. From the date of the ratification of this present Treaty there shall, God willing, exist a state of peace between the Spanish Crown and the Ottoman Empire, in the same wise as is enjoyed by the other allies, such that, between the Provinces and states in any part of the Spanish mainland together with Her adjacent islands, strongholds etc. ... and the inhabitants of the dominions of the Ottoman Empire, there shall be peace, both on land and sea, and all trade between the two shall be declared lawful, such commerce enjoying the same freedom as that accorded all the other allies: to buy and sell, to have any damage to merchant-ships occasioned by squalls or by any other agency repaired in each other's ports, and to purchase whatever is needed for such repairs in addition to all necessary supplies therein.

... Art. XVII. It shall be decreed and firm measures shall be taken to ensure that no subject of the Sublime Porte, and in particular none of those pirates who operate in the Adriatic* and from Albania, nor any other similar persons, shall commit any act of aggression against Spanish shipping, and that when Spanish boats arrive off their coasts, they shall meet with a friendly reception...

... The Sublime Porte shall inform the Berber Rulers of Algiers, Tunis and Tripoli of this present Peace-Treaty so happily concluded between the Court of Spain and the Sublime Porte, and, should they

* 'Dulciñotas' in the text = pirates operating from the port and area of Dulcigno (Montenegro).

each wish to enter into a separate agreement with the said Court, the Sublime Porte shall be pleased to look upon such a wish with approval...

... Constantinople, 14th September 1782. Don Juan de Bouligny, Ambassador Plenipotentiary of His Catholic Majesty. – Haj Seid Muhamed, Grand Vizir.'

(*Colección de tratados*..., pp. 269 ff.)

66

The Decree of Carlos III, removing all stigmas attaching both to work and those who perform it, underlines great social changes. The traditional idea of the Caballero is swept away

1783

'Permission for artisans and employees to hold state office on production of evidence of their integrity and respectability.

We do hereby decree that the trades followed by not only the tanner but the blacksmith, the tailor, the cobbler, the joiner and all other occupations of that ilk are upright and honourable, that such a trade does in no respect demean the family nor the person that adopts it, and that to follow such a trade does in no way disqualify such a person from holding public office in those quarters of the Republic peopled by artisans and workmen who practise such trades, nor does the exercise of such arts and trades disqualify such a person from the rank and privileges of a gentleman, should he have lawful right to such estate ... unless it be that such an artisan or workman desert his trade and that of his forefathers and not apply himself assiduously to some other honourable art or profession to his betterment, save that he do so because his financial state no longer demand that he work at all. In consideration of this Our decree, Our Council shall, in the case of persons whose families have exercised the same trade or calling for at least three generations, through father, son and grandson, to the benefit and profit of the State, prefer them to Us, as We have directed, as worthy of such a distinction being conferred on that person who can prove himself head and fount of the said family, and We shall grant such an application, including even a claim to noble estate, if We deem such persons worthy of it in virtue of their achievements in the crafts and trades...'

(Novísima recopilación..., Book VIII, Section XXIII, Statute VIII, Decree of Council, 18th March 1783.)

67

Conclusive Peace-Treaty between His Catholic Majesty and His Britannic Majesty, signed at Versailles on the 3rd of September 1783

1783

'... Article IV. His Majesty, the King of England, relinquishes all rights to the island of Minorca to His Catholic Majesty.

Art. V. His Britannic Majesty likewise relinquishes all rights to Florida, both East and West, and guarantees His Catholic Majesty in the possession of them...

Art. VI. It being the intention of the two major signatory Powers to remove all possible ground for complaint and discord between Their two countries over the felling of Log-wood or Campeachy-wood, to conduct which trade the English have set up many several installations on Spanish soil, it is herein agreed that the subjects of His Britannic Majesty shall enjoy the right to fell Log-wood, collect it and transport it in that region which is defined by the rivers known as the Hondo and the Belize... All English subjects at present residing in any other part of the Spanish American mainland, or on any of the islands pertaining thereunto, shall accordingly, over the next eighteen months, assemble within the territory so defined, and His Britannic Majesty shall ensure that all strongholds constructed by the British in the said lands shall be dismantled, and He shall instruct His subjects henceforth not to construct any such strongholds therein.

Art. VII. His Catholic Majesty shall restore to His Britannic Majesty all the Providence Islands and the Bahamas without exception, and shall restore them in the same condition which pertained when they were conquered by the forces of the Spanish King.

Dated, Versailles, 3rd September, 1783. – Count of Aranda. – Manchester.'

(Colección de tratados..., vol. III, pp. 295 ff.)

68

Since the punishment meted out the previous year proved insufficient, the Spanish fleet now appears before Algiers. This time Spain has brought allies with Her (Sicilians, Portuguese and some Knights of Malta), but in spite of their help, this year the attempt proves more difficult and the results less effective (12th to 20th July). They make six assaults before eventually withdrawing

1784

'Don Antonio Barceló, Vice-Admiral of the Royal Fleet, writes to the Comptroller of the Navy in the following terms:

... at four-thirty this morning (12th July), I gave the signal for my men to prepare the attack without further delay and instructed them to man the cannon and the boats that were to carry them and to occupy the positions we had pointed out to them so as best to silence the enemy cannon during the encounter. At five, the enemy in the city fired a salvo and revealed their launches which were all in position ... at eight-thirty I gave the order to open fire, and the whole line thereupon burst into action, maintaining a steady fire on the enemy, as I directed, until twenty minutes past ten when I gave the order to stand off, as the launches had by then run out of ammunition.

The action was most properly conducted by our lines, and they had the full support of the galleys of the Knights of St John, the galliot San Antonio, and all the sloops, Xebecs* and brigs of the Spanish and Neapolitan fleets which covered our flanks to right and left, many of them affording ample proof of their coolness, dash and bravery, as indeed did the officers in charge of the launches and small boats attached to the fleet and all the lighter vessels involved in the attack, and as indeed did that gallant gentleman, Rear-Admiral Forteguerni, who had command of His Sicilian Majesty's forces attached to this expedition.'

(*Gaceta de Madrid*, 20th July 1784.)

---

* Small three-masted vessel with some square and some lateen sails.

69

Peace-Treaty and Alliance between His Catholic Majesty and the Dey and Province of Algiers, agreed on 14th June

1786

'... Article 1. There shall be a permanent state of peace between that most powerful monarch, the King of Spain, and His Magnificence the Pasha Dey, the Divan, and all the soldiery of the city and Realm of Algiers, and between all Their respective subjects, such that all trade between Their two dominions shall be declared lawful, and that They shall give a mutual undertaking that all mercantile shipping of either party shall be able to sail without fear of attack or harassment, for whatever cause, from the other.

Art. 2. The corsairs operating from the Algerian coasts, and all private vessels owned by citizens of Algiers, shall be under an obligation not only to allow all Spanish vessels that cross their path the freedom of the high seas but also to go to the assistance of such vessels when requested to do so. It is agreed also that whenever any such persons require to board a Spanish vessel they shall not be permitted to send more than two men, besides the rowers in the launch, and that those two men, who shall be persons of prudent judgement, shall be the only persons permitted to board the said vessel. All such stipulations shall apply equally to Spanish men-o'-war when they encounter the said corsairs or any private vessels owned by citizens of Algiers. These last shall be required to be in possession of a passport issued by the Spanish consul in Algiers, so that there may be no mistaking their identity.

Art. 3. All ships flying the Algerian flag shall be admitted to Spanish harbours and roadsteads whenever they are obliged to put in there by bad weather, are in need of repair, or are fleeing from enemy vessels. All their needs will be supplied, and all charges made at normal prices. Such occasions apart, they shall only be welcome in Alicante, Barcelona and Málaga, and in each of these cases only for the purposes of trade or to take on supplies, and then only for the minimum necessary length of time, nor will they be permitted to blockade these harbours and thereby harass the traffic of other nations. The same will apply to Spanish shipping in the port of Algiers.

Art. X. A Spanish Consul will take up residence in Algiers and will enjoy exactly the same rights and privileges as the French consul ... and shall have absolute jurisdiction in all disputes arising between subjects of the Spanish Crown; the Municipal Judges in Algiers having no power to direct therein.

Art. XI. All Spaniards shall be free to practise their Christian religion in the Realm of Algiers, both in the Hospital Real de Redentores Trinitarios Calzados in Algiers itself, and in the residences of all the Consuls and Vice-Consuls wheresoever it prove necessary to set these up.

... Art. XX. The City of Oran, together with its castles and the fort at Mers-el-Kebir shall remain as heretofore without any overland links with Moorish territory, The Dey of Algiers undertakes never to attack them and the Bey of Mascara is not empowered to do so without his instructions. But, seeing that the Bey of Mascara rules despotically in His Province, the Dey of Algiers shall welcome any treaty between Spain and the said Bey of Mascara whom he herewith exhorts to safeguard the cities and fortresses in Spanish possession and ensure that they remain unharmed.

... Art. XXV. Out of consideration for His Catholic Majesty, the Algerians shall respect not only the coasts of Spain but also those belonging to the Holy See. Out of this same consideration the Dey of Algiers shall be pleased to welcome any persons travelling under the flag and protection of His Catholic Majesty, and, in return, His Catholic Majesty shall treat all those who journey to Spain under the flag and protection of the Dey of Algiers in like fashion. The Dey shall be ready and willing to open negotiations with those powers proposed by His Catholic Majesty who are at present at peace with the Ottoman Porte, by whose example the Dey shall ever be guided.

... Promulgated and ratified in Our palace on the seventeenth day of the crescent moon, one thousand two hundred, or, in the calendar of those who follow Jesus, the fourteenth day of June, 1786. – Mohamed Baxa.

... We have come to accept and ratify the said treaty ... At San Ildefonso, 27th August 1786. – We, the King. – José Moñino.'

(*Colleción de tratados* ..., vol. III, pp. 357 ff.)

70

The Nootka incident. Treaty between His Catholic Majesty and His Majesty, the King of England, settling various points arising over fishing and shipping rights, and trade, in the Pacific Ocean and the South Seas. San Lorenzo el Real, 28th October

1790

'Having agreed to settle the differences that have arisen of late between Their two Realms, His Catholic Majesty and His Britannic Majesty have decided that the speediest and most effective method of achieving this is by an Agreement ... which shall leave aside all retrospective debate over Their respective rights and claims, and consist simply of a friendly exposition of Their respective positions vis-à-vis the future ... and shall settle the issues amicably as best serves Their true interests and best ensures harmony and good understanding between Them.

Art. I. It is agreed that those buildings and that property on the north-east coast of North America, or rather those islands lying just off that coast, of which His Britannic Majesty's subjects found themselves dispossessed in April 1789 by a Spanish officer, shall be restored to the said British subjects.

Art. II. It is agreed that no harassment or interference with the subjects of either Crown who sail or fish in the Pacific Ocean or in the South Seas, shall be tolerated, and that all such persons shall be at liberty to disembark on the coasts of the said oceans, wherever there is no colony already established, and to barter with the natives there or to found a colony ...

Art. III. His Britannic Majesty undertakes to employ all the means at His disposal to ensure that His subjects do not abuse their rights to sail the Pacific Ocean and the South Seas and to fish therein, by indulging in unlawful trade with Spanish settlements ... no subject of the British Crown shall be permitted to sail or fish in the said seas within ten nautical leagues of those shores already occupied by Spain.

Art. IV. It is also agreed that no colonies shall be set up in the future on either the eastern or the western shores of South America, or on any of the offshore islands, to the south of these points presently occupied by Spain.

... In San Lorenzo el Real, 28th October, 1790. – The Count of Floridablanca. – Alleyne Fitz-Herbert.'

(*Colección de tratados* ..., vol. III, pp. 367 ff.)

71

The Death of Louis XVI and public pressure lead to the declaration of war on France (23rd March)

1793

'WE, THE KING

High among those objectives which We have held close to Our heart from the time of Our exaltation to the Throne, has been a wish to contribute to peace and well-being in Europe, and, in making such a contribution, We have not only striven for the general good of Mankind but have afforded Our faithful and beloved subjects tangible proof of the Fatherly care with which We do unceasingly toil to vouchsafe them the happiness We so greatly desire they should enjoy, and which they so richly deserve in virtue of their unswerving loyalty to Us and their noble and magnanimous character. The moderation which We have exercised in all our dealings with France, ever since the seeds of disorder, impiety and anarchy were sown in Her midst, and until the present time when that Nation is reaping abundant harvest with these turmoils and convulsions which have gripped Her people and are swallowing them up, is so well-known that it would be superfluous to furnish evidence of it. It will be quite sufficient, therefore, for Us to limit Ourselves to the events of these last months and to leave untold the whole host of horrendous incidents which We should gladly put out of Our mind and from which We should be pleased to spare Our beloved subjects' sensibilities. Of these We shall mention only the most atrocious, since it is unavoidable that We do so.

Our first instincts were to discover whether it would be possible to quell the French sufficiently, and bring their frenetic ambition to within reasonable bounds, hoping thereby to avoid a full-scale war in Europe and to manage to obtain, at the very least, the freedom of His Most Christian Majesty, Louis XVI, and his noble family, who were thrown in chains and daily exposed to the basest of insults and the greatest of perils.

To achieve this, which was a matter of such great consequence for the preservation of world peace, so intimately bound up with the dictates of humanity, so naturally pursuant upon the ties of kinship, and so absolutely vital, if the lustre of the Crown was to remain untarnished, We acceded to the manifold representations made to Us by the French Government, and passed them two notes containing a declaration of neutrality and stipulations for the mutual withdrawal of troops. When it seemed quite certain, after negotiation, that both these proposals would be accepted, they changed their mind about the withdrawal of troops and put forward the idea of leaving a force in the Bayonne area, under cover of fearing an invasion by the English, but in reality holding this army in readiness against any whim that might enter their heads, and, by keeping a large force in that area, occasioning a considerable drain on Our resources by obliging Us to match their force with one of Our own, stationed on Our border; that is, if We did not wish to expose Ourselves to surprise attack from an undisciplined and ungovernable rabble. They also were at pains to make frequent and very self-conscious mention (in this same note) of their "French Republic", in the hope that We would grant "de facto" recognition of such a "republic" by the very act of answering that note.

We issued strict instructions to our Ambassadors in Paris that, when they handed in the notes which We had penned from here, they should make every effort to secure some amelioration in the lot of King Louis XVI and His unfortunate Family; and, if We did not stipulate this as a necessary condition of the declaration of neutrality and the disarmament, it was because We entertained very real fears that to do so would only make their situation, in which We took such a lively and proper interest, very much worse. We were, moreover, quite persuaded that, unless the French Government was a total stranger to good faith, She could not fail to see in Our making this recommendation and intercession in such emphatic terms at the very time that We handed in these notes, an implicit connection between the two proposals which was none the less quite evidently a very vital one, and that She could not fail to conclude from this that We would not accept accession to the one without equal accession to the other, and that Our not having said so in as many words was no more than tactful and courteous, and was motivated by the hope that to make Our point in this way would stand the French Government in good stead – given the factions into which France was, and still is, divided – when they come to perform this good deed which they had led Us to believe they held close to their hearts. Their perfidy was shown up at once in its true colours, for, at the same time as they affected not to understand the recommendations and intercessions of a Sovereign placed at the head of a great and magnanimous Nation, they pressed for accession to their emended Notes and accompanied each attempt at persuasion with threats to the effect that, should their demands not be met, they would withdraw their Ambassador at Our Court. And while they were making these requests, interspersed with threats, they were committing the savage and unspeakable crime of assassinating their Sovereign, and, while We and the entire Spanish Nation stood horror-struck and filled with indignation before the spectacle of such a monstrous outrage, they still persisted in making attempts at negotiation; no longer, it is true, with any hope of securing what they sought, but as a calculated offence to Our honour and to that of Our subjects; they were not unaware that every approach they made in such a situation amounted to a twist of irony, a taunt that nobody could list to without demeaning himself and imperiling his honour. Their Ambassador requested passports, these were granted him; and at the same time a French ship was seizing a Spanish vessel off the coast of Catalonia and the Commander-in-Chief was crying out for reprisals to be taken; and at that same time reports began to reach Us of other captures made by the French, and news to reach our ears from Marseilles and other French ports that our ships were being detained there and their cargoes impounded.

Finally, on the seventh of this present month, they declared war on Us, – this same war they had been waging (in an underhand fashion) since, at the very latest, the twenty-sixth of February, which is the date on the warrant they issued, authorising attacks on Our men-o'-war and interference with Our mercantile shipping, and on the other documents which were found in the possession of the French pirate-ship "Le Renard", – Captain Jean-Baptiste Lalanne, – when he was caught by our brig "El Ligero", under the command of ship's-lieutenant Juan de Dios Copete, as she was carrying off a Spanish boat laden with gunpowder.

Having regard, therefore, to such behaviour and to the acts of aggression made by France, even prior to her declaration of war, and having taken all available measures to check, repulse and attack the enemy at every opportunity, on both land and sea, through Our Royal Decree of the twenty-third of this present month relayed to Our Supreme Council of State for War, We have determined that We shall forthwith publicly declare war on France, on Her possessions, and on Her peoples, and with no delay put into effect all measures and orders relevant and necessary to the defence of Our Realm and Our subjects, and to the defeat of the enemy: We have therefore resolved to declare unlawful, – which declaration We do hereby make – all trade, relations and communication between our two Kingdoms, on pain of those sentences laid down in the Pragmatic Laws and Royal Decrees issued against such eventualities, which sentences shall apply to all Our subjects and all the inhabitants of Our Realms and Domains, and from these may no man claim exemption no matter of what nature the privileges he enjoy. It is Our will that this Our declaration of war be made known to all Our subjects as speedily as is possible, so that they may both protect themselves and their possessions from the insults of the French, and begin to harass them forthwith by acts of piracy and by all the other means at their disposal under the articles of War; and We do hereby instruct Our captains and commanders to see that this our Royal Decree be promulgated in the regional capitals, the local administrative centres, townships, ports and other centres of population that fall within their respective areas of command, by the commanders and sergeants-at-arms, or in those places where such people are wanting, by the local justices.

Given at Aranjuez, on the twenty-fifth day of March in the year seventeen hundred and ninety-three. – WE, THE KING.

Manuel de Negrete y de la Torre (signed and sealed).'

(*Colección de tratados...*, vol. III, pp. 393 ff.)

72

Conclusive Peace-Treaty between His Catholic Majesty and the French Republic, signed at Basel

1795

'Our Lord, the King, who has lately been engaged in a savage and costly struggle to ensure the peace of His subjects, now enjoys the satisfaction of having obtained that peace on precisely those terms which, after giving them long and careful consideration, He dictated to His Ambassador Plenipotentiary; the which terms are those contained in this present Treaty which He has ordered to be published and divulgated among all His subjects, that they may also share His Majesty's pleasure in them.

Article I. There shall be peace, friendship and good understanding between the King of Spain and the French Republic.

... Art. III. Neither party shall grant passage through His territory to a force of any Nation which is at war with the other.

Art. IV. The French Republic hereby restores to the King of Spain all territories taken from him during this present war.

... Art. IX. In return for the restoration set out in Article IV, the Spanish King, in His Own Name and in that of His successors, does herewith renounce in favour of the French Republic all Spanish possessions on the island of Santo Domingo in the Antilles, and all rights thereunto. One month from the date of publication in that island of the ratification of the present Treaty, the Spanish forces at present occupying all the cities, ports and other establishments therein, shall be ready and willing to hand these over to the French troops as soon as they arrive to take possession of them. The said cities, ports and establishments shall be made over to the French Republic together with all the cannon, ammunition and effects existing therein for their defence.

... Art. XV. Wishing to afford His Catholic Majesty tangible proof of the friendship They profess towards Him, the French Republic have resolved to hearken to His intercession on the part of the Queen of Portugal, of the Kings of Naples and Sardinia, of the Prince-Duke of Parma, and the Rulers of the remaining Italian States, and have agreed to the restoration of peace between those Rulers and States and the French Republic.

... Signed at Basel on the 22nd day of July 1795. Fourth day of Thermidor, Year 3 of the French Republic. – Domingo de Iriarte. – François Barthélemy.'

(*Colección de tratados* ..., vol. III, pp. 393 ff.)

73

The French Directory attempts to turn Carlos IV's obsession with dynastic matters to their own political and economic advantage. This is how they brief their Minister of Foreign Affairs

1796

'The Directory forsees, Citizen Minister, that the victorious march of the Italian army will carry the theatre of war yet closer to the Duchy of Parma, and will force the Commander-in-Chief of the army of that Duchy to take the only recourse open to him and declare war on the advancing forces. The obduracy of the Duke of Parma in insisting on siding with the Coalition, and his blindness to his own interests can hardly induce the Directory to look favourably upon him, but the close links of the Court of Parma with that of Madrid offer us an opportunity to strengthen the harmony that now exists between France and Spain. We shall not hesitate to seize this opportunity, and we therefore suggest that you instruct General Pérignon to pass word to the King of Spain that, in the light of the non-aggression Treaty that binds our two Nations, we shall be pleased to look favourably upon any intercession He might care to make on behalf of the Italian States of the said Duke ...

There is one matter you must not permit yourself to forget in your dealings with the Spanish Court: you must press Her to permit our shipping in the Mediterranean to fly the Spanish flag, which, since they could then pass as neutrals and shake off the vigilance of the English, would afford us enormous advantages in transporting men, merchandise and supplies which are vital to the French war effort. Le Tourneur, Carnot, Revellière-Lépaux. – 11th day of Floréal, Year IV. 8th May 1796.'

[Translated from French.]

(*Receuil des actes du Directoire Exécutif*..., vol. II, p. 338.)

74

Treaty of Alliance between His Catholic Majesty and the
French Republic, signed at San Ildefonso on 18th August,
and treating of matters both offensive and defensive

1796

'His Catholic Majesty, the King of Spain, and the Directoire Exécutif
of the French Republic, fired with the desire to strengthen the bonds
of friendship and consolidate the good understanding between their
two Nations, happily reconstructed by the Peace-Treaty of Basel on
the 22nd day of July 1795 (4th day of Thermidor, Year III of the
Republic), have resolved to draw up a Treaty, covering both offence
and defence, and which shall comprehend all matters redounding
to the mutual benefit of both Nations, and all questions related to
their mutual defence.
    ... Article II. The two signatory Powers hereby undertake to
guarantee each other, without any caveat whatever, and in the
most comprehensive and binding manner possible, in the possession
of all those states, territories, islands and townships within their
jurisdiction, both now and at any time in the future, in such wise
that, should either of the parties find Themselves subjected to threat
or attack, the other shall, in virtue of this solemn undertaking, be
obliged to use Her every good office on behalf of the oppressed
party and come to Her assistance whenever such assistance be
required.
    Art. III. Within three months of any such request for assistance,
the Power requiring assistance shall be in receipt of fifteen ships of
the line, three of these either three-deckers or ships of eighty cannon, and the remaining twelve of from seventy to seventy-two
cannon, as well as six frigates of corresponding size and fire-power,
four corvettes or ships of small draught, every one of these equipped
with a full armament and with a sufficiency of stores for six months,
and rigging enough for one year, all provided by the other party.
    ... Art. V. The Power to whom such application is made shall
provide, in addition to the above, and also within three months
from the date of such a request being made, ... eighteen thousand

foot and six thousand horse, with proportionate allocation of arms and equipment; the which forces shall be employed solely in Europe or in the defence of territories possessed by the two signatory Powers in the Gulf of Mexico.

... Art. VIII. Such a request made by either of the two signatory Powers for assistance as defined in the aforegoing Articles shall of itself be sufficient evidence of the need for such assistance, and shall automatically constrain the other to provide it. All discussion of whether the war envisaged by the Power entering the request be of its nature offensive or defensive, and all demand for further explanation made in order to avoid swift and complete compliance with the said request, shall be declared of no validity whatever.

Art. IX. All troops and ships supplied in consequence of such a request for assistance, shall remain at the disposition of the Power entering the request for the duration of the war, and at no time may any charge be made to such a Power in respect of them. All expenses incurred in the maintenance of such forces, wherever the party to whom they have been assigned may choose to station them, shall be defrayed by the other entirely as though the latter were employing the said forces in Her own service.

... Art. XIII. Should the two signatories declare war by mutual consent on some other Power or Powers in the belief that actions of that Power or Powers constitute an equal threat to Them both, then the limits specified in the Articles above shall cease to have effect, and the two signatory Powers shall be under an obligation to throw all their forces, both on land and sea, against the common enemy ... and They do undertake also in such an eventuality ... not to treat for peace save by mutual consent and in such a way that They shall both obtain due satisfaction.

... Art. XVIII. Since England is the only Power involved in this war to make direct attacks on Spain, this present treaty shall, for the duration of the war, have effect only in respect to that Power, and Spain shall maintain a neutral posture vis-à-vis the other Powers presently at war with the French Republic.

... Signed at San Ildefonso on the 18th day of August, 1796. – The Prince of Peace.* – Pérignon.'

(*Colección de tratados* ..., vol. III, pp. 435 ff.)

---

* Title of Godoy.

75

The close alliance between Spain and France inevitably brings War with England in its wake. This was so much a sine qua non *of the Treaty that even the traditional list of outrages committed by the British Nation has the hollow ring of exaggeration about it*

1796

'His Majesty has sent a copy of the following Decree, addressed to His Council of State for War, to all His Councils.

One of the chief reasons which impelled Us to conclude a Peace-Treaty with the French Republic, once the latter's Government had settled down and its polity taken a solid shape, was the conduct of England towards Us throughout the war and the suspicion with which We had learned to view Her activities as the result of long experience of Her perfidy. This perfidy quickly became apparent right at the outset of the campaign in the treatment meted out to Our squadron in Toulon by Admiral Hood when his only concern was to destroy anything he could not carry off with him, and in that Admiral's occupation of Corsica not long afterwards, which he had kept a closely guarded secret from Don Juan de Lángara who was with him in Toulon. Further evidence of this perfidy was afforded by Her silence during all Her negotiations with other Powers, above all in the Treaty with the United States of America which She signed on the 19th November, 1794, wherein is not paid the slightest regard or respect for Our rights, rights of which She was only too well aware.

... In the days since We concluded our Peace-Treaty with the French Republic, We have not only been vouchsafed solid evidence for suspecting an attack from England on Our possessions in the Americas, but We have been insulted in so direct a manner as to lead Us no longer to hesitate in believing Her determined to force Us to adopt a position contrary to that We should otherwise have adopted – and contrary to the interests of all humanity who have been decimated by this bloody war that grips the whole of Europe in its jaws – and contrary indeed to the spirit of those representations We repeatedly made to Her to the effect that She should put an end to the sufferings of Europe and negotiate a peace-settlement, and that We were ready and willing to use Our good offices to hasten the advent of such an agreement. In effect, England has now revealed to all that She has set Her sights on Our dominions by mounting great expeditions to the Antilles, some of which were bound for Santo Domingo in order to prevent that island from being handed over to the French. All this is evident from the proclamations made by the English commanders in that island ...

By these repeated and unprecedented outrages, that ambitious and greedy Nation has once more proclaimed to the world that She recognises no law but that of aggrandisement of Her own trade, achieved by Her global despotism on the high seas; Our patience is spent, Our forbearance exhausted, and We must now turn Our gaze to the dignity of Our throne and to Our duty of affording protection to Our subjects, and We must declare war on the King of England and the English Nation. We do, accordingly command that throughout all Our Realms all measures be taken and no stone be left unturned to safeguard these Our Realms, to defend Our beloved subjects and to attack the enemy. The Council of State for War shall be fully informed of these Our wishes and shall act upon them as they deep fit. In S. Lorenzo on the fifth day of October, 1796. – Witnessed by Our Royal Hand. – To the Secretary of Our Council of State for War.'

(*Gaceta de Madrid*, 11 October 1796.)

76

Rout of the Spanish off Cape St Vincent. Reading between the lines of the excuses he offers, one can see quite clearly that, in comparison with the polished technique of the British, the Spanish were quite inexperienced in handling the fleet. Losses: six ships of the line

1797

'Admiral-in-Command of the Ocean Fleet, Don José de Córdoba, from Cádiz bay on the second of this present month to His Excellency Don Juan de Lángara, giving the following account of the action against the English which took place on the fourteenth of last month off Cape St Vincent:

... At about nine o'clock in the morning some of the smaller craft on our left signalled that they had sighted a suspicious looking sail, and I ordered the "Príncipe de Asturias" to give chase, since she was the best suited of our vessels to such a task. Shortly afterwards the "San Fermín" and the frigate "Perla" reported that the number of such suspicious-looking sails now in sight had risen to eight, and, although the overcast weather meant that nothing could be seen from the "Trinidad", the whole fleet crowded sail and, when at ten o'clock I could make out from fifteen to eighteen enemy ships and several frigates, I gave the order for the ships to haul the wind and come into line as best they could by veering to port, both because I wanted to leave our starboard free, and because, given the disposition of our vessels, this manoeuvre could be executed far more swiftly than could have been a corresponding tack to starboard. In the event, the "Príncipe", the "Regla" and the "Oriente" fell off so far to leeward during the luffing that they could no longer rejoin the line without our running a great risk of having our line cut by the enemy who had crowded on sail and were fast approaching us already drawn up in formation. I accordingly signalled these ships to veer round and join the tail of our line, which the first two managed to do; the "Oriente", however, could not manage this and finished up to leeward of the enemy.

The lines met, and, at a quarter past eleven, the leading ship in the enemy opened fire on the ship immediately in front of the "Trinidad", from which point our rearguard fell off increasingly to leeward.

... The enemy rearguard was some distance astern of their van and, in order to turn this to our advantage, and also to profit somewhat from the fire-power of our van, I ordered our ships of the van to come about, and coming round behind the enemy and outflank them. I adopted this tactic for many reasons of great moment, but when the ships to whom I directed these orders failed to understand my signal and consequently did not carry out this manoeuvre, I gave up the "Príncipe", the "Regla" and the rest of our rearguard for lost. When it was no longer timely to effect such a manoeuvre, I ordered the whole fleet to fall off to leeward in the hope that we should thereby be able to put more clear water between ourselves and the enemy, and bring more ships of our centre and rearguard into the thick of the battle, thereby carrying the day by taking the fight over on to the tack to which the enemy already seemed committed. When the moment arrived for us to fall off to leeward,

the "Trinidad" found herself going astern and closing with the
enemy. So close did she come that she lay within range of the enemy
rifles and there, pounded by the whole English line, she was sorely
crippled.

Just as the front ship in the enemy line came round our tail, she
veered about, this move being followed smartly by another five or
six of the enemy ships, who doubled round our line to leeward. As
soon as the last of these ships had completed this outflanking
manoeuvre, all the remainder wheeled about so that, where they
had been coming round ten degrees to starboard of us, they now
appeared on our port side in tight formation, their guns blazing.
This manoeuvre swung the balance in their favour and enabled them
to carry the day. I was not slow in reading their intentions and
accordingly ordered the ships of the van to turn about and come
round to leeward of the enemy rearguard, and if another six or
eight ships of the van had been able to join up with the aforementioned vessels, the "Príncipe", the "Regla", the "Oriente" and
the "San Fermín" at the crucial moment, they would have trapped
the enemy in a cross-fire, and the outcome of the action would
have been somewhat different.

... At two in the afternoon, with our vanguard still lying too
far off to leeward, the signals were hoisted to fall off, run down the
sails and mount a full attack on the enemy.

... Any reader who has attentively followed the chain of events
and the series of misfortunes that befell us from the moment we
sighted the enemy will hardly be surprised at the outcome of the
action, the more so when he grasps that their line was cruising
in a formation much more easily translated into a line of battle
than any we could manage, caught as we were in convoy formation
and completely at the prey of cross-winds. No sooner did their
strategy become plain to see than they were lined up in battle-
formation, and so close to us that I had to scramble out an order to
form up into some sort of line without being able to pay any attention to the deployment of our vessels and having to make do with
a line that was not balanced either in ships or in commanders. In
consequence of this, the "Pelayo" and the "San Pablo" were left to
leeward of both lines, the "Príncipe" and "Regla" ... were unable
to join our lines until the evening, and neither could the "Firme",
who had lost her topmast. So it was that a mere seventeen of my
squadron were in a position to take part in the action, one of which
was the "Santo Domingo", who was shipping water fast and therefore of precious little use. Of the seventeen ... some only joined
in the fighting from time to time and many were never in a position

to fire a single shot, leaving the whole enemy force to concentrate
their fire on six Spanish ships and the resistance offered by these
is all the more worthy of praise since there was not a single one
of them that had enough hands on board to man her properly.'

(*Gaceta de Madrid*, 10 March 1797.)

77

*Britain is still mistress of the waves. Her fleet shells Cádiz.
The strange kind of bomb-ketch or bomb-barge they have
with them has to have the protection of an escort. All this
in July. Nelson saves a Spaniard's life*

1797

'Continuation of the report of the Admiral of the Ocean Fleet, Don
José de Mazarredo, to His Excellency the Prince of Peace and to Don
Juan de Lángara giving a detailed account of the behaviour of the
English fleet which can be seen cruising outside Cádiz harbour:
Despatches as from the 4th of this month:
    ... The English squadron was joined in the early morning of the
2nd by a strange kind of bomb-barge and several other vessels of
small draught which were fitted out in Gibraltar. On the morning
of the third they were seen together with their vanguard tacking
out by the sandbanks off Rota, and before nine that night this
bomb-ketch was towed by the English fleet towards San Sebastián
lighthouse.
    [Boarding of the defence launches] ..., and Irigoyen could not
save them ..., but he did manage to stage a resistance, staving off
the boarding-parties on five of the launches until he succumbed to
two wounds inflicted with pikes, one of them in the chest. He
dropped unconscious and when he came round he found Rear-
Admiral Nelson propping him up by the shoulders. Nelson saved
him from the boarding-party who wanted to finish him off.
    ... the shelling began at eleven-thirty and the bomb-barge lay at
anchor in the shelter of a frigate and many other armed vessels ...
while it fired thirteen or fourteen rounds at the city, three of which
landed on target, while three or four more fell short, and the rest
exploded in mid-air.

... on the fifth, they were seen to make preparations to repeat their shelling of the city the following night. The enemy fired their first shell at five and twenty minutes past ten and from then on they kept up a steady fire, some of the shells falling over towards the wharves and the quay. They kept up a simultaneous fire from another bomb-vessel and a ship carrying howitzers. The tide which was still coming in both helped the enemy to bring the barge up quickly and delayed the arrival of our auxiliary launches on the scene. At a quarter past midnight the barge fired for the last time.

(*Gaceta de Madrid*, 24 July 1797.)

78

Representation to Carlos IV on the nature of the Holy Office by G. M. de Jovellanos

1798

'Sire:

The jurisdiction of the Holy Office is not privative, but rather accumulative; its power not inherent, but delegated; its authority not absolute, but limited, both in application, since this must be exercised jointly with the bishop or his nominee, and in purpose, which is restricted to questions of the Faith.

Even in these questions, its power is limited, for it must concern itself only with matters of heresy and apostasy. It can only take action after two denunciations, it can arrest individuals only when these denunciations are substantiated, and it can only punish when the defendant has confessed or been justly convicted.

The right to settle all disputes arising in questions of dogma, which was invested in the Holy Office, did safeguard the original rights of of the Bishops (in the Bulls of Pius IV and Gregory XV). Although it is claimed that this right has been revoked, revocation has not been made public, and does apply to neither the Prelates nor to anyone else, since the documents cited by the Inquisitor-General prove that the question had arisen of abolishing this right, and the fact that it was not done affords tangible proof that such revocation was held to be neither just nor opportune. Moreover, the Bull of

Benedict XIV reaffirmed the previous Bulls and safeguarded the episcopal rights.

Besides this, the Holy Office was never entitled to publish these edicts on its own initiative: Firstly, since it is not in its jurisdiction to resolve or pronounce on questions of the Faith but rather is its task to punish and correct: it can inflict punishment on heretics but it cannot pronounce on heresy; secondly, since it cannot pass sentence without the sanction of the Bishop, even less can it command and direct without such sanction; thirdly, since the offences mentioned above do not pertain to its fundamental mission, that is, to direct in all matters pertaining to offences committed against the Faith, but rather to all offences not directly jeopardising the Faith; fourthly, because temptation does presuppose the existence of lust, and if lust were to be a contravention of the Faith, then, My God, countless myriads would indeed fall into the clutches of the Holy Office; and fifthly, since its foundation, or rather its right, is not existential or geographical, but rather personal, and therefore, its decisions should not pertain to property or places but to people.

The Holy Office was founded at the end of the fifteenth century, at the same time as the expulsion of the Jews. Its aim was to try those who had publicly forsworn the Hebrew faith but did continue to profess it in secret. The clandestine nature of its procedures derived from the fact that its formulas were specifically designed to fit this purpose. This was what gave rise to the ignominy in which the descendants of these converts were held: they were ever to be derided by the people. This was confirmed by law when the "limpieza de sangre"* statutes were approved. These not only removed many innocent people from honourable offices and positions of trust, but also proved an insuperable barrier to their taking Holy Orders, and entering universities, convents, and even the brotherhoods and trade guilds. As a result of this, there has been unceasing hatred directed not only at the Holy Office but also at religion itself, and also as a result many have obstinately held to their old faith, as was discovered when the Moors were expelled at the beginning of the last century and as we have seen ever since that date.

Faith has now little to fear from heretics and nothing to fear from the Jews, but a great deal, nay, everything, to fear from those who flaunt their impiety. Moreover, it has not only to fear those who are nurtured in the bosom of this Nation, and who, by the grace of God, are but few, but also must it fear many who do not belong to this our Nation, for all the foreign gazettes, newspapers, books and broadsheets come crammed with impious doctrines, and

* 'limpieza de sangre': racial purity.

these ungodly thoughts are also smuggled into this country by the many propagandists among those who travel here, among the persons engaged in diplomatic affairs and among the members of the commercial and industrial missions which visit our shores.

The Inquisition is but a flimsy bulwark against the multitude of its enemies: firstly, because its members are ignorant and cannot pass judgement without the censors; secondly, these latter are also themselves ignorant perforce, because these are posts which are unremunerative and therefore are taken up by friars, who only perform these tasks in order to acquire sustenance and avoid the duties of the choir, who do not have the gift of tongues and who know but a little scholastic theology and a touch of moral casuistry and even in these matters they follow the well-established tenets of their school; thirdly, because decisions which demand resolutions and despatch are of necessity slow and dilatory; fourthly, because only the jurisdiction of the Bishops could provide more effective remedy, for it would carry more authority and would be more welcome and more readily respected by the people and more replete with humanity and charity, since their power has been given them by the Holy Ghost; fifthly, since the Bishops, aided and abetted by the deans, their chapters and their parish priests, could extend their watchfulness to the very last corners of their dioceses, track down impiety in its lair, and enforce the swiftest and most effective remedy against it; sixthly, because this is even more necessary in matters pertaining to the censorship of books since rapid measures are required to stop the spread of impious ideas, and the procedures of the Holy Office are not equal to this task; and seventhly, because the Inquisitor-General himself recognises this in his letter to the Minister of State, of which I received a copy sent to me ... this present month, in which he proposes the establishment of a censor's office.

Everything cries out for the restoration to the Bishops of the rights they have lost and the jurisdiction which has been unlawfully taken away from them, and, more than all this, the circumstances of today, when the preservation of the Faith hangs upon their zeal and authority. On the death of His Holiness, a horrendous schism will threaten the Church. If this should come about, the flocks of every Nation will have to gather and unite under their shepherds and only move and graze to the sound of their whistles.

Even if the schism is avoided, the same need will still exist. The Popes will no longer have any temporal power, and they will nevertheless fight to retain their Cardinals, their Curia, their Councils, their Authority, their Bulls, their Dispensations, and they will even struggle to extend their sway and thereby swell their exchequer, since this is human nature and the human condition.

So, what is required of States in such a situation? To convince them to restore the quintessential functions of the Church, those which it exercised through eight long centuries; to restore to Bishops their authority, to place under their jurisdiction the friars, and those who boast exemption from the jurisdiction of their ordinary; in a word, to seek nothing outside the religion of Jesus Christ which cannot be found within, in accordance with the recognised Canons of the Church, and Her old and venerable discipline; that is, to seek all this in the Bishops and the shepherds who are the ministers of the Faith, and in His Majesty who was born to the defence of the Church, to the wardenship of its Holy Canon and to be the Father and fount of consolation for all His peoples.

To sum up, therefore, I shall propose to Your Majesty various drafts for decrees, so that Your Majesty can look over them, search through them, ponder upon them, and then choose whichever is more in accordance with Your Royal and pious intent.

Jovellanos.'

(Jovellanos, Gaspar Melchor de, *Representación a Carlos IV sobre lo que era el Tribunal de la Inquisición* (*Obras de Jovellanos*, t. v, Bibl. Autores Españoles, t. lxxxvii, pp. 333–4).)

79
Treaty of San Ildefonso

1800

'Article 1. The French Republic shall be obliged to obtain for His Royal Highness, the Prince-Duke of Parma, an increase of territory in Italy such that his estates may be increased from one million to one million two hundred thousand inhabitants and to grant him the title of King ... and it shall be binding on the French Republic to obtain the consent of His Majesty the Emperor and King in this matter as well as the consent of all the other interested parties ...

2. The territory that is to be added to the lands of His Royal Highness the Duke of Parma may be the province Tuscany ... or equally it may be the three Roman legations or any other Italian continental province which forms an estate by itself.

3. His Catholic Majesty for his own part promises and enters into an obligation to return to the French Republic, six months after

the completion of all the conditions and stipulations laid down above, the colony or province of Louisiana which shall be at that time as large as it is now under the Spanish flag and as it was when a French possession.

... 5. One month after the completion of all those clauses referring to the Duke of Parma, His Catholic Majesty shall be obliged to hand over to the French Republic in Spanish European ports six fully equipped warships in good condition with provision for seventy-four cannon and ready to receive French munitions and supplies.

6. Since there is not among the stipulations of the present treaty any which is inequable, and since the individual rights of all signatories are to be left inviolate, there can be no grounds for fear that any power might feel resentment. However, should events belie this and the two powers find themselves either under attack or threatened as the result of fulfilling their obligations under this treaty, they shall undertake to join forces to repel the aggressor and also to take whatever conciliatory steps may prove necessary to maintain a state of peace with all their neighbours.

7. The obligations contained in the present treaty in no way annul those laid down in the treaty of alliance signed in San Ildefonso on the 18th August, 1796 ...'

(Lafuente, *Historia general de España* ... (ed. de Barcelona, 1879), vol. IV, p. 344.)

80

War with Portugal. Spain and France sign the Convention prior to the ultimatum

1801

'Art. 1. His Catholic Majesty will outline for the last time his intentions to the Most Faithful Queen and will give her fifteen days to make up her mind. After this period has elapsed, if she refuses to make peace, a state of war shall be understood to exist.

2. If Her Most Faithful Majesty should prove to want peace with France, she shall undertake: 1. To secede utterly from the alliance with England; 2. To open all her ports to French and Spanish shipping and to close them to the British Navy; 3. To make over

to His Catholic Majesty one or more provinces equal in population to a quarter of all her European possessions, as a surety against the return of the island of Trinidad, Malta or Mahón or to pay reparation for all hurts and losses suffered by the subjects of His Catholic Majesty.

... 3. If peace is not realised, the First Consul shall furnish His Catholic Majesty with 15 000 infantry, complete with all their equipment, together with a task force (supplied and paid for by France) for the servicing of this equipment ...

... 5. In the case of the conquest of Portugal, His Catholic Majesty shall undertake to put into effect the terms offered to the Most Faithful Queen at present by France ...

... Art. 8. The French army shall, from the moment of its entry into Spain, obey the directions of the Spanish general, the commander-in-chief of the combined armies. The French generals shall not be empowered to countermand his orders. His Majesty, knowing the wisdom and experience of the First Consul, trusts that he will give the command of the said troops to individuals who well understand how to adapt themselves to the customs of the towns through which they will pass, and to endear themselves to the people, and thereby contribute to the maintenance of peace; but if there should be any incidents (which God forbid) provoked by a single individual or by many French soldiers, the French commander shall order them back to France to any place deemed suitable by the Spanish general, without any idle debate and argument; for agreement is the basis of that well-being which both parties so earnestly desire.

... 10. Since the work under discussion is of such great importance, even more for France than for Spain, since all depends on the former's being at peace, and since the political balance is weighted in her favour, the sending of troops will not be delayed until the expiry of the period laid down in the treaty of alliance but will be straightway effected since the ultimatum gives Portugal only fifteen days.

Madrid, 29th January, 1801. Pedro Ceballos: Lucien Bonaparte.'
(Carlos Pereyra, Cartas confidenciales de la reina María Luisa y don Manuel Godoy, pp. 388–9.)

81

Peace of Amiens

1802

'Conclusive Peace-Treaty between, on the one hand, His Majesty the
King of Spain and the Indies, the French Republic and the Republic
of Batavia, and on the other, His Majesty, the King of the United
Kingdom of Great Britain and Ireland, signed in Amiens on the 27th
of March, 1802. The First Consul of the French Republic, in the
name of the French people, and His Majesty the King of the United
Kingdom of Great Britain and Ireland, being equally imbued with
the desire to put an end to the horrors of the war, laid the foundations of peace by means of the preliminary clauses signed in London
on the 1st Oct. 1801 ...
  The plenipotentiaries ... have agreed to the following articles:
  I. There will be peace, friendship and good understanding between
the King of Spain ... French Republic ... the Republic of Batavia
on the one hand, and Great Britain on the other.
  II. All those taken prisoner of war by both one party and the
other, on land or on the sea, and all hostages taken or given during
the war up to the present time shall be returned without ransom.
  III. His Britannic Majesty restores to the French Republic and
to each of her allies – that is to say to His Catholic Majesty and to
the Republic of Batavia, – all those possessions and colonies previously belonging to them which have been occupied or conquered
by British forces during the war, excepting the island of Trinidad
and the Dutch possessions on the island of Ceylon.
  IV. His Catholic Majesty surrenders Trinidad.
  V. The Republic of Batavia surrenders Ceylon.
  VI. The Republic of Batavia retains absolute sovereignty over the
Cape of Good Hope as before the war. Ships of all kinds belonging
to the other signatories to the treaty shall have the right to put in
there and buy necessary supplies as before.
  ... VIII. The territories, possessions and rights of the Sublime
Porte shall remain exactly as they were before the war.
  IX. The Republic of the Seven Isles is hereby granted recognition.
  X. The islands of Malta, Gozo and Cominho shall be restored
to the order of St John of Jerusalem.

... XIII. In all cases of restoration agreed under the present treaty, the fortifications shall be handed over in the state which they were in at the time of signing the preliminary agreements and all constructions undertaken since the occupations shall be left intact.

Dated, Amiens 27th March 1802. 6th Germinal, year 10 of the French Republic.

Signed: J. Nicolás de Azara, Joseph Bonaparte, Schimmelpenninck, Cornwallis.'

[The only languages used were French and English.]

(*Gaceta de Madrid*, 14 May 1802 *et seq.*)

82

Treaty of Neutrality between Spain and France

1803

The first article refers to the fact that the English had captured French ships in Algeciras and the Military Governor had done nothing to prevent this. The Governor of Cádiz had wanted to press some Frenchmen, and the governor at Málaga had not protected other French citizens from ill treatment.

'Article 1. His Majesty the King of Spain shall give orders to the effect that the governors of Málaga and Cádiz, and the Commander of Algeciras, who have, in the course of exercising their functions, done injury to the French government, shall be deprived of their posts.

Art. 2. His Majesty the King of Spain undertakes to look to the safety of Republican ships driven into the ports of El Ferrol, Coruña and Cádiz by events at sea and to that of any which might be driven in future into these ports. He will give orders to advance all the money that may be needed for the repair and rearmament of these ships and the victualling of their crews, providing everything out of his own warehouses against the account of the French Republic.

Art. 3. The First Consul agrees to the conversion of all obligations incurred by Spain in the course of all treaties uniting the two nations, into a financial subsidy, given by Spain to her ally, which

shall amount to six million per month, counting from the renewal
of hostilities up to the end of the present war.

... Art. 6. Taking into account all stipulated clauses, France will
recognise Spanish neutrality as soon as these conditions are complied
with, and undertakes not to oppose any measures that may be taken
in the future concerning the belligerent nations as a result of general
principle and of the laws governing neutrality.

Art. 7. His Catholic Majesty, wishing to forestall any difficulties
which might arise about the neutrality of his country, undertakes,
in the event of a war between the French Republic and Portugal,
to force the latter power, by means of a secret agreement which
shall be effected, to pay the sum of a million per month ... and this
subsidy shall guarantee French acceptance of the neutrality of
Portugal.

Art. 8. His Catholic Majesty shall permit free passage of French
textiles and manufactured goods bound for Portugal and exempts
them from duty ...

The present treaty shall be ratified by exchange of copies in
Paris, 18 days after signing. Paris, 26 vendémiaire, year 13 of the
French Republic (9th October 1803). José Nicolás de Azara – Ch.
Maurice Talleyrand.'

(Lafuente, *Historia general de España*..., vol. IV, p. 367.)

83

The battle of Trafalgar. The 'battle log' received and published in Madrid

1805

'Rear Admiral Antonio de Escaño, Admiral of the ocean fleet, has
written from Cádiz harbour to His Excellency the Prince of Peace.
His despatch is dated 22nd October and is as follows:

My most excellent Sir: The condition of Captain Federico Gravina,
who was wounded in his left arm by grapeshot right at the close
of the action yesterday, prevents him from sending Your Excellency
news of this bloody encounter ... That sad duty falls to me ... I
have to inform you that all our endeavour and heroic unconcern
for our own lives did not prove sufficient to prevent our sustaining

losses which would have been overwhelming had we not been convinced to a man that there was nothing more we could do and so come off with honour unscathed.

I know that ... on the 18th Captain Gravina recounted in his letter to you how Admiral Villeneuve had expressed his resolve to set sail the next day and how the Admiral had wanted to know whether the Spanish fleet was in a position to carry out such an order. Your Excellency is not unaware of the reply the captain gave, which amounted to the assurance that his fleet would follow promptly and eagerly in the wake of the French and that Your Excellency had repeatedly commanded him to do so ... On the morning of the 19th some of the ships put to sea ... [those left] followed suit on the morning of the 20th.

... At seven thirty in the evening, we had a report from a French ship that the "Aquilés" had sighted 18 enemy ships drawn up in battle formation and we ourselves straightway made out several patches of light not far off, which could not have been but those of enemy frigates which lay between the two fleets. At nine, the English fleet fired a salvo and by the lapse of eight seconds between the flash and the report of the cannon, we reckoned them at two miles from ourselves. We used our signal lanterns to suggest to the French Admiral that we should draw up our line of battle over against those ships which had fallen to leeward, and he confirmed this later with a salvo. The morning of the 21st saw us lined up in this formation with 28 enemy ships, 8 of them three-deckers, lying within sight.

... At seven in the morning, the enemy ships fell off to leeward and, drawing up into separate lines, made for the centre and rearguard of our fleet. Seeing this, Admiral Villeneuve ordered an immediate wheel, leaving Captain Gravina's observation squadron in the rearguard. There followed another order from the French Admiral to the effect that the first ship of the van should haul the wind and the others should follow in her wake. This had the effect of making the whole fleet fall to leeward in order to regroup. Captain Gravina gave timely signals so that these movements could be effected as quickly and as speedily as circumstances demanded, and, as the enemy came up, he ordered his ships to spread out and come into line.

... At eight minutes to twelve in the morning, an English three-decker, with pennant flying at her topmast, cut our line at the centre with the support of those ships following at her stern. The leading vessel of each enemy column did likewise; one of them came round our rearguard and a third crossed between the "Aquilés" and the "San Ildefonso" and, from that moment on, the action was restricted to particular encounters, ship to ship, of a very bloody nature, and the greater part of them carried on by an exchange of pistol-fire. This between the whole of the enemy fleet and but half of our own, with the inevitably consequent boarding of some ships. At the moment of writing, I am not in possession of the necessary and indispensable information about each of these separate actions that I would need to give Your Excellency a full account, nor can I say anything about the movements of the vanguard, which I am assured came round right at the beginning of the action to sail to the aid of those under attack. What I certainly can assure Your Excellency is that every single vessel that I could see, be it French or Spanish, carried out its duty to the full in battle, and that this ship, after engaging three or four of the enemy in horrifying combat, was relieved just in time, all her rigging in shreds, her stays cut adrift, and in a sorry plight, her masts and her mainmast riddled by shot and quite unable to set sail. Her rescuers were the Spanish "San Justo" and the French "Neptuno", whose coming together made the enemy stand off and made it possible for the "Rayo" the "Montañés", the "Asis" and the "S. Leandro", which had been ill used, to be recovered along with some other French ships whose fate had been no more fortunate.

As soon as this ship found herself free from enemies the order was given to those which had regrouped to go to the aid of those who were hard pressed ... and at dusk, once the firing had ceased completely, the frigate "Temis" was made ready to tow us back to harbour at Cádiz.'

And the *Gaceta de Madrid* adds:

'...News received after this goes up to the 25th. On the 23rd Captain Escaño ordered the French and Spanish ships, which had come into Cádiz the night before, to put out again to help any demasted vessels of the fleet which might heave into view and to attack their escorts. In this way, the "Santa Ana" and the "Neptuno" have been recovered.... Commander Cayetano Valdés lies gravely wounded from three balls he caught during the battle, as does Captain Ignacio María de Alava. The English have also suffered important losses in the battle, during the course of which Lord Nelson and other officers of distinction perished, according to a report from Gibraltar.'

(*Gaceta de Madrid*, 5 November 1805.)

84

Letter from Fernando, Prince of Asturias, to the Emperor Napoleon

1807

'Sir: The fear of disturbing Your Imperial Majesty in the middle of those great deeds and weighty affairs of state which occupy you unceasingly has until now deprived me of the pleasure, which I have long wished to indulge, of expressing at least in writing, the feelings of respect, esteem and affection I have for a hero greater than any who has gone before and who has been sent by Providence to rescue Europe from the total devastation that threatened her, to put her tottering thrones back on solid foundation and to give to all nations peace and happiness.

... The condition in which I have existed for a long period and which I am unable to keep secret from Your Majesty's keen intelligence has been up to now a second barrier which has restrained my hand in its yearnings to write to you making my ambition plain to you. But fired with the hope that I shall find in the magnanimity of Your Imperial Majesty the most powerful protection of all, I am resolved not only to bear witness to the feelings of my heart but to entrust my most intimate secrets to Your Majesty as to a tender father.

... Imbued with respect and filial love for my father (who is most upright and bountiful of heart), I would not presume to keep from Your Majesty something which Your Majesty knows better than I do myself: that these very qualities are often the instrument of cunning and malicious persons whose wish it is to hide the truth from their sovereign, especially when they are dealing with someone in whom these qualities are readily to be found, as in the case of my worthy father.

If the men who surround my father were to allow him to become familiar with the character of Your Imperial Majesty, as I am myself, how anxious my father would be to do everything to tighten the bonds which ought to unite our two nations! And what more fitting way could there be to do this than by entreating

Your Imperial Majesty to do me the honour of bestowing a princess of your noble line on me as a wife? This is the unanimous desire of all my father's subjects, and I do not doubt that it will be his own (despite the efforts of a small clique of malevolents) as soon as he finds out what Your Imperial Majesty's real intentions are. This is what my heart desires, but at the moment I fear for its happy fulfilment because of the perfidious and selfish people who surround my father and who might get to hear of it.

Only the weight of Your Imperial Majesty's good name could upset their plans and open my beloved parents' eyes to the truth, assuring, at one and the same time, the happiness of the Spanish nation, that of my parents, and my own. The whole world will be struck with admiration daily more and more for the goodness of Your Imperial Majesty who will find me a most grateful and affectionate son.

I beg therefore, with hopeful heart, for the paternal protection of Your Imperial Majesty, not only so that you may deign to bestow upon me the hand of a princess of your line, but also so that all the difficulties and obstacles which might be put in the way of the fulfilment of this, the sole object of my desires, may be removed.

This effort of goodwill on the part of Your Imperial Majesty is all the more vital for me, since, for my own part, I can make none, as it would be interpreted as an insult to parental authority, reduced, as I am, to the situation in which the only act of freewill left to me is that of resistance which I shall offer with insuperable constancy to any other proposal of marriage, with whomsoever, without the consent and positive approval of Your Imperial Majesty from whom alone I hope for the choice of a wife.

This happiness is what I seek to obtain from Your Imperial Majesty, wishing as I do that God may grant that your precious life be a long one. Written and signed with my own hand and sealed with my seal at El Escorial, 11th October 1807. – Your Imperial and Royal Majesty's most affectionate servant and brother, Fernando.'

[Translation made by Llorente in his memoirs and taken from the original inserted in the *Moniteur* of 5 February 1810.

(Toreno, *Historia del levantamiento* ..., 1835, vol. I, appendix 8, p. 11.)

85
Treaty of Fontainebleau

1807

'Article 1. His Majesty the King of Etruria shall be given complete ownership and sovereignty of the Province of Entre-Douro-y-Minho together with the city of Oporto, and be known as King of North Portugal.

Art. 2. The Prince of Peace shall be given complete ownership and sovereignty of the Province of Alentejo and the Kingdom of the Algarve and shall enjoy them with the title of Prince of the Algarve.

Art. 3. The provinces of Beira, Tras-os-Montes and Portuguese Extremadura shall be held over until a general peace is declared, at which time they shall be disposed of depending upon the situation and in accordance with whatever terms are arrived at between the two major powers to the agreement.

...Art. 11. His Majesty the Emperor of the French guarantees His Majesty the King of Spain possession of all of his estates which lie to the south of the Pyrenees.

Art. 12. His Majesty the Emperor of the French undertakes to recognise His Majesty the King of Spain as emperor of the two Americas as soon as all has been prepared for His Majesty to take this title, which could be either at the time of the general peace or at a later date within three years of this.

Art. 13. The two major powers to the treaty shall come to an understanding and divide the islands, colonies and other overseas possessions of Portugal equally between themselves.

... Made in Fontainebleau, 27th October, 1807. Duroc–Izquierdo.'
(Barado, *Museo Militar* (1889), vol. III, p. 486.)

86

Carlos IV explains the imprisonment of his son to the nation

1807

'God, who watches over his creatures, does not tolerate acts of atrocity when innocent people are the victims. Our people, all our subjects know us to be a Christian man of decent and regular habits; all love us and, from all we receive proof of their veneration: the kind of veneration demanded by the respect of a father who loves his children. We lived persuaded of the truth of this when suddenly an anonymous person taught us a lesson by uncovering the most outrageous and reckless plot which was being hatched against our life even within our own palace. Our life, which has so often been at risk, had already become an intolerable burden for our heir who, totally taken up with this obsession, and casting aside all the Christian principles inculcated in him by our paternal love and devotion, had gone along with a plot to dethrone us. We wanted to investigate the truth of the matter for ourselves and, catching him unawares in his own quarters, found in his possession the code for messages and the instructions which he received from the villains. We invited the provisional governor of the Council to the inquiry (together with some other ministers) so that they might take charge of the proceedings of the investigation. All this was done and, as a result, we have ordered the imprisonment of several criminals and the detention of our son within his own quarters. This grief comes on top of all the other sorrows which afflict us; but, just as it is the most painful of them all, so also is it the most important to set to rights. We therefore order the results to be published in the meantime as we do not wish to leave our subjects unaware of our displeasure when they can mollify it by proving their loyalty. Make sure this is published in a suitable fashion. At San Lorenzo, 30th October, 1807. To the provisional governor of the Council.'

(Lafuente, *Historia general de España* ..., vol. IV, p. 427.)

87
King Carlos pardons his son

1807

'The voice of nature sheathes the avenging sword, and when an oversight calls out for mercy, a loving father cannot refuse the plea. Our son has already given the names of the perpetrators of the horrible plot who persuaded him to accept the idea; he has put his name to this in the form of a legal document, and all this has been done with the scrupulousness which the law demands in such trials; his repentance and dread have guided his hand in the following statement which he has written to us:

Sir,
   My Father; I have erred, I have failed in my duty to Your Majesty both as King and as father; but I am filled with contrition, and offer Your Majesty my humble obedience. Nothing should have been done without Your Majesty's knowledge, but I was taken unawares. I have given evidence against the guilty parties and I beg Your Majesty's forgiveness for having lied the other night and that you will give your grateful son leave to kiss your royal feet. Fernando.

Madam,
   My Mother; I am filled with remorse for the enormity of the offence I have committed against my parents and my monarchs, and I therefore most humbly beg that you will deign to intercede for me with father and persuade him to give his grateful son leave to kiss his royal feet. Fernando.

Because of these letters and the entreaties of our beloved wife, the Queen, we grant pardon to our son and restore him to our grace provided that his behaviour furnishes proof of a real reform in the frail vessel of his self-government.' San Lorenzo, 5th November, 1807.
   (Lafuente, *Historia general de España*..., vol. IV, pp. 428–9.)

88

Carlos IV tries to calm Spanish distrust of Napoleon's army

1808

'Beloved subjects: your noble agitation in the present situation bears fresh witness to the feelings of your hearts. This we find reassuring, and we, who love you as a tender father, hasten to comfort you in the anguish which besets you at the present. You can breathe again: We assure you that the army of our beloved ally, the Emperor of the French, is crossing our kingdom in a spirit of peace and friendship. His plan is to move his forces to those places which lie under threat of enemy landings. We assure you also that the mustering of the troops of the royal bodyguard has not been occasioned either by a threat to our person or by the impending journey on our part which malicious tongues have led you to suppose we are being forced to make. Surrounded by the untarnished loyalty of our subjects of which we have irrefutable token, what can we have to fear? and should we need to make use of them, can we possibly entertain doubts about the forces their generous hearts would offer us? But no; our peoples will not have to face up to such a necessity. Spaniards; calm your spirits; behave towards the forces of your good King's ally as you have done up to now, and soon you will find peace restored in your hearts and see us enjoying the fruit of heaven's dispensation in the bosom of our family and the shelter of your love.

Given in the royal palace of Aranjuez, 16th March 1808. We, the King. To Don Pedro Ceballos, First Secretary of State and Cabinet.'

(*Gaceta de Madrid*, 18 March 1808.)

89

Proclamation of 19th March. Imprisonment of Godoy

1808

'Proclamation: By Royal Command issued this afternoon by His Excellency Marquis Caballero to His Excellency The Provisional Governor of the Council, the latter is notified that His Majesty the King has been graciously pleased to authorise His Majesty the Prince of Asturias to institute legal proceedings against Don Manuel Godoy, who is already under arrest. The Council, informed of this at the house of His Excellency, has agreed that this order of His Majesty's should be announced publicly, together with another in which it is decreed that all goods and effects now in the Court apartments of the said Don Manuel Godoy shall be the property of His Majesty. His Majesty commands this order to be published so that the people, trusting in His justice and that of His Council, might be placated, as he hopes they will be as loyal citizens, and return forthwith to their dwellings. There will then be no reason or pretext to doubt the signal loyalty of this law-abiding neighbourhood, nor to require the Supreme Court to take further measures.

Madrid, 19th March, 1808. Signed and Sealed.

This is a copy ... etc, etc. Don Bartolomé Muñoz.'

(*Gaceta de Madrid*, 25 March 1808.)

90

Abdication of Carlos IV

1808

'Since the attacks from which we suffer do not permit us any longer to bear the great burden of governing the affairs of our kingdom, and since our poor health demands a kinder climate and the peace and quiet of private life, we have, after the most searching deliberation, decided to abdicate in favour of our dear son and heir, the Prince of Asturias. It is therefore our wish that he should be recognised and obeyed as King and natural sovereign of all our Kingdom and domain. And, in order that this our Royal decree of abdication, arrived at of our own free-will, may have issue and due fulfilment, we communicate it to the Council and to all other relevant persons. Given in Aranjuez, 19th March 1808.

(*Gaceta de Madrid*, 25 March 1808.)

91

Letter from Napoleon to his brother Louis dated 27th March, offering him the throne of Spain

1808

'The King of Spain has recently abdicated following the imprisonment of the Prince of Peace. There had been the beginnings of an insurrection in Madrid while my forces were still forty leagues distant from that capital. The Grand Duke of Berg entered the city on the 23rd, with forty thousand men, to find the inhabitants crying out for my presence. Persuaded that I shall never achieve a lasting peace with England without doing great deeds on the continent, I am resolved to place a French Prince on the Spanish throne*... Let me have a definite decision on this idea. You must understand that it is no more than an idea, and that, although I have 100,000 men in Spain, it is possible that events may induce me to go there at once, or that the whole matter may be cleared up in a fortnight, or else that things may evolve more slowly and operations carry on in secret for several months. Let me have a definite answer: am I to crown you King of Spain? Do you accept? Can I count on you?'

(Toreno, *Historia del levantamiento* ... (1835), vol. I, p. 107.)

---

* '... This being so, I thought of you as an incumbent for the said throne...'

92

Letter from the Emperor of the French to Fernando

1808

'My brother: I have received Your Royal Highness's letter; you will
already have been convinced from what you have seen of the documents of the King, your Father, of the concern I have always shown
you. In the present circumstances, Your Highness will allow me to
speak with candour and devotion. I was hoping, on my arrival in
Madrid, to induce my illustrious friend to bring about some necessary reforms in his domains and go some way towards satisfying
public opinion. The removal of the Prince of Peace seemed to me an
essential move both for his happiness and that of his peoples. Events
in the North have delayed my journey; the events at Aranjuez have
now taken place. I would not set myself up as a judge of what has
happened, nor of the conduct of the Prince of Peace; but what I do
know only too well is that it is very dangerous for kings to allow
their subjects to get into the way of spilling blood by taking the law
into their own hands. I hope to God that Your Highness does not
experience this some day. It would not be in the interests of Spain
to prosecute a Prince, who is married to a princess of royal blood,
and who has for so long held the reins of government in your Realm.
He no longer has any friends: Your Highness will have none in
your turn if one day you should fall from grace. The people are eager
to exact reparation in return for the respect they grant us. Furthermore, how could you try the Prince of Peace without also trying the
King and Queen, your parents? This trial would foment hatred and
sedition which would have dire consequences for your throne. Your
Royal Highness has no other rights to the throne besides those invested in you by your mother; if the trial blemishes her honour, Your
Highness will sabotage your own rights. Do not lend an ear to
treasonable and morally weak advice. Your Highness has no right to
try the Prince of Peace. The crimes, which are attributed to him,
disappear along with his claim to the throne. I have on many occasions expressed my desire that the Prince of Peace be removed; if I
have not insisted on this, it has been because of my love for King

Carlos which induced me to turn a blind eye to his weak indulgence of favourites. Oh, pitiful humanity! Weakness and error, these are your escutcheon. But all this can be sorted out. Exile the Prince of Peace and I will offer him asylum in France.

As for Carlos IV's abdication, this took place at the very time my armies were going into Spain; and to the eyes of Europe and of posterity, it could seem that I had despatched all those troops with the sole aim of toppling my ally and friend from his throne. As a neighbouring sovereign, I must know all the details about this abdication before giving it my official recognition. I say to Your Royal Highness, to the Spanish nation and to the whole world that if King Carlos' abdication was of his own free will, and his hand was not forced by the insurrection and riots in Aranguez, I see no obstacle to accepting it and recognising Your Royal Highness as King of Spain. I would, therefore, like to discuss this matter with you.

Your Royal Highness is not entirely free from blame; sufficient proof of this is that letter you wrote me and which I have always tried to put out of my mind. Being a King, you will know how sacred are the rights of the kingship: any gesture in the direction of a foreign power by an heir to a throne constitutes a crime. I deem a marriage between Your Royal Highness and a French princess to be in the interests of my peoples...

Your Royal Highness must learn to view popular emotion with suspicion; there could be a few random assassinations of my soldiers, but these would only lead to the downfall of Spain.

... I have several plans in mind but these have yet to consolidate themselves, but you may rest assured that I shall conduct myself towards your Person as I have always done towards your father, the King. You may rest assured of my wish to sort everything out and to find an opportunity to offer you proof of my affection and unbounded esteem. With which, I pray God extend to you his Holy protection, my brother. Bayonne, 16th April, 1808. Signed: Napoleon.'

(Pedro Ceballos, *Exposición de los hechos y maquinaciones*..., n.d.)

93
The Second of May

1808

'Orders of the day [in French and in Spanish in two columns]:

Soldiers: The population of Madrid is up in arms, and there have even been some killings. I know that all good Spaniards have raised their voices against these riots, and I am very far from confusing these citizens with those wretches who seek no more than crime and plunder, but French blood has been spilt and it cries out for vengeance. As a consequence, I issue the following orders:

Article I.

General Grouchi will tonight convene the military commission.

Article II.

All those arrested during the disturbances and found to be carrying arms will be shot.

Article III.

The State Council shall disarm the local people in Madrid. All the inhabitants and all other people in the city, who are found either carrying or owning arms without special licence, after this order is put into effect, shall be shot.

Article IV.

All gatherings of more than eight persons shall be held to be a treasonable meeting and shall be broken up by gunfire.

Article V.

Any place where a Frenchman is killed shall be burned down.

Article VI.

Heads of households shall be held responsible for their servants: overseers of factories for their workers and other staff, parents for their children, and heads of monasteries their religious.

Article VII.

Authors, purveyors and distributors of libellous pamphlets provoking sedition, be they printed or circulated in manuscript, shall be held to be English agents and shot.

Given in our Madrid headquarters, 2nd May, 1808. Signed

Joachim, on the orders of His Royal and Imperial Highness. Chief of
the General Staff, General Balliard.'
  (*Diario de Madrid,* 4 May 1808.)

94
Resignation of Fernando VII

1808

'We have today handed our beloved father a letter couched in the
following terms: Sir, our venerable Father and Lord: As a token of
our love, our obedience and our submission, and so that we may
accede to the wishes Your Majesty has on so many occasions revealed
to us, we renounce our throne in favour of Your Majesty, in the
hope that Your Majesty may enjoy it for many years. We recom-
mend to Your Majesty those who have served us since 19th March.
May God bless you with a long and happy life. Bayonne, 6th May,
1808. To Your Royal Majesty.
  Your most humble son, Fernando.'
  (*Gaceta de Madrid,* 13 May 1808.)

95
Treaty between Carlos IV and the Emperor of the French

1808

'Carlos IV, King of Spain and the Indies, and Napoleon, Emperor of
the French, King of Italy and Lord Protector of the Confederation of
the Rhine, imbued in equal part with a desire to put a timely stop to
the anarchy which reigns supreme in Spain and to free this courageous nation from factious strife, thereby salvaging her from the
convulsions of civil and international war and placing her without
political upheaval in the only position in which, having due regard
for the extraordinary situation in which she finds herself, she can

maintain her political unity, guarantee her colonies and gather together all her resources to work alongside those of France to achieve
peace on the seas, have resolved to join forces and make a secret pact
to protect their considerable interests.

Art. I.

His Majesty King Carlos, who, all his life, has had no other aim
in view than the happiness of his subjects, constant to the notion
that a sovereign's every act should have this object only as its goal,
and seeing that the state of affairs at present can be nothing more
than a source of dissension, all the more grave as it has brought
division and strife into his own family, has taken the resolve which
he hereby carries out to hand over the Spanish throne and that of
the Indies to His Majesty the Emperor Napoleon, since as matters
now stand he and he alone is capable of restoring law and order. He
makes this transfer of power on the understanding that it shall have
the effect of allowing his subjects to enjoy the following conditions:
1. The unity of the kingdom shall be inviolate: The prince that
Napoleon shall choose for the Spanish throne shall be independent
and the frontiers of Spain shall be in no way altered. 2. The Roman
Catholic Faith shall be the only religion in Spain. No reformed faith
will be tolerated in her lands, even less any set of beliefs held at
present to be heretical.

Bayonne, 5th May, 1808. – The Prince of Peace* – Duroc.'

(Toreno, *Historia del levantaniento*..., vol. I, appendix 26, p. 82.)

96

Resignation of Carlos IV

1808

'We are pleased to give our beloved subjects this last proof of our
fatherly love. Their happiness, peace and prosperity, and the safeguarding of the integrity of the lands which Divine Providence has
placed under our rule, have been throughout our reign the sole
object of our continual anxiety ... Today, in the extraordinary situation in which we find ourselves, our conscience, our honour and the
good name it is our duty to preserve for posterity, emphatically

* i.e. Godoy.

demand that the final act of our reign should be directed only towards our expressed goal: that is, the peace, prosperity, security and
integrity of the throne which we now vacate; – that is, the greatest
happiness of our subjects on both sides of the Atlantic.

We have to this end, by a treaty duly signed and ratified, ceded all
our rights both to Spain and to the Indies to our ally and dear friend,
the Emperor of the French; it being agreed that the sovereignty of
Spain and the Indies shall be for all time respected as a separate
entity, as it has been under our sovereignty, and also that our holy
religion shall not only be the dominant faith of Spain but indeed the
only religion that shall be observed in all the lands of this monarchy.
You will communicate this to all the other councils, to the courts of
the kingdom, to all provincial governors, and their military, civil and
ecclesiastical authorities and to all the magistrates of our people so
that this, the last act of our reign, shall be made known to all who
live in our domains both in Spain and in the Indies, and so that you
and they may meet to carry out to proper effect the wishes of our
dear friend the Emperor Napoleon, which are directed to the maintenance of peace, to the friendship and union of France and Spain,
and to the avoidance of disorder and popular uprisings, for these are
ever the cause of havoc, of the affliction of families and the ruin of
everybody. Given at Bayonne in the imperial palace known as Government House, 8th May, 1808. – We, the King. – To the Provisional Governor of our Council of Castille.'

(*Gaceta de Madrid*, 20 May 1808.)

97

Proclamation of the General Council of the Principality of Asturias, 24th May

1808

'Loyal Asturians and beloved compatriots: Your first wishes have
now been fulfilled. The Principality, discharging those duties which
are closest to man, has now formally declared war on France. Are
you perhaps discouraged by so great an undertaking? But what
other course of action could we or should we have taken? Is there a
single one among you who would prefer the ignominious and despic-

able death of slavery to meeting his end in the field of honour, sword
in hand, in the defence of our unfortunate monarch, our homes, our
wives and families? If, at the very moment that they were regaled
with the greatest courtesy and triumph by the people of Madrid,
these soldier-bandits executed more than 2000 people in cold blood
for no other crime than that of coming to the defence of their out-
raged brethren, what could we hope for from them once they had
conquered us? Their treason towards our King and all his family,
tricking them into crossing into France with the promise of a
permanent armistice, only to throw them all in chains, has no equal
in history. Their behaviour towards the whole nation is more
iniquitous than that we should expect from a horde of hottentots.
They have profaned our temples, they have insulted our religion,
they have broken every last word of their promises and there is no
principle of justice which they have not trampled under foot.

To arms, to arms, Asturians!

Let us not forget that it was Asturias which, in another time of
invasion, surely less unjust than the present one, restored the
monarchy. Let us hope for equal glory in our own day. Let us remember that no foreign nation in history has managed to rule over us, no
matter how hard it has tried. Let us invoke the God of the Armies,
let us entreat Our Lady of the Battles to intercede for us; her image
is worshipped in the most ancient temple of Covadonga and, in the
certainty that she cannot abandon us when our cause is so just, let
us hasten to throw this treacherous and execrable nation out and to
wipe them from the face of our Peninsula. This is what the attorney
general of the Principality asks of you, in the name of your representatives. Álvaro Flórez Estrada.'

(Rodriguez Solís, Los guerrilleros de 1808 ... (1930), vol. I, p. 58.)

98

*Proclamation of the General Council to the King of Great
Britain*

1808

'The Principality of Asturias, assembled in the General Council of
Representatives, in whom all power is invested because of the particular situation of which Your Majesty shall be informed, finding herself

threatened with slavery at the hands of a conqueror who plans to increase his domain by the use of treachery rather than of lawful valour, and spurred on by her grief at seeing her unfortunate King, Fernando VII, and the rest of the royal family thrown into the chains of a tyrant who usurps all rightful laws, has this day taken up arms with great intrepidity in her defence in order to restore the monarchy, even while she cannot recover the royal family. The resolution, sir, is a great one; but equally great are the spirit and the justice with which this province has made her resolve and the faith which she has in the help and support of your great nation and its magnificent sovereign, who is of course aware of the terrible affects of the French government's unbounded ambition. Their aspirations to power, hugely increased by the annexation of Spain, will not stop short of world domination.

So it is that the Principality, acting through her delegates plenipotentiary, approaches Your Majesty to beg timely help in the present situation, and prays, along with her Commander-in-Chief, the Marquis of Santa Cruz de Marcenado, appointed, recognised and sworn in as such, that Your Majesty will deign to accede to her most courteous entreaties.

May God grant that Your Majesty's precious life be long and prosperous, Oviedo, 26th May 1808. The representatives of the Principality of Asturias. – The Marquis of Santa Cruz to Marcenado, – Count Marco de Peñálva. – Don Alvaro Flórez de Estrada, attorney. – By consent of the General Council of the Principality of Asturias, Juan Argüelles Toral, ambassador and secretary.'

(Rodriguez Solis, *Los guerrilleros de 1808*... (1930), vol. I, p. 58.)

99

Proclamation of Napoleon to the Spanish

1808

'Napoleon, Emperor of the French, King of Italy ... etc., etc., to all who read this, greetings.

Spaniards: after a long illness, your nation was on the point of death. I have seen the ills that afflict you and I am going to remedy them. Your greatness and your power is at one with my own.

Your princes have made over all their rights to the Spanish crown to me; I have no desire to reign over your provinces; but I do seek an everlasting claim on your love and the recognition of generations to come in Spain.

Your monarchy is ancient; my mission is to give it new life; I shall improve your institutions and I shall give you the benefit of reform which you can enjoy without sorrow, without disorder and without upheaval.

Spaniards: I have convoked a general assembly of the delegates of all provinces and all cities. I myself want to know what your wishes are and what are your needs.

Then I shall lay aside all my rights, and I shall place your glorious crown on the brow of another Me, guaranteeing you at the same time a Constitution which shall reconcile the holy and healthy authority of the Sovereign with the liberties and privileges of the people.

Spaniards: remember what your fathers were like and look at what you have become. It is not you who are to blame but the bad government which ruled you. Have complete confidence and full hope in the present situation: for it is my wish to be remembered by all future generations of Spaniards and to have them exclaim: He was the rejuvenator of our country.

Given in our imperial and royal palace at Bayonne, 25th May 1808. – Signed: Napoleon. – On behalf of the emperor, the Secretary of State, Hugues B. Maret.'

(*Gaceta de Madrid*, 3 June 1808.)

100

Decree of Napoleon conferring the Spanish Throne on his brother, Joseph

1808

'Napoleon, by the Grace of God, Emperor of the French, King of Italy and Lord Protector of the Confederation of the Rhine, to all those who read this, greetings.

Having been informed by the Council of State, the Council of Castille, the city of Madrid, etc., etc., through their representatives, that the good of Spain demands that a prompt halt be put to the interregnum, we have taken the decision which we hereby carry out to proclaim as King of Spain and the Indies our dearly beloved brother, Joseph Napoleon, at present King of Naples and of Sicily.

We guarantee to the King of Spain the independence and unity of his states in Europe, Asia, Africa and America.

We command the Lieutenant-General of the Realm, the Ministers and the Council of Castille to publish the present proclamation with the usual formalities of expression, so that no one can plead ignorance of it. Given in our imperial palace at Bayonne, 6th June, 1808.'

(Lafuente, *Historia general de España...*, vol. V, pp. 573-4.)

101

Seville declares war

1808

'Fernando VII, King of Spain and the Indies and the Supreme Council acting in his name.

France, or rather Emperor Napoleon I, has violated the most sacred pacts with Spain; he has carried off her royal family and has forced them into manifestly abrupt and invalid abdications and resignations; just as outrageously, he has made a gift of the sovereignty of Spain, which is something nobody is entitled to do; he has declared that he has appointed the King of Spain, the most horrible crime recounted in the annals of history; he has ordered his troops into Spain, taking over her strongholds and her Capital and scattering his troops over the whole face of the country where they have committed all kinds of murder, robbery and unheard of atrocities against the Spaniards; and to accomplish all this he has not had recourse to force of arms, but excuses his actions by claiming that he is effecting their happiness. This bears witness to the most heinous ingratitude for the services that the Spanish nation has rendered him, and a disregard for the friendship which we enjoyed. He has used deceit, treachery and the most horrible perfidy on a scale never chronicled as having been employed by any nation or any monarch before, however ambitious and barbarous, against any King or any people in all the world. He has recently declared that he intends to throw the Monarchy and its fundamental laws into disarray and threatens the

downfall of our Catholic Religion which we Spaniards have kept
alive since the time of the great Recaredo;* he has forced us to take
the only course of action open to us to remedy such afflictions – to
expose them to the whole of Europe and declare war on him.

And so, in the name of our King Fernando VII and all the Spanish
nation, we declare war on land and on sea against the Emperor
Napoleon I and against France for as long as she continues under
his despotic yoke, and we command all Spaniards to treat the French
with hostility and to occasion them the greatest possible hurt
consonant with the laws of war, to impound all French ships lying
at anchor in our harbours and all property, possessions and goods,
in whatever part of Spain, which belong either to that government
or to any individual citizen of that nation. We likewise command
that no harm or harassment should be given to the English, neither
to the government, nor to their ships, neither to their goods, nor to
the property of the government and the individual citizens of that
nation. We declare that we have entered into open and frank
diplomatic relations with England, and that we have come to an
agreement with her and that there exists between us an armistice
which we trust will end by becoming a lasting and stable peace.

Furthermore, we declare that we shall not lay down our arms
until Emperor Napoleon I restores the King and sovereign, Fernando
VII, and the rest of the royal family to Spain, and pays homage to
the sacred rights of the nation which he has violated, – to her freedom, her sovereignty and her independence. For the information of
the Spanish nation, we command that this solemn declaration be
printed, published, distributed and posted in all townships and
provinces of Spain, and be made known in Europe, Africa and Asia.

Given in the Royal Palace of the Alcázar at Seville. June 6th, 1808.'
(*Demostración de la lealtad española*...)

---

* *Recaredo*: King of the Visigoths in Spain from 586 to 601.

102

Proclamation of Joseph I on entering Spain

1808

'Joseph Napoleon, by the grace of God and the Constitution of the State, King of Spain and of the Indies.

Spaniards: As we enter the territory of the nation which providence has entrusted to our care, we must declare our feelings to her people.

Coming to the throne, we count upon men of good will to aid us in restoring Spain to her past glories. The Constitution to which you shall swear allegiance, assures the practice of our sacred faith, civil and political liberty, and sets up a system of nation-wide representation; it breathes new life into your ancient parliament, which, now placed on a more secure footing, shall, instituting and guaranteeing the liberty of the individual, be an honourable place of refuge where eminent service to the state shall be rewarded with the right to membership.

Blind passions, voices of deceit and intrigues perpetrated by the common enemy of Europe, whose sole aim it is to split asunder the Indies and Spain, have thrust some of you headlong into the most frightening anarchy, our heart bleeds at the thought of it, but such enormous evils can be wiped out at a stroke.

Spaniards, unite, close your ranks about our throne, see to it that internal strife does not waste our time nor stand in the way of measures which are but the instruments we would use to ensure your happiness. We have enough respect for you not to doubt that you will for your part do everything within your power to bring this happiness about, and this is our fondest wish.

Vitoria, 12th July, 1808. Signed, We, the King. For His Majesty, the Secretary of State, Luis de Urquijo.'

(*Gaceta de Madrid*, 16 July 1808.)

103

*Bailén. Terms of surrender agreed between the Spanish
and French armies*

1808

'Their Excellencies the Count of Tilly and Don Francisco Javier
Castaños, Commander-in-Chief of the Andalusian army, desirous of
tendering proof of the height of their esteem for His Excellency
General Dupont ... and for the army under his command, for the
brilliant and glorious defence that they offered in the face of an
army far outnumbering them and which had them surrounded on
all sides, and General Chaves, representative plenipotentiary of His
Excellency the Commander-in-Chief of the French army and . . .
General Marescot, ... have agreed to the following conditions:

    1. The forces under the command of the most illustrious General
Dupont shall be prisoners of war, with the exception of the division
under Vedel and all other French troops also in Andalusia.

    2. General Vedel's division and all other French forces in
Andalusia who do not fall within the terms of the previous clause,
shall withdraw from Andalusia.

    3. Those troops covered by Clause 2 shall generally retain all their
equipment, and, to allay all apprehension during their journey, they
shall leave behind their artillery train and other arms in the hands
of the Spanish army who will undertake to return them as soon as
they embark.

    4. The forces covered by Clause 1 of the treaty shall leave the
field with full military honours, two cannon at the head of each
battalion, and the soldiers carrying their rifles which they will surrender and hand over to the Spanish army at 400 toises* from the
field of battle.

    5. General Vedel's troops and the others who are not obliged to
surrender their arms, shall stack them in pavilions against the line of
the colours, leaving their artillery and train in the same manner,
while officers of both armies make an inventory of it all. It shall then
be returned as agreed in Clause 3.

* About 800 metres.

... 7. The French troops will embark as soon as they arrive at the port of Rota, (bound for France) and the Spanish army shall guarantee their passage against all hostile attack.

... 15. Since, in several other places, particularly in the attack on Córdoba, many soldiers, despite the orders of the generals and the efforts of the officers, committed atrocities, and these are inevitably pursuant upon the fall of cities which have put up resistance, generals and officers will take the necessary steps to recover sacred vessels which may have been stolen and to return them should this be the case.

(Toreno, *Historia del levantamiento* ..., vol. I, appendix, p. 123.)

104

The First Manifesto of the Supreme Council of State to the Spanish Nation

1808

Spaniards:

The Supreme Council of State, in which the highest authority has been provisionally vested, has dedicated the first moments following its inauguration to the urgent measures which the circumstances surrounding its creation have dictated. It has held the firm belief since its very inauguration that one of its first duties was to address itself to you, to speak to a glorious and magnanimous nation with the dignity meet and proper to it, to inform you of your situation and, openly, sincerely, to establish the mutual confidence which is the foundation of every just and prudent administration. Without this relationship, those who wield power cannot accomplish the great mission which is incumbent upon them nor can the true interests of those over whom they rule be realised.

Twenty years of despotism, under the most incompetent control ever known to man, had taken our country to the brink of the abyss. The jackal of Europe had realised that the moment had come to pounce on a prey which he had coveted for so long and to add to an already bloodstained crown a jewel which would be its most brilliant and precious ornament. The omens all predicted success for him. The nation was split away from a government which it hated and scorned, the royal family was divided among itself and the long-awaited heir to the throne was censured, slandered and even reviled, the forces of law and order were scattered and in disarray, and all the means at your disposal were of no avail since French troops were already on Spanish soil, where they were in control of the strongholds along the frontier. Sixty thousand men were ready to enter the capital, from where they would dictate to the nation.

At this critical juncture, you suddenly rose from the sloth in which you wallowed, ousted a favourite from the eminent position he had unlawfully seized and placed a Prince that you revered on the throne. This innocent King of yours was then wrested from you in the greatest act of treachery ever recorded in the annals of human deceit. The Madrid massacre of the second of May told of the treason at Bayonne and of the French invasion. The blood and death of the innocent and valiant folk who were there gave an ominous and awful warning of the fate that Napoleon had in store for us.

By this time, the council in which our deluded King had vested supreme power had already been sold out to our enemies, all the other bodies in authority were now in shackles and an usurper was on the imperial throne. After that memorable day the second of May, the French thought they would meet with no resistance. They did not realise that by giving offence to and taunting the nation here on earth which is most conscious of her honour, they were heading towards inevitable doom. The provinces of Spain were provoked into a sudden, massive uprising. They came to grips with the invaders, swearing to die rather than submit to the opprobrium of a foreign despotism. An astonished Europe heard of the insult and of the revenge at almost the same time. A nation which only a few months previously had hardly had a shadow of influence, suddenly became an object of concern and wonder for the whole world.

The event is unique in our history, unforseen in our laws and almost completely foreign to our habits. The forces of law and order needed a hand to guide them, a hand worthy of the will and the sacrifices of the people. From this need were born the supreme councils of the provinces, who took upon themselves the whole responsibility of keeping danger at bay, by holding back the enemy, and of keeping peace in their region. The tale of their struggles, of the way they discharged their public duties and of the gratitude owed them by the nation, is told by the battlefields, which are littered with French corpses, and in our churches, where French military insignias are kept as trophies. It is told in the preservation of activity and independence in nearly all the institutions of the realm, and it is told in the thanks of thousands who owe their freedom and their revenge to these institutions.

As soon as the capital was rid of her enemies and communications restored between the provinces, then an authority which had been divided between all the provisional councils had to be united under one banner, to work with all the necessary strength and energy. This was the will of the people and this is the course that the provinces took. Each Council named deputies who were to come and form the central authority and in less time than it took the Machiavellian scheming of the French to destroy our former government, a new government, which the French shall fear much more, was formed in the Central Council which is speaking to you now.

Spaniards, your greatest enterprise, your finest victory, has been both the agreement of the public will of the paramount importance of the good of the nation, and the selflessness which the provinces have shown in giving authority and power over into other hands. Both at the present time, when all eyes are on you, and in the future, when you will be a fount of wonder and a subject of study, these decisions of yours will be seen as the most convincing proof of your moderation and caution. Our enemies had already selected the moment for our destruction. They had already seen the breaches which civil discord would work in our defences. They had anticipated that the provinces would be split by ambition and greed and were enjoying the thought that some would come to them for protection and aid, in an attempt to establish a supremacy over the others. Then, suddenly, a central authority was peacefully established and accepted by the majority under their very eyes. The ship of State was sailing on a single, even keel, gathering speed and momentum until it crushed under it, once and for all, every foreign pretention and every hope in their iniquitous souls.

Once the Council had taken up the mantle of authority, it turned its mind immediately to a consideration and evaluation of its duties. The principal objectives which the Council believes itself empowered by the nation to fulfil are twofold: to throw our enemies back across the Pyrenees, and to force them to restore to us our noble King, his brother and his uncle, thus recognising our freedom and independence. The Council found that much of this had been done before its creation. Public enthusiasm had been quickened, armies had been formed almost from scratch, important victories had been won, our enemies thrust back to the frontiers, with their military pride crushed: the laurels which had wreathed the brows of the conquerors of Europe were transferred to our warriors.

All this had been done and it was everything that could be expected from the first enthusiastic impulse. It is necessary now, following these achievements of impetuosity and courage, to follow the counsels of caution and perseverance for the rest of the road we must travel. It has to be said and repeated over and over again: the path we must tread is long and hard. Spaniards, the great enterprise we have embarked on must whip up all your enthusiasm and channel all your virtues.

This you will understand, when you cast your mind back over affairs of state both at home and abroad at the time when this Council began to wield authority. Our armies were full of courage and anxiously awaiting a march towards victory, but they were unarmed and bereft of all the necessary provisions. Over and against them were the French forces, waiting for reinforcement, along the banks of the Ebro, laying waste old Castille, the province of Rioja and the Basque country. They had occupied the fortresses of Pamplona and Barcelona, they had command of the castle of San Fernando and were thus masters of almost all Navarre and Catalonia. The churlish, lying French tyrant, restless on his throne, was working up his minions to fever pitch. His aim was to appease other nations in order to throw the whole weight of his military strength against us. Meanwhile other European powers, either subdued or riled by France, were anxiously awaiting the outcome of this first struggle. Though longing to stand up against their common enemy, experience had afforded them harsh counsel that they should proceed in this with timid prudence.

It is clear that the only way they had of keeping their independence was through a confederacy. It will have to come to this, for both self-interest and necessity dictate that it shall. Where is the state that can have any confidence in its dealings with Napoleon? Who believes his words or his promises? Who trusts him to be loyal and friendly? The destiny of Spain should be a lesson and a warning to them, its resolve an example, its victories an incentive. By disregarding the principles of justice and the sanctity of a promise, this senseless tyrant has placed himself in the awkward situation of having to possess greater strength than everyone else put together or of being entombed under the mountains thrown up by his own fury.

The fact that an alliance, which is both just and necessary, will provide security and the sureness of victory, is underlined by our first successful struggles and by the cautious way we have proceeded. When we have created a military force which has numbers and means enough to make it dreaded, when we are able to follow up a success and recover quickly from a reversal, when we always control our acts and aspirations with the good sense and integrity which distinguish the Spanish nation from all others: then the whole of Europe will be sure of success and will unite with us to exact revenge for outrages perpetrated on themselves and on us. Spain will take the glory for having saved the countries of Europe. Our wishes restrained and righteous, our position one of strength, we will be accepted as the friend and loyal ally of all, the slave or tyrant of none.

We must now harness all our resources, as if we were alone in sustaining the onslaught of France. With this in mind, the Council has deemed it necessary to keep a standing army of five hundred and fifty thousand men and fifty thousand cavalry. It might be thought that this enormous number of troops is disproportionate to our former position and needs. Be that as it may, it is by no means disproportionate in the present circumstances. The three armies which must guard the frontier and the reserves which must back them up and supply their losses will easily take up the whole of this number. It might be asked if even this number or the sacrifices we must needs make will be sufficient for the enterprise which we are to undertake, even with the enthusiasm that drives us forward. Spaniards, our enemy's strength is colossal, his ambition is greater even than his strength and his very existence is incompatible with our freedom. His exertions must be judged by his barbaric character and by the extremity of the dangerous situation in which he has placed himself. But his exertions are those of a tyrant and must surely break when pitted against the total strength of a nation which is both great and free and which has selected for this conflict no other ends than total success or death in the attempt.

Having first paid heed to this great and momentous enterprise, the Council turned its attention to the immense expedients which would be needed to bring it to fruition. The profligacy of our last government (if its continual, hideous, squandering makes it worthy of the name of government) had dried up every source of prosperity, had obstructed all the channels through which life and food flow to all members of the body politic, had drained all our financial resources, had scattered the forces of law and order and had exhausted our every means of defence. As the Council has already told the people, all that was lost can be recuperated by the great savings that come from the abolition of the expenses of the royal family, the huge sums that were taken by the court favourite, with his sordid and insatiable greed, the income of his many large estates and also by the goods taken from those renegade Spaniards who have fled with the invader. To this we must add the advantages that the state will gain from being able to make free use of shipping and trade and from the communications with America which have now been established. The principal source of finance for our enterprise must be a well-run economy, and a well-organised tax system. The Council will be turning all its attention to reform and order in the tax system. We can add to these resources the generous help which the English people have given us and will carry on giving us. But even though this help came at the right time and has been received gratefully and used to such good effect, much of it must be reciprocated with all the honour and propriety due to a great and powerful nation. The Spanish monarchy must always be on equal terms of mutual interdependence with its allies.

The yield from the sources of income outlined above will doubtless be great but it will only come slowly and then too late. It is therefore not enough for the extremely urgent needs of the state now. Will even it be enough to supply at one and the same time everyday needs which must be met, a huge debt which must be paid and an immense army which must be maintained? But in cases of extreme necessity, when diverse events or the force of circumstances might cause the funds in the exchequer to dwindle, the Council will turn straightways to the nation, in the certain knowledge that they can count on the patriotic zeal which is everywhere in evidence and on the widely recognised need for self-denial. Desperate ills like those of today require desperate remedies. And as the government takes it as a bounden duty to give the nation an exact account of the way it uses the funds and resources which are to be given it, there can be not the least doubt in its mind that its apparently arbitrary demands might be disliked or disregarded through mistrust.

So much for the defence of the realm and for the means of preparing for it. This was the first and most urgent aim entrusted to the Council. But there is another aim, Spaniards, which is just as valuable and important. Without regard for it, the Council would be doing no more than fulfil half the number of its tasks: this is the great reward for your enthusiasm and your sacrifices. Political independence is nothing if it does not go hand in hand with personal happiness and security of the individual. You must turn your eyes back to the time when you were unaware of your own strength because you were harassed, oppressed and abused. When you could not find a safeguard against the evils in the administration of the state or the evils in the law; then you counted foreign domination more acceptable than the mortifying bigotry which had taken hold of your country. It is our misfortune that for so long Spain was under the control of an unjust man of fickle purpose. Your patience, your love of order and your magnanimous loyalty have been abused for long enough. It is high time that the word of the law, based on the principle of the common good, should be alone in governing your affairs. This is what our good but unfortunate King wanted and this is the path which He pointed out for us from the window of a cell where an iniquitous traitor had confined Him. Spaniards, the word Fatherland must no longer be a vague, empty word for you. In your ears and in your hearts it must signify the place where law and custom are inviolate, a place where talent is allowed to flourish and virtue is rewarded.

Indeed, Spaniards, the day will soon dawn when the monarchy is given a solid and lasting foundation, in accordance with the unanimous wishes of the King's loyal peoples and of the King Himself. You will then possess basic rights which will be advantageous for all, which will hinder the growth of arbitrary power and foster law and order. When your true rights are established and secure you will take delight in viewing a monument worthy of you and of the King who will mount guard over it, and who will give it his blessing, knowing that it stands for the way in which His people have fought for its construction through so many trials and tribulations. This Council has absolute power over the forces of the realm, to secure in every possible way its honour, defence and happiness. This Council has already acknowledged publicly that influence in the government shall be wielded by the people, who, in the name of the King and for His cause, have been the authors of all that we see today and have achieved this with the help of nobody. So this Council is duty bound to see that you, the people, are given this Nation, to which you have rallied so enthusiastically and which you have defended, or rather conquered, so courageously.

Although our military operations have at first to be slow, in order to make success doubly sure, they give us the opportunity and the calm which are necessary for the solemn and momentous congress which is hereby announced to you, where the Government will draw up and discuss, in private sessions, their proposals for reform and for new laws, which they will present to the people for ratification. The stately edifice of legislation is the work of men who have no learning, no expertise, no precedents and has resulted from will operating in the dark, with neither experience nor directions. It is therefore exposed to mistakes, inconsistencies and derision. To be perfect, it needs amendments, and this must be the work of those Spaniards among you who are distinguished by their wisdom, who have devoted their lives to researching into social principles and who join love of humanity to love of the fatherland and marry education with devotion to duty. Far from rejecting your advice, the Council desires it and looks to you for it. Understanding and elucidation of our long-standing constitutional laws, and the alterations they should undergo

224 SPAIN UNDER THE BOURBONS

when restored, consequent upon changes of circumstances; the reforms which must be made in our civil, penal and commercial codes; proposals for an improvement in the standard of our public education system, which is so far behind that of other nations; economic arrangements for the better collection and distribution of state funds: all this calls for your attention and makes up a long list of problems and tasks in which to show your learning and your abilities. The Council wishes to employ you in various committees, each one of which will be in charge of a certain, specific section of the economy. You will be freely given access to all the documents concerning matters of government and administration in which the various aims of public policy requiring scrutiny are discussed. Your work will help to keep public opinion on a virtuous and wise path. You will help to place the nation in the position of being able to establish its happiness on a firm and peaceful foundation.

In this way revolution in Spain will assume characteristics which make it completely different from the French Revolution. The latter began with the private, petty intrigues of courtiers. Ours with our need to throw out an iniquitous and mighty enemy. In theirs there were as many theories of government as there were factions, or rather as there were individuals. In ours there is only one unanimous opinion and desire: an hereditary monarchy with Fernando VII as King. Rivers of blood were spilt in France at the height of chaos, and the French proclaimed no theory which was not subsequently disavowed, they made no law which they did not themselves break. In the end they submitted to a tyrant and his despotism. The perfidious invasion of Spain by the French left us without a government and without communications between the provinces, but Spaniards have been able to restrain themselves within the confines of the prudence which is characteristic of them. They have been bloody and merciless only with their enemies and they will show themselves capable of improving their laws and consolidating their freedom without sabotaging the ship of State.

Spain! In front of us there is the beautiful prospect of honour and wealth, if we can take advantage of this exceptional period of our history and if we can fulfil the great project to which Providence has assigned us. Instead of being objects of pity and scorn, as we have been up to now, we are to be the envy and the wonder of the world. Our beautiful climate, the fertile land in which we live, our geographical position, the riches which nature in her bounty has showered on us and the noble and generous qualities with which she has endowed us, will not be gifts which are wasted on a base, enslaved people. The name of Spaniards is already pronounced respectfully throughout Europe, where the people who have been crushed by the French see their hopes dependent upon our fortunes. The very slaves of the tyrant, groaning under an intolerable yoke, pray for us. Let us stand firm and we shall pluck the fruits of victory. A day of reckoning will come for the outrages perpetrated on religion. Your King will be returned to his throne or avenged. The basic laws of the monarchy will be restored. Civil liberty will be solemnly and permanently assured. The streams of national prosperity will spontaneously flow, spilling wealth without let or hindrance. We shall have more brotherly and therefore more beneficial relations with our colonies. Energy, industry, ability and virtue will be quickened and rewarded. These are the pinnacles of splendour and fortune to which we can raise our country if we live up to the magnificent opportunities which surround us.

These then are the plans and purposes which the Council has had before it since the moment of its inception. The two principal and essential objectives are thus to be accomplished. The members of the Council have been given such high authority and have become responsible for such seductive expectations yet they realise the difficulties which they must overcome in order to fulfil their tasks and they are not unmindful of the weight which they must bear and the dangers to which they are exposed. But they will count themselves well paid for their travails and the sacrifice of their persons to the Fatherland if they succeed in inspiring in Spaniards a confidence without which no public good is achieved. The Council makes bold to say that it is deserving of such confidence in virtue of the uprightness of its principles and the purity of its intentions.

Aranjuez, October 26, 1808. Given with the agreement of the Supreme Council on November 10, Martin de Garay, general secretary.

(Toreno, *Historia del levantamiento* ...)

105

Joseph complains to the Emperor

1809

'Madrid, 19th February.

Sir, It pains me to see from your letter that you lend an ear to those who would deceive you about the events in Madrid. You do not have the complete confidence in me without which this office is untenable. I cannot count on a penny to give to anyone. I am now in the fourth year of my reign and I still see my guards in the dress I gave them four years ago ... The power of my throne extends no further than Madrid, and in Madrid I am daily contradicted by others ... I am accused of over-indulgence.

... if you think it necessary to surround me with niggards who make me blush at myself, if I am to be insulted even in my own capital, if I am not to have the right to appoint my own governors ...

... I am not King of Spain except by the force of your arms; I could become King through the love of the Spanish people, but, to achieve that, I must govern according to my own lights.'

(A. du Casse, *Mémoires et correspondence politique et militaire du roi Joseph*, Bayonne, n.d.)

106

Surrender of Zaragoza

1809

'Article 1. The Zaragoza garrison will come out at noon tomorrow by the Portillo gate with their arms and will leave them at one hundred paces from the said gate.

2. All the officers and men of the Spanish army will take an oath of allegiance to His Catholic Majesty, King Napoleon I.

3. All officers and men who have taken the oath of allegiance may, if they so wish, enter into His Catholic Majesty's service.

4. Those who do not wish to enter the service shall be taken to France as prisoners-of-war.

5. All inhabitants of Zaragoza and all outsiders, if there are any, shall be disarmed by the justices of the peace and their arms shall be handed over at Portillo gate at noon on the 21st.

6. All persons and property shall be respected by His Majesty the Emperor and King.

7. Their religion and its ministers shall be respected. Sentries will be posted at the doors of all important buildings.

8. Tomorrow at noon, French troops will occupy all the gates of the city and the palace of Coso.

9. Tomorrow at noon, all artillery and all munitions of every kind shall be handed over to the forces of His Majesty the Emperor and King.

10. All members of the civil administration and all employees of whatever kind shall take an oath of allegiance to His Catholic Majesty.

11. Justice will be carried out as heretofore and will be practised in the name of His Catholic Majesty Joseph Napoleon I.

... Garrison headquarters before Zaragoza, 20th February, 1809. Lannes.

(Toreno, *Historia del levantamiento* ..., vol. II, appendix, p. 26.)

107

Jovellanos' reply to General Sebastiani

1809

'General: I am not working for a particular party. I am working in the just and holy cause of my country, a cause adopted by all those who receive from her hand the imposing task of defending her and running her affairs, a cause which we have all sworn to serve and to maintain at the cost of our own lives. We do not go into battle, as you are suggesting, for the inquisition, nor for some dreamy ideal, nor in the interests of the Spanish grandees; we do battle for the precious rights of our King, our faith, our constitution and our independence. Nor should you think that the urge to maintain these is a far cry from the urge to destroy any obstacles that may get in their way; in fact, the opposite is true, and, to borrow your own phrase, the design of regenerating Spain and lifting her to the level of former glories and the desire to do this are seen by us as one of our first priorities. Perhaps it will not be long before France and the whole of Europe recognise that a nation which can, with such valour and singlemindedness of purpose, keep the cause of her freedom and her King alive in the teeth of aggression which is all the more unjust as it was unlooked for, coming from those who called themselves her best friends, is zealous enough, purposeful enough and wise enough to set about reforming those evils which led her unconsciously to the dreadful fate with which they were preparing to greet her. There is no sensitive heart which does not weep at the evil atrocities which this aggression has unleashed on an innocent people, who, branded with the infamous name of rebels, are now denied those human rights which the laws of war demand and which are countenanced even by the most barbarous of enemies. But who is to blame for these evils? Those who have brought them about with their violation of every principle of nature and of justice, or those generous hearts that are doing battle to beat them off and throw them out once and for all from this great and noble country? For you, General, should not labour under any misconceptions: these sentiments which it is my honour to express to you are those of the whole nation: there is not a single good man and true among those oppressed by your arms whose breast is not alive with the noble flame which burns in the hearts of the defenders of this country. To speak of our allies would be an impertinence were it not for your letter to which your honour demands a reply. The designs which you attribute to them do them great calumny; they are far removed from the spirit of magnanimity in which the English Nation offered her friendship and support to our land, when we went to her, unarmed and impoverished, right at the outset of the oppression which our friends were threatening, and begged for her help.

In short, General, I shall be only too ready to respect the humane philosophical principles which you say your King Joseph professes, as soon as he leaves our lands and recognises that a country which your soldiers are at present laying waste in his name is not the proper stage on which to expound them. This certainly would be a triumph for his philosophy, and you, General, if you are imbued with the ideals which it inspires, must also be proud that your role in this triumph will entitle you to some small part of our respect and place us in your debt. Only if this should happen, will my honour and my ideals allow me to be a party to the communiqué you suggest, assuming that the Supreme Central Council agrees. Meanwhile, General, please accept my sincere gratitude for the honour you do me personally, and rest assured of the esteem in which I hold you. Seville, 24th April, 1809. Gasper de Jovellanos. To the Most Excellent General Horace Sebastiani.'

(Toreno, *Historia del levantamiento...*, vol. II, pp. 327–9.)

108

The first session of the parliament of the Supreme Council. Royal decree of His Majesty

1809

'The Spanish people must come out of this bloody struggle in the certainty that they will leave for posterity a heritage of prosperity and of glory, which shall be worthy of the marvellous efforts they have put in and the blood which has been shed. The Supreme Council has never lost sight of this end and it has been, throughout the continual stirrings of the events of the war, its main aim in all it has done. The advantageous position of the enemy, due less to his valour than to his superiority in numbers has taken up all of the attentions of the Government, but at the same time it has heightened the bitterness of the thought that the disasters which rack the nation are the fruit of having allowed healthy institutions, which were in happier times the sources of the nation's prosperity and its strength, to sink into oblivion.

The ambitions of the usurpers and the abandon of the idle have gradually reduced them to nothing, and, from the moment of its setting up, the Council has been solemnly pledged to their re-establishment. The time has already arrived to set our hand to this great task, and to think out what reforms are called for in the administration, basing them on the fundamental laws of the monarchy which alone can lend them real solidity, and giving ear, as has already been publicly announced, to all those men of wisdom who would like to express their thoughts on the matter so that the best solution may be found.

It being the wish of Fernando VII and of the Supreme Governing Council of the Realm acting in his name, that the Spanish nation should appear to the eyes of the world with the dignity due her heroic struggle, and determined that the basic rights of the citizen should be free from fresh attack, and that the fount of the common weal, should have the blockage which has hitherto held it in check cleared away, and it should gush forth unimpeded, as soon as the war is done, over lands parched by the unkind glare of fate and over the devastation wrought by the present whirlwind; they have decreed the following:

1. That legal representation in parliament as of old under the monarchy shall be restored; the first parliament being convened all next year or before if the situation allows:

2. That the Council shall forthwith devote itself to the study of the kind, number and station of members to be called to the august assembly bearing in mind the present situation. To this end it will appoint a committee of five ...

3. That, besides this, ... The Council shall extend its considerations to take in the following items so that it can put these as an agenda before the nation in parliament:— Means and resources for continuing the holy war in which it finds itself most justly involved until such time as it shall have achieved the glorious aims it has set itself. Means to ensure that the fundamental laws of the realm are obeyed. Means of improving our laws, getting rid of the abuses which have crept in and making perfection of the laws possible ... Necessary reforms in the public education system ... The part which the Americas should play in parliament.

4. In order to bring together the necessary men of learning to take part in such important discussions, the Council will consult with its advisers, with the upper regional assemblies, and with tribunals, municipal councils, chapters, bishops and universities and will pay heed to all learned and illustrious persons.

... You will pay attention to this and take the necessary measures to ensure that it is carried out.

The Marquis of Astorga, President. – The Royal Alcázar, Seville. 22nd May, 1809. – To D. Martín de Garay.'

(Toreno, *Historia del levantamiento* ..., vol. III, appendix, p. 6.)

109

Communiqués on the Battle of Talavera

1809

'Last night I communicated to Your Excellency from the left bank of the Alberche that, in the event of my being cut off from the English troops, I would fear attack from the enemy forces massed in Talavera. This factor persuaded me to re-cross the river ... and take up the position agreed with General Wellesley, so that both our armies formed a line opposite Talavera ...

Yesterday, at five in the afternoon, when we had only just formed up, the enemy came into sight, numbering, according to our estimate, forty thousand men, five thousand of whom were horse. These troops immediately attacked our line with the utmost tenacity, directing their major assault upon our left, which was held by the English, trying to surround them on that flank.

Both attack and defence were equally tenacious, so much so that the fighting became hand to hand, but eventually the enemy were twice repulsed, losing many dead and wounded. The action lasted until eight thirty in the evening and the English suffered heavy losses especially among the officers.

Our losses have not been great, and generally speaking, our men displayed great valour and steadfastness, except for three or four detachments who left something to be desired. I shall give details of all this later.

Very early this morning, the enemy renewed their attack which is still going on now, at seven in the evening, but it has been repeatedly repulsed and will continue to be so, I trust. Joseph Napoleon was with his troops up to this evening and we know that he withdrew with his guard to Santa Olalla and that 98 cartloads of wounded crossed the Alberche with him.

I cannot for the moment go into more details, as I have been with all my troops on battle alert in the field for three days, during which time we have had no supplies at all, nor even the means to obtain them, seeing that the victuallers and their staff deserted from both armies as soon as they heard the first shot.

Communiqué 2.

Last evening at seven, I informed Your Excellency from the battle field that the enemy attacks and our defence were continuing relentlessly. When night fell the hostilities eased, but the enemy did not leave its positions until it began to withdraw a little before dawn, and has now re-crossed the Alberche heading in the direction of Casalejas and Santa Olalla, having given up hope of being able to force us to retreat or even to dislodge us from our position ... They have suffered appalling losses which would have been greater had the exhaustion and hunger of our troops not prevented us from giving them chase.

Talavera 29th July, 1809. Gregorio de la Cuesta. His Excellency D. Antonio Cornel.'

(J. Canga Argüelles, *Documentos pertenecientes* ... (1835), vol. I, pp. 238 *et seq.*)

110

The first surge of Mexican Independence

1810

[Father Hidalgo proposes the surrender of Guanajuato to Superintendent Riaño]

'Military Headquarters, Hacienda de Burras, 28th September, 1810. The vast army under my command elected me Captain-General and Lord Protector of the Nation on the battle-field of Celaya. This choice was ratified by some 50,000 in that city and has been endorsed in all the towns I have passed through. This will show Your Honour that I have the proper authority of my Country to put into effect those plans which have seemed to me to be in their interests. These are to the benefit and in the interests alike of Americans and of those Europeans who have had the spirit to take up residence in this country, and amount to a proclamation of Independence and natural freedom. Thus it is that I do not view Europeans as enemies but rather as an obstacle standing in the way of the success of our undertaking. Your Honour will be pleased to communicate this to the Europeans who have mustered there in Alhóndiga and invite them to decide whether they will come out against us or agree to be taken prisoner and receive the sort of humane and kindly treatment which those we have brought with us are now tasting. They will remain prisoner until the liberty of the Nation, which we have hinted at, and its independence is achieved, at which time they will become full citizens and their rights of ownership of those posses-sions of which we temporarily deprive them in the pressing interests of the nation, will be recognised. If, on the other hand, they should reject this request, I shall spare no force nor any pains to destroy them utterly, nor can they expect any quarter. May God grant you a long life; such is the wish of your humble servant, Miguel Hidalgo y Costilla, Captain-General of America.'

(V. Riva Palacio, *México a través de los siglos*, vol. III, pp. 115–16.)

III

Marshal Soult opens the war to the death, 9th May

1810

'There is no Spanish army apart from that of His Catholic Majesty, Joseph Napoleon. All factions now in existence anywhere in the country, whatever their size and whoever leads them, shall there-fore be treated as gangs of bandits ... All individual members of these groups caught sword in hand shall be summarily tried by the local army commander and shot: Their bodies shall be put on public exhibition in the streets.'

(Toreno, *Historia del levantamiento* ..., vol. III, pp. 265–6.)

112

News of the Revolution in Venezuela

1810

'Events in Caracas.

One of the saddest effects of the sorry pass to which the affairs of state had come last January was the regrettable effect the news from the metropolis must have had on other American colonies.

Exaggerated by distance and distorted by malicious tongues, this news could have led the natives to despair of the well-being of the state and induced them to hasty action which might have proved their downfall. They have, however, proved steadfast in their loyalty, and only in Caracas, where some turbulent parties already known to be restless and lawless and not properly held in check by previous directives, found in the crisis the opening they were seeking for their ambitious designs. They turned the credulity of the people who were filled with anxiety and worry by accursed news coming out of the metropolis, to their evil ends and with all their friends and faction notified in readiness about the insurrection, Thursday of Holy Week, the 19th of April gave them just the chance they were looking for to set their work in motion ...'

(*Gaceta Extraordinaria de la Regencia de España e Indias*, 8 August 1810.)

113

Proclamation of 20 April of the Council of Caracas to the 'inhabitants of the United States of Venezuela'

1810

'The Spanish nation, after a bloody and passionate war which has been fought for two years in defence of her liberty and independence, is on the brink of collapse in Europe under the tyrannical yoke of her conquerors ... The Central Council of the Government of the Realm which united the will of the nation under its absolute authority, has in this turbulent struggle been scattered in disarray and its sovereignty, legally constituted to protect the realm, has been finally destroyed. During the conflict, the inhabitants of Cádiz have set up a new style of government, under the title of Regency, which can at present have no other aim than the protection in the short run of the few Spaniards who have managed to escape the yoke of the conqueror and to look to their future safety. It is in no way representative of the general wishes of the nation, even less of those inhabitants whose legitimate and unalterable right it is to watch over the safe keeping and security of these areas as integral parts of the Spanish monarchy. Could you succeed in such an important endeavour, with a power which is illegal, intermittent and excitable? Is it sensible to waste precious time chasing after vain figments of hope instead of acting promptly and joining forces in a union which is the only possible guarantee of political survival and of obtaining the release of your beloved Fernando VII from the gloom of his captivity? Is this the way we shall carry on in these beautiful lands the tradition of the magnificent and sacred faith which we were given by our parents? No, our beloved countrymen. Already, in Caracas they have learned how vital it is that we pursue our cause vigorously and energetically, if we want to preserve all those interests so dear to us. To this end, having learned of the sorry state of things in the war in Spain from the latest ships to arrive from Spain on our shores, we have taken the decision to constitute a provisional government here in the capital to take charge of the affairs of this city and of all other townships in this province who care to join forces with her. This shall be done with traditional loyalty to King Fernando VII.'

(*Gaceta extraordinaria* ..., 8 August 1810.)

114

Declaration of independence by the Congress of Venezuela

1811

'In the name of Almighty God. We the representatives of the provinces ... which make up the American Confederation of Venezuela on the Southern Continent, meeting in session to consider the complete and absolute possession of our rights which has been justly and legitimately ours once again since the 19th April, 1810, as a result of the journey to Bayonne and the occupation of the Spanish throne by conquest and the succession of another dynasty arrived at without our consent, wish, before making use of these rights of which we have been forcibly deprived for over three hundred years and which have now been restored to us by the political order of human events, to make plain to the whole world the rationale which has emerged from these very events and which empowers us to make full use, as we intend, of our own sovereignty.

We do not want, nevertheless, to start by alleging the right which every conquered nation has to recover its own country and its independence ... we shall only present the true facts which are well known and which were bound to split the old world from the new, as indeed they have done, through the upheaval, disorders and conquest which now have the Spanish nation in a state of disunity.

It is against natural order, is impossible for the Spanish Government and has dreadful effects for America, that a country so much more vast and with an incomparably greater population should be dependent on and subject to a peninsula at the corner of the Continent of Europe. The surrenders and abdications of Bayonne, the journeys from El Escorial and Aranjuez and the orders of Lieutenant the Duke of Berg to America, must induce Americans to make use of those rights which they have until now forsworn in the interests of the unity and integrity of the Spanish nation.

We have for three years lived in a state of indecision and political uncertainty of so dire and dangerous a nature that this alone would be sufficient justification for our taking this resolve which our promises and our family ties led us to postpone until necessity forced us to go further than we had intended, driven by the hostile and unnatural conduct of the Spanish authorities, which conduct has released us from the limited oath with which we were called to the awesome office of representatives, which office we are now filling ...

... We, therefore, the representatives of the United Provinces of Venezuela, with the Supreme Being as a witness of the justice of our proceeding ... in the name and with the support of the virtuous people of Venezuela, solemnly declare to the world that our provinces are and shall be from this day forward de facto and de jure free, sovereign and independent nations, owing allegiance to no one and independent of the Spanish crown and from all who claim either now or at any time in the future to be her proxy or her representative.

... Given in the Federal Palace at Caracas, signed by our hands and sealed by the great provisional seal of the Federation and countersigned by the Secretary to Congress, the fifth day of the month of July, 1811, the first year of Independence. Juan A. Rodríguez Domínguez, President, etc.'

(D. F. O'Learey, *Bolívar y la emancipación de América* (1915), vol. I, pp. 107 *et seq.*)

115
First news of the Argentinian Revolution

1811

'When the Royal High Court in Buenos Aires demanded that the
Council which had been set up there should recognise the authority
of the Supreme Council of the Regency about June of last year,
1810, the Council replied that it would do so as soon as official
advice of the constitution of that body reached it, since it only
knew of the existence of that body through the accounts of
individuals, and none of the formalities usually observed in such
cases had been observed in this instance. This reply did for a little
while allay the fears of those well intentioned persons who looked
for the restoration of the monarchy and who hoped for the unity
of all Spaniards to safeguard untarnished the rights of the King
during the bitter days of his captivity ... But they soon had cause
to view the Council of Buenos Aires with suspicion when they
saw how intent it was on distorting events in Europe, painting
an absolutely desperate picture of the situation and heaping in-
crimination on the conduct of those who were for the union of the
Provinces on both sides of the Atlantic, and who, it claimed, could
be suspected of wanting to hand over these enormous and wealthy
lands to the thief of Europe. Finally unmasked, the dissidents kid-
napped the Viceroy, D. Baltasar Hidalgo de Cisneros, and the
Ministers of the Realm and expelled them from the country. They
deposed the Ministers that made up the cabinet of the city and
sent them into exile because they had, in secret session, given
recognition to the Council of the Regency, and they appointed
another cabinet from among their own supporters, without any
reference to the people, not even for the election of the attorney
general. They exiled the most respectable citizens, confiscated all
their property and ordered the execution of many who were not
happy with the changes, under the pretext that they were plotting
a revolution.'
   (*Gaceta Extraordinaria...*, 20 July 1811.)

116

Political constitution of the Spanish Monarchy

1812

In the name of Almighty God, Father, Son and Holy Ghost, Creator and Supreme Law-giver of society.

The Extraordinary National Parliament of the Spanish nation, firmly convinced, after the closest examination and the most weighty deliberation, that the ancient and fundamental laws of this Monarchy, given timely good fortune and proper precautions which will ensure that they can be exercised fully in a stable and lasting manner, can lead to the complete fulfilment of the great aim of realising the fame, prosperity and well being of all the Nation, decrees the following political constitution for the good government and proper administration of the State.

Section I
On the Spanish nation and the Spaniards

Chapter I
On the Spanish nation

Art. 1. The Spanish nation shall be defined as the sum total of all Spaniards on both sides of the Atlantic.

Art. 2. The Spanish nation is free and independent and it is not nor can it ever be the property of any family or person.

Art. 3. Power resides essentially in the nation, and, as such, the right to establish the fundamental laws is exclusively of the nation.

Chapter II
On the Spaniards

Art. 5. Spaniards are:
First: All free men born and residing in lands belonging to the Spanish crown, and their descendants.

Secondly: Foreigners who have a certificate of naturalisation issued by Parliament.

Thirdly: Those who, while not officially naturalised, have resided for ten years in any city of the realm.

Fourthly: Freed men from the moment of their being granted their liberty within Spanish territory.

Art. 6. Love of one's country is one of the chief duties of all Spaniards as are those of being upright and charitable.

Art. 7. It is the duty of every Spaniard to keep faith with the Constitution, obey the laws, and respect the established authorities.

Art. 8. It is also incumbent upon every Spaniard whatever he may be, to contribute proportionately of his wealth to the expenses of the State.

Art. 9. It is also the duty of every Spaniard to defend his country in battle, when the law demands it of him.

Section II ...
... Chapter II
On Religion

Art. 12. The religion of the Spanish people is, and ever shall be, the only true faith of the Roman Catholic Church. The Nation offers it protection with wise and just laws and outlaws the practice of any other.

Chapter III
On Government

Art. 13. The aim of the Government is the happiness of the nation, since the political aim of any society is none other than the well-being of the individuals that make up that society.

Art. 14. The Government of the Spanish people is a conservative hereditary monarchy.

Art. 15. The power to make the laws is invested in Parliament and the King.

Art. 16. The power to put the laws into practice is invested in the King.

Art. 17. The power to enforce the law in both civil and criminal cases is invested in courts established by the law.

... Section IV
On the King

Art. 172. The restrictions on the power of the King are as follows: First: For no reason of any kind may the King prevent Parliament sitting at those times and for those reasons laid down in the Constitution nor may he suspend or dissolve it, nor may he in any way interfere with its sittings and debates. Those who counsel him or abet him in any attempt he may make to do this are declared to be traitors and shall be prosecuted as such.

Second: The King may not absent himself from the realm without the consent of Parliament and should he do so he shall be understood to have abdicated.

Third: The King may not transfer, surrender, resign or hand over to any other person his royal authority, nor any of his prerogatives
    If for any reason he should wish to abdicate in favour of his immediate successor he shall not be able to do this without the consent of Parliament.

Fourth, Fifth, Sixth and Seventh; The King cannot hand over ... any province or town, etc. which lies in Spanish territory, make an alliance or trade agreement ... give financial aid to foreigners ... surrender national assets ... without the consent of Parliament.

Eighth: He cannot demand taxes in his own name.

Ninth: He cannot give exclusive rights to any individual or group of individuals.

Tenth: He may not ... confiscate the property of any individual or group of individuals, nor interfere with their tenure, use and enjoyment of it.

Eleventh: He may not ... deprive any individual of his liberty.

Twelfth: The King, before entering into any marriage contract, shall inform Parliament of his intentions and should he not do so, he shall be held to have abdicated.

Art. 173. On his accession to the throne, or, should he not be of age, at the time of taking over the government of the realm, the King shall take an oath before Parliament as follows:

'I, X (Here his name), by the Grace of God and the Constitution of the Spanish Monarchy, King of Spain, Swear by God and the Holy Apostles that I shall defend and maintain the Holy Catholic Faith, outlawing any other from my Realm; that I shall keep and ensure the safe keeping of the political Constitution and the laws of the Spanish Realm, having no other aim in all I do but the good and profit of the realm: that I shall not divide up the realm nor transfer or surrender any part of it: that I shall exact no tribute in commodities, money or any other form, except that laid down by Parliament: that I shall not confiscate anyone's property and that I shall above all respect the political liberty of the nation and the personal freedom of every individual citizen, and if I in any respect depart from that which I have sworn I shall do, I shall not expect to be obeyed and that which I order in contravention of my oath shall be null and void. May God be my aid and defend my realm, and if I fail, may He be my judge.'

(*Colección de los decretos y órdenes de las Cortes generales y extraordinarias* (1820), p. 101.)

117

Wellington, Commander-in-Chief

1812

'Decree of Parliament, moved by Don Francisco Ciscar, Member of Parliament for Valencia, and other members,

It being indispensable for the rapid and certain destruction of the enemy that there should be unity in the plans and operations of the allied armies in the Peninsula, and it not being possible to achieve this vital state of affairs without there being a single Commander-in-Chief of all the Spanish troops stationed there, the common extraordinary Parliament, aware of the pressing need to follow up the glorious triumphs of the allied forces and to take advantage of the favourable situation which is speeding up the arrival of the day when the evils which beset the nation will be done, and greatly

appreciative of the distinguished ability and pertinent services of the
Duke of Ciudad Rodrigo, Captain General of the national army,
who has agreed to the decree, which is hereby promulgated, that, for
the period of allied co-operation in the defence of the Peninsula,
the overall command of all the forces shall be entrusted to him in
accordance with general statute, (article 6, section I, agreement 7).
The sole difference which is made by this present decree in the
respect of the said Duke that this command should be valid for all
regions of the Peninsula, the illustrious Commander-in-Chief being
under the obligation to deal with the Spanish government through
the Secretariat of the Ministry of War. This shall be made known
to the Regency of the Realm ...

Given at Cádiz, 22nd September, 1812.'

(Toreno, *Historia del levantamiento* ..., vol. V, p. 144.)

118

Abolition of the Inquisition

1813

'The Common and Extraordinary Parliament, desirous that the
stipulations laid down in Article 12 of the Constitution shall be
completely effective and that the strict observance of this wise
measure shall be ensured in the future, declares and decrees:

Chapter I

Art. I. The Roman Catholic Faith shall be protected by laws
compatible with the Constitution.

II. The Tribunal of the Inquisition is not compatible with the
Constitution.

III. Consequently, Law II, Section XXVI Item VII will be rein-
voked with all its previous weight. It shall fall to the Bishops and
their deputies to decide in matters of faith in accordance with sacred
canon and common law, and to the lay magistrates to pronounce and
determine sentence on heretics according to the punishments laid
down by the law, now and in the future. Both ecclesiastic and lay
judges shall proceed in their respective courts in accordance with the
Constitution and the law.

IV. Every Spaniard has the right to bring a case of heresy before the ecclesiastical court. In the absence of a prosecutor, or even where there is one, the ecclesiastical prosecutor will move the case.

IX. After the ecclesiastical trial is over, the transcript of the trial shall be handed over to the lay magistrates, and the defendant shall pass in to his hands so that he may proceed against him and sentence him as the law demands.

Given at Cádiz, 22nd February, 1813.'

(*Coleción de los decretos...*, p. 190.)

119

Decree of Valencia (4 May) annulling the previous liberal one of the Cádiz Parliament

1814

'... to this Parliament – constituted in a way never before seen in Spain even for the most thorny of issues and at the most turbulent of times, during the minority of a King when the number of members has generally been larger than during an ordinary Parliament – neither the Lords Temporal, nor the Lords Spiritual were summoned, although the Central Council had ordered that they should be, this decree having been artfully concealed from the Council of the Regency as was the fact that The Council had assigned to it the presidency of the Parliament, a prerogative of sovereignty which the Regency would never have left to the decision of the Council had it known anything about it. With that, everything was left to Parliament, which, on the very day on which it met for the first time and as its first piece of legislation, stripped me of my sovereignty which these self same representatives had recognised but a few days before, giving it in name only to the nation so that it could take it for itself and then, after this coup, give the country laws of its own making. It then forced it under the yoke of a new Constitution which it drew up, agreed upon and published in 1812, without the authority of any region, any township or any council and without taking into account any of the cases made out by the replacement members for Spain and the Indies.

I abhor and detest absolutism: neither men of discernment in

Europe nor her civilisation will any longer tolerate it, nor do her goodly laws and constitution permit it – although unfortunately from time to time, as is always the case in human affairs, there have everywhere been abuses of power which no Constitution imaginable could completely prevent. These were not the result of defects in the particular constitution of that nation, but rather of defects in particular individuals and of the changeability of mean persons, but they can only arise very rarely when circumstances conspire to that end. Still, in order to prevent them as far as human foresight allows – that is, by maintaining the decorum and dignity of the royal family which are proper to its very nature, and by keeping its rights inviolate, and by looking after the rights of the people, which are equally inalienable, – I shall negotiate with the Members of Parliament for Spain and the Indies, and, as soon as the law and order which this country used to enjoy and which was maintained with its consent by its Kings, my august predecessors, have been re-established, I hope, with the help of a Parliament legally constituted by Members both from Spain and the Indies, to set about passing a number of sound laws which will work to the good of the nation and towards the creation of an ideal state where my subjects shall live in the prosperity and happiness of a Faith and an Empire closely knitted together in indissoluble harmony. On this and on this alone does the happiness on this earth of a King and a Kingdom, graced with the lofty title of Catholic, depend, and we shall put our hand at once to preparing and working out whatever seems best for the summons of Parliament where I trust that we shall lay the foundations of the prosperity of my subjects right across the world.

The freedom and safety of both private citizens and the King shall be firmly guaranteed by laws which, ensuring peace and order in the realm, shall give to all that welcome freedom in the enjoyment of which – the hallmark of a moderate government as against an arbitrary and despotic regime – all the citizens under its sway shall live. Everybody shall taste the same justice and freedom to communicate his ideas and thoughts through the press, provided, of course, that he keeps within the limits prescribed by the ruling canon of reason which are drawn to stop degeneration into licence – for no civilised government can reasonably allow the respect due to religion and authority, and that men should show to one another, to be disregarded and flaunted with impunity. A halt will be called to any suspicions about profligacy with the Exchequer by keeping the moneys used to meet the expenses incurred in maintaining the decorum of my royal person and of my family and of the nation over which it is my glory to reign, separate from the treasury funds accrued from taxes with the consent of the realm and set aside for the maintenance of the State, and all the various branches of its administration. Also, the laws which shall in future regulate the actions of my subjects shall be arrived at by agreement with Parliament. So it is, that this outline may serve as a definite foretaste of my royal intentions in the government which I am about to assume, and make it known to everyone that he can expect not a despot nor a tyrant but a King and a father of his subjects. So it is that, basing my actions on what every person well known for his experience and devotion has told me, and on the representations which have been made to me from all corners of the realm and which tell of the repugnance and disgust with which the Constitution drawn up by the Common and Extraordinary Parliament and all the new political institutions recently introduced are viewed in the country, and of the evils and injustices which have sprung from them and which would be only on the increase if I were to give the royal consent to the Constitution and swear an oath on it; and, acting upon such widespread and incontrovertible proof of the wishes of my people, because these representations are so deeply rooted in the reality of the situation, I declare that my royal intentions are not only not to put my name and give my consent either to the said Constitution or to any decree of the Common and Extraordinary Parliament, or of the ordinary Parliament now in session — that is, to any decree which may detract from the rights and prerogatives of my sovereignty established by the Constitution and the laws which have for so long held sway — but to declare that Constitution and such decrees null and void, whether now or at any time in the future, as though such acts had never been passed, thereby exempting all my peoples and subjects from any duty to obey them or keep to them.

And, since anyone who upholds them and in so doing goes against this my royal declaration, taken with due accord and of my own free will, shall undermine the prerogatives of my sovereignty and the happiness of the nation and shall be the cause of disturbances and unhappiness in my realm, I declare any person who dares to attempt this to be guilty of "lèse-majesté", and I sentence him as such to death, whether he does this by his actions or his writings or by what he says, inciting or in any way exhorting and persuading others to keep and observe the said Constitution and decree.

[After having ordered the dissolution of Parliament and put all its documents into store, sealing and locking up even the books, he orders all those prosecuted for their hatred of the Constitution to be set free.]

These are my wishes, because they are demanded by the good and the happiness of the nation. – Given in Valencia, 4th May, 1814 – We, the King. – The King's secretary for decrees, with special licence for this one. – Pedro de Macanaz.'

(M. Ferrer, D. Tejera y J. F. Acedo, *Historia del tradicionalismo español* (1941), vol. I, pp. 303 *et seq.*)

120

Declaration of the Assembly of Angostura convened by Bolívar on 20 November in the knowledge that Spain was seeking the help of the European Powers

1816

'The Republic of Venezuela is by both divine and human right free from the Spanish nation and constituted as an independent, free and sovereign state. Spain has no right to claim back her dominion over her nor Europe to try to bring her under Spanish rule. She has not sought nor ever shall seek incorporation within the Spanish nation; she has not sought the mediation of the great powers to reconcile her with Spain; she will never have any dealings with Spain save on an equal footing both in peace and war as is the practice of all other nations. She only desires the intervention of foreign powers so that they might use their good offices to intercede for humanity's sake, inviting Spain to conclude a treaty of peace and friendship with the Venezuelan nation, and to recognise her and treat her as a free independent and sovereign nation. Lastly, the Republic of Venezuela declares that since the 19th April 1810 she has fought for her rights, that the greater part of the blood of her sons has been shed, that she has sacrificed all her wealth, all her pleasures and all that is dear and sacred in the world in her quest to recover her sovereign rights and to keep them as untarnished as on the day divine providence made her the gift of them, and that the people of Venezuela are resolved to perish among the ruins of their own country if Spain, Europe and the world insist on bending her back under the Spanish yoke.'

(J. Gil Fortoul, *Historia Constitucional de Venezuela* (2nd ed., 1930).

121
Act of Independence of Chile

1818
'... The Regency had informed us* that we would for ever associate that name with the period of regeneration of monarchy and restitution of happiness both in the old world and the new.

... the peoples of the Peninsula have not built their revolution save on the demands of necessity – why cannot the people's of America just as equally be judges of whether they are or are not faced with the same demands? Since the Regency and Parliament have proclaimed that the only basis for their authority is the sovereignty of the people, they have lost all pretext for giving orders to any people who wish to exercise their sovereignty for themselves. If their authority emanates from the Spanish people and they have no power over the peoples of America who, like them, are an integral and chief part of the nation, why cannot we ourselves represent the King and act in his name as they do themselves when they declare us rebels?

... let us look at the map ... Twenty two thousand square leagues and one million people ... are these to remain dependent on a speck of the old world which begs all its resources from them? ... in a Parliament with equal representation we find one member for every thirty thousand people in the Peninsula while we have to have nearly a million for ours.

... Free peoples of the world ... convince her (Spain) of her powerlessness and the mutual advantages which would accrue from our independence ... and persuade her to make close appraisal of the outcome which threatens her and to lay down her arms and make a sacrifice, in the interests of justice and freedom, of those trappings which hasten her down the road to obliteration. Cry out to her on our word of honour that Chile The Magnanimous will open her heart to the friendship of her brothers and will share with them, in due observance of the law, the benefits of her undying independence.

* By the Decree of 14 February 1810.

Presidential Palace of Chile, 15th February, 1808 – Bernardo O'Higgins.'

(Carlos Calvo, *Anales históricos de la Revolución de la América*, vol. IV, pp. 37 *et seq.*)

122

Liberal revolution. First proclamation of the army of Cádiz

1820

'The national army, in its proclamation of support for the Constitution of the Spanish monarchy promulgated in Cádiz by its lawful representatives, is not in any way bent upon sabotaging the rights of the lawful monarch recognised in the Constitution, but, persuaded that all the moves by the Government have been ill fated, in a way as sad as it is incomprehensible and have led to the downfall of a nation which made so many sacrifices to sanction the monarchy, believes that only this coup can rescue both it and the Prince from the impasse in which they find themselves. The army has no designs upon property or persons, nor does it seek to make innovations which equity, justice and the religion of our fathers do not countenance; this is not a spirit of sedition; the motives which provoke it are not mere ephemeral babblings. The purest of patriotism, the most ardent of desires for the happiness of the country have dictated the solemnest of oaths that the last drop of blood shall be shed to see these goals fulfilled. The rest of the Spanish militia which has spared no sacrifice in the salvation, honour and glory of the nation, and the whole nation which has given such shining examples of heroism to the world, will not be able to forbear to applaud the sentiments and steadfast resolve of her citizens. This satisfying ideal will be the reward for their labours and their example will be followed by all those in whom a noble and generous heart lies beating.

Spanish people: it is up to you to follow it, it is up to you to relive your past glories or to sink for ever into an abyss of ignominy. The alternative is not in doubt, and all Europe, whose gaze is fixed upon you, will not lose the illusions it entertains of the nation which six years ago shook it out of its lethargy and then decided its destiny. – By order in the absence of the Commander-in-Chief at headquarters. – Chief of the military staff, Felipe de Arco Agüero.'

(*Correo Universal de Literatura y Política*, no. 1 (April 1820), pp. 18–19.)

123
Declaration of the King to the Nation

1820

'Spaniards: When your heroic struggle finally succeeded in putting an end to the captivity in which we were held as a result of the most unheard of treachery, everything we saw and everything we heard, almost as soon as we set foot on our native soil, conspired to persuade us that the country wanted to see a resurrection of the old style of government, and this persuasion decided us to go along with what seemed to be the almost unanimous wishes of a magnanimous people who, having overcome their foreign enemy, feared even more terrible evils from internal strife.

We were not unaware, however, that the rapid progress of European civilisation, the universal spread of culture to include even the less elevated classes, the increases in frequency of communications between the different countries of the world and the astonishing events of the present generation had given rise to ideas and aspirations unknown to our parents, and to fresh and pressing needs. Nor were we unaware how vital it was to shape political institutions to accommodate these factors so as to produce that desirable harmony between Man and Law on which the stability and peace of society depend.

But while we were giving due consideration, with that solicitude which is natural to our paternal nature, to what changes in our basic form of government would appear to be the most adaptable to the national character and to the present state of the various parts of the Spanish monarchy as well as most nearly analagous to the organisation of learned peoples, you gave us to understand your desire for the reinvocation of that constitution which was promulgated in Cádiz in 1812 in the middle of the turmoil of hostilities at a time when you were fighting to the astonishment of the world for the freedom of your country. We have heard your supplications and, as a loving father, we have deigned to accede to what our children hold to be in the interests of their happiness. We have sworn to the constitution which you were hoping for and shall always be its most constant supporter. We have already taken the necessary measures for a speedy recall of Parliament. There, working alongside your representatives, it will be our pleasure to attend to the great task of promoting national prosperity.

Spaniards, your glory is the only one our hearts yearn for ... our heart's desire is to see you around our throne in unity, at peace, and happy. Trust your king, then, who speaks to you in that sincere confidence which the situation in which you find yourselves and the intimate awareness of the lofty duties which Providence has placed on his shoulders inspire in him. Your good fortune shall from today onward depend in great part on yourselves. Be wary of allowing yourselves to be led astray by the mirage of an ideal good which so often proves an obstacle to the achievement of real well being. Avoid the exultation of passion which tends to turn the person who should be a brother and who is at one with you in faith, language and custom, into an enemy. Turn a deaf ear to the treacherous suggestions of your rivals which are masked so flatteringly. Let us march openly together with ourself at your head along the path of the Constitution, giving to Europe a model of wisdom, order and proper self-control at a time of crisis which in other countries has been accompanied by tears and afflictions. Let us make the name of Spain admired and revered and at the same time forge our happiness and our glory for centuries to come.

Madrid Palace, 10th March 1820. – Fernando.'

(*Correo Universal de Literatura y Política*, no. 1 (April 1820), p. 7.)

124

Declaration of the Provisional Council

1820

'The moment has finally arrived, which all good men have longed for, when our constitutional King, recalling with full solemnity the representative body of the nation, puts an end to all our anxiety, and, laying the foundation of trust between the Government and the Spanish people, builds on the sacred Code of Rights and leaves us to watch in peace as the storm-tossed ship of state comes into harbour. Yes, Spaniards, your representatives, working together with the King, shall inspect her and, examining each area where she is damaged and applying suitable repairs, shall once more float her, majestic and strong, atop the waves, fearless of fresh squalls. Then, indeed, the hour of glory, fortune and peace shall be upon us; then shall you reap the harvest of all the blood with which you watered the countryside; then shall you be a Nation and, ever in harmony with her voice, worshipping as true brothers in the only true religion, subject to her laws in the noble pride of free men and in constant loyalty to the King you snatched from the claws of a tyrannical beast, you shall be the chosen people, the envy of all nations and the pride of the human race.

... Happy, a thousand times happy, if we come to serve our country and if our names are spoken with gratitude by our compatriots. Madrid, 24th March, 1820. – Luis de Borbón, Cardinal of Scala, Archbishop of Toledo, President.'

(*Correo Universal de Literatura y Política*, no. 2 (May 1820), pp. 76 *et seq.*)

125

Declaration of the King to the Americas

1820

'Spanish Americans: When, in 1814, we announced to you our arrival in the capital of the Spanish empire, Fate so disposed that some institutions which antiquity and custom had made to appear better than others were being re-established and, being ancient, they fell into oblivion and were classed as prejudicial since they had been resuscitated under a different form. The sad experience of six years in which evil and misfortune have been piled one on top of another by those same measures which had been thought the cradle of happiness, the widespread outcry of the people on both sides of the Atlantic and their energetic demonstrations finally convinced us that we had to turn back from that road which we had taken so impetuously, and, seeing the common wishes of the people driven by the instinctive urge which compels them to rise to stature they should enjoy among the other nations in the theatre of world affairs, we have identified ourself with their feelings making their dearest wishes sincerely and cordially ours: these are to adopt, recognise and swear allegiance to the Constitution drawn up in Cádiz by the Common and Extraordinary Parliament and promulgated in the city on the 19th of March 1812, and this we have done of our own free will.

Americans, who find yourselves wandering far from the path that leads to prosperity, you now have what for so long you have been seeking at the cost of enormous efforts of ceaseless suffering, of bloody war, of awful desolation and of widespread destruction. Your schism has brought you nothing but tears and grief, disillusion and bitterness, disturbances and rancour, bloody struggles, famine, conflagrations, devastation and unheard of horror: even just to point to your misfortunes will be enough to chill the hearts of future generations. So what are you waiting for? Harken to the gentle voice of your King and father.

... We have adopted a more widely based system (in the country) and one which is compatible with the system you yourselves have outlined to us. Let it be a distinctive feature of our character to deal with each other openly and faithfully, condemning the tenets and the counsel of that misguided and twisted policy on whose deceitful compoundings Fortune smiled for a brief period.

... But if you turn down the sacred advice which comes from the depths of our heart and if you do not shake the hand which your loving country offers you and embrace this country which gave life to many of your fathers who, were they still living, would use their authority to order you to accept, then have no fear for all the fury unleashed by civil war ... and you will feel besides the terrible effects of a nation's indignation at seeing its Government insulted: a Government now strong and powerful as it has the support of the people and runs the country according to their lights. Oh, may the fatal day of such thoughtless obstinance never dawn! Never; that we may never experience the terrible grief of having even for the shortest space of time to refrain from calling ourself your loving father, Fernando.'

(*Correo Universal de Literatura y Política*, no. 2 (May 1820), pp. 94 *et seq*.)

126

The Provisional Council to the people

1820

'Citizens:

The Provisional Council has, from the moment of its inauguration, followed unhesitatingly the course of action dictated by the trust of the people and the steadfast love of all its representatives for the letter of the Constitution where there are set down all the inviolate rights of the heroic Spanish nation and those of the glorious constitutional throne which shall lead her to the heights of splendour which are being prepared for her. Far from the involutions of adulation and self-interest, and free from timidity and weakness, it has given no counsel in which any of the rights of the people or those of its beloved monarch can be seen to be infringed ... it has watched with pleasure as the system of constitutional government here at the seat of the Realm has been provisionally introduced in all branches of the judiciary and the Government ... Given these beginnings, the political freedom of the press established, the tribunal of the Inquisition done away with, their wealth restored to the credit of the nation, and this set aside from the general funds of the Treasury, and the managers appointed by Parliament back in office ...

... The setting up of any new system on the ruins of one that has passed away is the greatest, most difficult and most arduous task known to Man ... the history of revolution and the experience of the French revolution should make you cautious and temper your impatience, for it teaches you by its awfulness, that any revolution that is carried out in a hurry and which indiscretion has demanded be effected in a single day, has been the cause of centuries of grief ...

... Citizens: let us carry on our sublime progress in the same order and peace that there has been up to now. This will make us the objects of admiration and respect in Europe, and furnish positive proof of how worthy we are of our freedom. – Madrid, Chamber of the Provisional Council, 19th March, 1820. – Luis de Borbón,

Cardinal of Scala, Archbishop of Toledo, President, etc., etc.'
(El *Censor*, t. I, p. 230, 19 de agosto de 1820.)

127
The assault on Madrid

1822

'Madrid, Monday 8th July.

... After some words had been uttered close by the Palace* on
the 30th June which were thought insulting by a few soldiers, there
was a skirmish between some of them and several civilians during
which a lieutenant named Casasola fell wounded when, as it seems,
he tried to settle the dispute.

This minor incident of almost no importance whatsoever which,
had it not been for the misfortune of the officer, would have passed
unnoticed, should have had no ill effects, and indeed it did not.
But the reports of the incident ... could not but give rise to gossip
which had its effect upon public opinion ...

On the 30th – that same evening – there was a scandalous incident
which set in motion all the events which were to follow. Several
members of the Royal Guard, forgetful of their duties, made a
dreadful attempt on the life of their first-lieutenant, D. Mamberto
Landaburu, within the royal palace itself. A crime of this nature
was bound to arouse universal indignation ... from that moment
on, disobedience and indiscipline were the order of the day among
the Royal Guard inside the palace.

... Early on the morning of the 1st, it was made known that
those battalions of the Royal Guard who were in their barracks
had decided to leave their posts and make for the Pardo.†

... then came the 7th – on the one hand, a fateful day; on the
other, a glorious one in the annals of Spanish liberty ... The battalions of the Royal Guard who had raised the standard of revolt
took it into their heads to attempt a daring surprise attack on the
capital and disarm the militia.

And indeed before dawn they entered the city through the Conde

---

* Palacio de Oriente.   † Not the Prado.

Duque gate and launched a three-pronged attack. The battalion to whom it fell to attack the arsenal was completely and quickly routed, and as it scattered, its officer, D. Luis Mon, was taken. He tried to buy off the civilian who had captured him with some ounces of gold and a watch, but in vain. The noble countryman refused and led his prisoner to the munitions depot.

The attack on the main square* was much more bloody ... The enemy's main target was to take the square and especially the Bakery house from which they could hold the whole square. The attacks were incessant and tenacious, but the lively fire kept up by the Grenadier company under D. Juan Muguiro, a gentleman employed in court business, the bravery and inconceivable heroism of our light infantry, and the dexterity of our artillery ... frustrated enemy plans. They sustained heavy losses and were forced to withdraw in disarray.

Before the battle for the square began, one of the enemy divisions had already taken over the Puerta del Sol, but without managing to get into the Provincial building where the guards shut the doors and, having no key to the lock, made them fast with a huge slab of stone which the burly Imperial grenadiers prised free from the staircase.

The enemy lost no time in abandoning this position because they found themselves under attack from the rear and were forced to withdraw in great haste. One of their columns started to go up Montera Street in formation shouting "Long live the King!", with great ferocity, and filling the people who lived there with consternation as they thought them victorious; but then they turned back and withdrew along Arenal Street.

... Those who had attacked the square and been routed made for the palace where they sought refuge.

The people had been on edge for many hours, awaiting the outcome of this morning's victory, when, about three in the afternoon, the happy news was announced that the battalions from the Pardo had agreed to surrender their arms. But in the event, far from granting this favourable outcome, the obdurate troops went out of the city and across the river. The people straightway gave chase ... and, catching up with the fugitives near the wastes of Alcorcón, destroyed them and routed them utterly ...'

'Yesterday, the 7th, the Constitutional City Council published the following:

People of Madrid: Spanish blood has run through the streets of Madrid, shed by traitors to the country and to the sacred oaths they

* Plaza Mayor.

had taken to defend her liberty. The mutinous battalions of the Royal Guard who were out at the Pardo have this night secretly invaded the capital of the monarchy and attacked her defenceless people, the gallant National Militia and the no less gallant soldiers of the garrison. Dearly have these traitors paid for their folly. They have been routed on all sides and scattered in every direction. Those who managed to come off with their lives have had to take refuge in the monarch's palace.

The cause of the nation is triumphant. Long live the Nation! Long live the Constitution! Long live Liberty. – Madrid, 7th July, 1822. – On the instructions of the Most Excellent City Council, Francisco Fernández de Iborra, Secretary.'

(*Gaceta de Madrid*, 9 July 1822.)

128

Resolution of the Congress of Verona

1822

'The undersigned plenipotentiaries, authorised especially by their sovereigns to make some additions to the treaty of the Holy Alliance ... have agreed on the following articles.

1. The great powers who are signatories to this treaty, fully convinced that a system of representational government is as incompatible with the principle of monarchy as is the idea of the sovereignty of the people with principle of divine right, formally undertake to use all the means at their disposal to destroy the representational system of government in every European state in which it now exists and to prevent its introduction into those countries where it is unknown.

2. As there can be no doubt that the freedom of the press is the most powerful weapon in the armoury of those who pretend to defend the rights of the people in their struggle against their kings, the great powers who are signatories to this treaty promise to take every measure to suppress it, not only in their own states but also in every other European country.

3. Persuaded that the principles of religion are still the most powerful factors in the preservation of that state of passive obedience to the monarchy which is right and proper in a nation, the great powers

who are signatories to this treaty declare that it is their intention to uphold in their countries all the authority invested in the clergy... to maintain the authority of the monarchs...

4. Since the state of affairs in Spain and Portugal at the present time brings together all the unfortunate circumstances which are referred to in this treaty, the great powers who are signatories to this treaty, entrusting to France the task of reforming them, assures her of their support in that form which will least compromise her with their own peoples and with the French people – that is, in the form of an annual subsidy of twenty million francs each, effective from the day of ratification of this treaty and valid for as long as the war shall last.

5. In order to restore the Peninsula to the state pertaining prior to the Cádiz revolution, and to ensure complete fulfilment of the aims set out in the clauses of the present treaty, the great powers who are signatories to this treaty ... do mutually undertake to issue ... orders in the roundest possible terms to establish perfect harmony between ... the four signatory powers...

... For Austria, Metternich. – For France, Chateaubriand. – For Prussia, Bernstorff. – For Russia, Nesselrode. – Given at Verona, 22nd November, 1822.'

(Lafuente, *Historia general de España*..., vol. V, pp. 416–17.)

129

European Intervention. With the disapproval of Britain, the four powers agree to send an ultimatum to Spain through instructions to their respective ambassadors. As an example, here follows that from Metternich

1822

'The situation of the Spanish monarchy which has resulted from events in Spain over the last two years was a matter of sufficient gravity for the cabinets meeting at Verona to give their undivided attention ... the Spanish revolution has right from the outset been condemned by us ... even before it came to a head it had already given rise to major catastrophes in other countries; it was from its virulent principles and example and through the intrigues perpetrated by its main agents that the revolution in Naples and in Piedmont arose, and had it not been for the intervention of those powers which have rescued Europe from this fresh conflagration, it would have made these the order of the day throughout Italy, threatening France and compromising Germany. The regrettable methods employed in Spain to foment and carry out revolution have served as a blueprint everywhere else for those who flattered themselves they would win by it new victories; the Spanish constitution has everywhere been the standard and war-cry of factions pledged to the destruction of the security of kingdoms and the peace of their inhabitants.

... The harsh language which conscience and the force of truth use with Your Imperial Majesty is not directed against Spain either as a nation or as a power; it is only directed against those who have wrought her ruin and troubled her countenance, and who persist in prolonging her suffering.

... The King of Spain shall be free as soon as he can put an end to the traumas which visit his people and re-establish peace and order in his realm, surrounding himself with men worthy of his trust both in their principles and in their cultivation, and as soon as he can replace a régime, recognised as unworkable by those who, for reasons of selfishness or pride, uphold it, with one in which the rights of the monarchy are harmoniously reconciled with the true interests and lawful wishes of his subjects at every social level.

... Count, you will make the best use of this communiqué you can in the situation which pertains at the time you receive it. You are hereby authorised to read it to the Minister of Foreign Affairs and even to give him a copy should he ask for one.

Metternich.'

(Lafuente, Historia general de España..., vol. V, p. 418.)

130

Reply of the Constitutional Government to the signatories of the Convention of Verona

1823

'His Catholic Majesty's Government has just received a communiqué and diplomatic note from the government of... This despatch, filled with misleading facts, with lying imputations, with incriminations as unwarranted as they are libellous, and with ill-defined proposals cannot expect a definite formal reply to every one of the points it makes. The Spanish Government, postponing until a more auspicious moment the formal public declaration to other peoples of its principles and intentions and of the justice of the cause of the great nation at whose head it is placed, shall restrict itself to stating: First: the Spanish nation is at present governed by a Constitution formally recognised by the Emperor of all the Russias in 1812; Secondly: that the Spaniards who, at the beginning of 1820, proclaimed in their love for their country this Constitution which had been forcibly overthrown in 1814, were not traitors but enjoy the undying glory of having been the mouthpieces of the wishes of the people; Thirdly: that the Constitutional King of Spain enjoys full exercise of the rights laid down in the Basic Code, and those who say otherwise are enemies of Spain who libel her in order to bring her into disrepute; Fourthly: that the Spanish nation has never interfered in the institutions and internal affairs of any other country; Fifthly: that no one is more concerned to cure those evils which beset her than she is herself; Sixthly: that those evils are not the effects of the Constitution but of the efforts of those who are trying to destroy it; Seventhly: that the Spanish nation shall never recognise the right of any power to meddle or interfere in her own internal affairs; Eighthly: that His Majesty's Government will not depart from the demands of its duty and its honour nor from its unflinching fidelity to the Basic Code sworn to in 1812.

   ... Evaristo San Miguel. – The Palace, 9th January, 1823.'
   (Lafuente, *Historia general de España...*, vol. V, pp. 420-1.)

131

Fernando VII declares the acts of the liberal Government to be null and void

1823

Well known to all our subjects – indeed, notorious – are the scandalous events which preceded, accompanied and resulted from the establishment of the democratic Constitution of Cádiz in March, 1820; events of the most criminal kind, the most shameful cowardice, the most profane disrespect for our Royal Person, and the ensuing violence which was inevitable – these were the instruments used to revolutionise the paternal government of our realm and to replace it with a democratic code: a prolific source of catastrophe and misfortune. Our subjects, used to living under wise, conservative laws, finely tuned to their ways and customs, laws which have been for so many years a source of happiness to their ancestors, were very quick to show widespread public scorn, disaffection and disapproval of the new Constitutional régime. People of all classes joined in their resentment against institutions which they foresaw would mean their wretchedness and misery.

The public cried out on all sides against the tyrannical Constitution and called for an end to a code which was null and void in its creation, illegal in its formulation and inequitable in its content; and it cried out lastly for the preservation of the Holy Faith of its parents, for the re-institution of its fundamental laws and for the safeguarding of the lawful rights which we inherited from our forefathers and to which our subjects had sworn with due solemnity.

... Having been reinstated on the throne of San Fernando by the wisdom and justice of the Almighty, by the magnanimous resolve of our powerful allies and by the valiant efforts of our cousin, the Duke of Angoulême, and wishing to furnish a remedy for the pressing needs of our peoples and to show all the world the reality of our liberty, we have decided to make the following decrees:

1. All acts (of whatever kind and on whatever issue) of the so-called Constitutional Government which has held sway over our people from 7th March, 1820 until today, 1st October, 1823, shall be null and void since, as we here declare, we have been deprived during the whole of that period of our freedom and been forced to give our consent to laws and carry out decrees and regulations which were thought up and put into effect by this same Government against our will.

2. We hereby give approval to all the decrees of the Provisional Council of State and of the Regency of the Realm ... until such time as, being in possession of all information concerning the needs of our people, we can make laws and order the necessary measures to bring about their true prosperity and happiness, the constant objects of our desire.

You will give this your attention and communicate to all Ministers. – Signed and sealed by the Royal Hand. – Puerto de Santa María, 1st October 1823. – To D. Víctor Sáez.

(M. Ferrer, D. Tejera y J. F. Acedo, *Historia de tradicionalismo español* (1941), vol. II, pp. 257–8.)

132

Letter of Quintana to that English sympathiser with liberalism in Spain, Lord Holland

1823

... You have so often shown your great interest and regard for the affairs of Spain and have shown so much friendship for the author of these letters, that I am confident that we can enter into a sincere and unprejudiced study of the events which have befallen our two countries. I believe that destiny has brought me to London and that we can do the same here in your study or in your library as we did in former times in Madrid: talk of art, philosophy and politics. Let us cast an eye over the latest events of our revolution and contemplate the events which have led our political affairs into the abyss which has just swallowed them up. A man who is both a Spaniard and a friend is sure to find a careful and friendly hearing when he talks with you about the affairs of his nation....

... Let us turn our attention to what has happened in our own time and not look for the causes of the present situation in the distant past. Let us take as a first point, the reign of Carlos III. As you know, his ministers were never more than mediocre. His government was absolutist and there were both abuses of power and mistakes of administration which it would be futile to deny. Yet the King possessed an ability to order and foresee events and a certain composure and wisdom which characterised his political decisions. Under his rule the state reached a level of prosperity and culture which augured well for the future. When he died, these hopes went with him to the grave. Spain had been accustomed to a moderate and prudent administration and had accepted that the good of the nation was the yardstick, or at least the pretext, of the acts of authority. They must have been scandalised by the foolhardiness and the arrogance which the new government began to show.

Even if the central government wields absolute and despotic power, its authority is readily obeyed and respected as long as it matches the interests of the people. This is not the case when power becomes orientated towards personal gain or sectarian interest, since then, if it is strong it is hated and vilified, and if it is weak it is neither respected nor obeyed. The twenty years during which Carlos IV reigned saw only an uninterrupted series of governmental blunders, outrages against public opinion and travesties of justice. The sole aim of authority was the senseless aim of creating a public idol: * everything was sacrificed to bring this about. The whole nation genuflected to him, women lost all sense of decency and men all sense of propriety. One glance could make or destroy a man. He used the public purse for his own ends. War and peace were made at his bidding. Could even ability and success have justified the scandalous affairs that led to his assumption of power? Though this might be true, an incompetence which boded ill for the nation was stamped in indelible letters in the infelicitous results of the affairs to which he put his hand. A war with France in 1793 which was against our best interests was followed by a shameful peace in 1795. There followed an absurd alliance, which was beyond the understanding of mortal man; there followed the two maritime wars with England. In all these hapless, self-defeating enterprises, the energies of the army were spent to no purpose, the fleet squandered until not a vessel was left, and the funds of the Treasury, all credit and financial means drained utterly dry. An army of one hundred thousand men, one hundred and twenty ships of the line and forty frigates and a buoyant economy had sheltered the greatness and independence of the Spanish monarchy against the acquisitive designs of foreign nations and then everything was destroyed by a minion. So it was that when that cunning Machiavellian schemer Napoleon attacked the Peninsula with all his colossal might, he found it without an army, without a navy, with neither munitions nor money nor means, in short, as he himself declared, a nation which was his for the asking.

This was the high price that Spain paid for the frivolity of María Luisa.† Yet if Carlos IV had died on the throne and His rightful heir had succeeded Him, then we would have left our new king to find the remedy for our sickness and, far from thinking of revolution, we would have pinned our hopes on the changes at court, which always follow the death of kings, for a halt to earlier disorders and punishment of their instigators. We were far from possessing the revolutionary maxims which have been charged against us. We had seen the military despotism which had resulted in France from so much social upheaval. The enthusiasm of the most revolutionary among us had been dampened and the eyes of the most deluded had been opened. Since Spain was used to the chains of absolute power, she

* Godoy.   † Consort of Carlos IV and Godoy's mistress.

would have worn them again just as patiently and submissively. Instead of troubling and scandalising the courts of Europe, as is now believed to be the case, we would have been for them still an object of pity and scorn, as we were then.

Under the heavy yoke of Napoleon, we cast off our lethargy and found ourselves jolted into looking to our future. It is unnecessary to make a list here of the treacherous way in which French troops were brought to Spanish soil, of the royal family's attempted flight to Andalusia and the Aranjuez revolution which stopped them, of the deceits which Napoleon used at Bayonne to get his way and the arrogance with which he dictated his terms to us from there and proclaimed a new dynasty. May I, Milord, be permitted to ask a question of those who have so self-confidently set themselves up as attorneys entitled to discuss infractions of the law? A nation finds itself between a rapacious usurper and an inane, cowardly government which leaves it, tied hand and foot, at the mercy of its enemy. Does this nation not have the right to ask its government how it used the authority vested in it and what it did with the immense wealth entrusted to it? Might I ask whether the champions of passive resistance say we should have accepted the terms which our own leaders sent us from Bayonne? In their decrees we were bidden to yield to the conqueror and submit to his will. We made bold to resist this cowardly command and hold for our King, in His own despite, the sceptre and crown which He himself had relinquished. And what followed? Bonaparte and his henchmen accused us of being rebels, calling us Jacobins, whilst those who believed in the law of rightful succession applauded our uprising and realised that on our resistance and our sacrifices depended the stability of monarchy, the re-establishment of the Bourbons and the independence of Europe.

It would be foolish to suppose that Spain faced up to the trials and tribulations of this cruel war with no other aim than securing its independence and re-establishing its King. We were bound to think of reaping a full harvest for our struggles and of finding a remedy for the abuses that had brought us to such a grievous pass. To believe that this would not be the case, is totally to misconstrue the human condition and the ways of the world. We may be ignorant and backward but we are not so stupid as that. Whipped and flailed, this unhappy country learnt its lesson of future duty in grief and blood. Quite obviously, the idea of reforming our political and civil institutions could not have been the suggestion of a few hot-headed troublemakers nor the criminal plotting of agitators. If this is the way our noble ideal has been debased by impudent hypocrisy, base ignorance and supercilious political chicanery, every event since 1814 gives the lie to such an insolent re-writing of history.

The members of the provincial councils were neither 'agents provocateurs' nor Jacobins; and neither were the members of the central
government nor those of the first regency, for there are authentic
documents extant of all these bodies, in which one finds the will
expressed and the ways prepared for the re-establishment of the
Cortes; nor were the councillors of Castille 'agents provocateurs' or
Jacobins, for they agreed with the central government in claiming
for the Cortes the sole right to institute a government in the circumstances; neither were all the political commentators who presented
one and the same opinion with incontrovertible arguments and one
and the same desire with unswerving faith. It was certain in everyone's mind that reform of the monarchy was expressly tied up in
the re-establishment of the Cortes. If proof is needed, one only has to
remember the open letter of Don Juan de Villamil, where it was
clearly stated that the King should be welcomed and a Constitution
straightway handed him to the effect that governing well is synony-
mous with governing less. To apply to Don Juan de Villamil the
epithet 'doctrinaire liberal' would involve a contradiction in terms
at which he would laugh aloud – and we even more.

At long last, the Central Council, after many long thoughtful
debates and discussions, gave to the world its famous decree of the
22nd of May 1809, in which it was agreed to convene the Cortes,
and where were pointed out the aims for public welfare contained
in this momentous decision. These aims took in every branch of
public administration, for everything was deemed to be in need of
reform. The social structure of hereditary monarchy (Fernando VII
and His family), and of the Catholic religion as the state religion,
remained inviolate. Everything else was to be treated pragmatically,
according to the good of the nation. The economy, the army, the
navy, the courts, the laws, public education: all came under review,
and the healing hand extended across the whole social spectrum. It
is well worth remarking here that the renovatory aspects of this
decree seemed to be based in toto on the opinion of Don Antonio
Valdés, Commander of the Order of Malta. Your Lordship knows
this worthy individual. You know how great was his ability as a
public figure, you know the nobility and loftiness of his character
and the dignity, I might also say the haughtiness, of his speech and
of his manners. You more than anyone know the value of the word
of a man such as Don Antonio Valdés and how far he was from the
base, senseless motives that one would expect from a rabble-rouser.

I should also point out that our remarkable, indeed peerless friend
Jovellanos, held the same opinion. It is expressed in his works, which

will last as long as virtue and the Castillian tongue, with such fervour that it seems superfluous to record the fact here. To take examples from the context of his work would be to weaken them immeasurably.

In short, Milord, not one educated, intelligent Spaniard was against the restoration. You know much better than I how much it was supported too by all the foreign politicians who took an interest in our affairs. Since those events, diplomatic relations have not extended to those who wedded liberty, but at the time, a note was sent to the Central Council, showing both friendliness and favour, to the effect that the Council was threatened with the displeasure of the people of England if it did not give to the people of Spain the fruits of their unbelievably tenacious struggle: political and civil freedom, which it was meet and proper they should enjoy in the future.

My talk here is of this end itself, not of the means used to bring it about: the latter have been a bone of contention among those who at the beginning were unanimous in their assertion of the need for such innovations. But we will talk of these differences and their causes later. Here, it is enough to assert my basic proposition, that Spanish and European opinion was agreed on the idea of political reform in Spain. Everyone concurred that the time was ripe, and even more, that we Spaniards had the right to place our monarchy on a constitutional footing. It follows that to impeach the Spanish liberal party with recklessness and disorder is a gratuitous insult levelled by injustice triumphant and is not the severe, impartial sentence of justice.

We seized boldly on the chance that fortune had given us. The Cortes were convened, the deputies gathered together and a year and a half after its establishment, the Constitution of 1812 was published and proclaimed. It seems to me unnecessary to enter here upon a philosophical discussion of the Constitution. So many people have done this already, mainly to point out and protest against its defects. Whether it was defective or not, the Spanish Constitution is for me here simply a question of fact. The Cortes could have chosen any of a thousand different combinations to give form to the new Constitution. The one that came forth from its debates and discussions could have been better or it could have been worse, but this is the one we have, because we had to have one. If you like, it could well have been imperfect, but it could not have had more authority and prestige, since it came from our sole legislative body and was accepted and solemnly ratified by us, unanimously and unshrinkingly. Our Constitution was received neither as a scandal nor as an outrage. Indeed, in many parts of Europe it was greeted with praise and approval.

The people of Spain have not forgotten yet that the monarch who is now pitted against them expressly recognised the new Constitution when opening diplomatic relations with the then Spanish Government. The structure which was established then grew up in the provinces as the French were being thrown out. Not a single voice of protest was heard and the structure was calmly accepted by the state when the war ended. This surely, Milord, is enough cause for respect, or if not for respect at least for appreciation; at the very least, a cause for clemency. To see the extraordinary mutation which self interest has suddenly wrought in both words and deeds must surely both surprise and infuriate. Might I be permitted to ask under what heading or on what pretext this welcome innovation is called a transgression and its authors branded as rebels and agitators? How is it possible to treat a nation which deserves so much from Europe as if it was a mutinous galley mob, whipped into line by the rod and the lash of the boatswain?

I am not trying to say that we were unaware of the difficulties which some Spaniards would doubtless find in taking a constitutional system to their hearts. The ancient maxim that no law satisfies everyone,* must surely be mainly applicable to political statutes. The bigger the abuses which are to be corrected and the longer they have lasted, the greater is the displeasure and opposition they occasion. At first in Spain, where everyone thought themselves the hapless prey of Napoleon, there was revealed to them the bottomless pit where the excesses of arbitrary rule had brought them. They denounced their government violently and clamoured for redress. But after the danger had disappeared and the rights and privileges of each class had to be relegated below the question of common good, the early zeal rapidly cooled. The clergy saw its influence and riches whittled away by any liberal order. The justices of the realm saw the waning of their influence on governmental and administrative business. The army command saw itself as having exclusive right to political control in the provinces. The aristocracy saw themselves losing the privileges they had had under the 'ancien régime'. The regular soldiers saw themselves on short commons and housed in cramped quarters. None of these classes could agree freely with the new laws. It was inconceivable that any of them would fail to use all the physical and moral means at their disposal: their immense wealth and their powerful influence over public opinion.

But all their struggles would have been in vain without the active support of the supreme authority. The disposition of Spanish intel-

* 'Nulla lex satis commoda omnibus est: id modo quaeritur, si majori parti, et in summum prodest', Livy, Book 34, Ch. 3.

lectuals towards reform, and the long habits of obedience of the masses, if they had been helped by the government, would have restrained discontent and asserted the word of the law. When the King threw his weight into the struggle, the balance was tilted in the favour of the enemies of freedom. At the beginning they did not realise this, and when they knew that the King had come into His own, their melancholy quite clearly showed that this event did not come within the scope of their plans. Doubtless they supposed that it was impossible for the King to refuse to swear to the Constitution which the nation placed before Him when they handed Him the crown which they had shed so much blood to preserve. Moreover, the moral instincts of these classes were stronger than their desires and they disliked the whole idea of such a dereliction of duty. But when they learnt of the preparations of Fernando VII and his favourites against the Constitutional party, then they regained their breath and at one and the same time the clergy, the aristocracy, the military and the magistrature all agreed on the wisdom of unreservedly handing over the whole power and authority of the state to the King, thus stripping the nation of all the rights it had so recently acquired.

I am well aware, Milord, that even among those politicians who love Spanish liberty there is a general consensus against the Cortes of Cádiz, who are accused of foolhardiness and excessive greed and ambition. It is generally thought, first, that because they aspired to more than could be realised, even their moderate wishes did not come true, and, secondly, that freedom would have lived on without the declaration of national sovereignty, without a unified representative body and without the ostentatious apparatus of a rewritten Constitution. It is said that Spanish politicians made the same mistake as their French counterparts: they wanted everything at the same time. The representative system had to be re-cast, and the privileged classes involved in it, since they had been irritated and offended by ministerial despotism for quite a long time. With the system itself already safe, the opportunity should have been afforded for the remedy of society's ills and progress in administrative reform. The upper classes were astounded that so little note was taken of them and their spirits were troubled by so many innovations. This is where the reaction set in and the arrival of the King swept all before it. No trace was left of what had been done for the good of the people. I will not try to justify everything the Cortes did. Without any doubt, they made wide-ranging blunders. It would be difficult for men who were for the most part new to the affairs of the state not to do so. They had not been rehearsed for the great role they had to play in the theatre of the world and they were placed in an extraordinarily difficult position. But let us be frank and open-minded about this, Milord. Were these mistakes and misuses of power the real cause of the destruction of freedom at this period? I would deny this completely. The true cause of this misfortune was that the party which held the power then was the party which desired neither Cortes nor the rights of the people nor any reform whatsoever. Those who were in the fore-front of the drive to destroy freedom in 1814 were those who in 1809 had opposed the re-establishment of the Cortes when the Central Council had begun to turn its mind to this possibility. This was even before the form of its meetings and its political standpoints were known. It must be stated categorically that there would have been no question of tampering with the Constitution or the sovereignty of the King and no question of interfering with either the Holy Office or the Council of Castille. But at the very least, certain points would have come under scrutiny: questions of the security of the individual, freedom of the press, regular meetings of the Cortes, the accountability of ministers to the public and the economy. Was it not certain that those who hated liberty would attack these innovations as fundamentally opposed to the rights and privileges of the King and equally certain that we would be branded as rebels and agitators?

Those who accuse the Spanish people of not re-establishing their former political institutions fall into a very great error. They suppose that these institutions, proved by experience and accredited by tradition and history, would not have been exposed to the dangers and dislike with which new ideas are always greeted, and would have been respected by Spaniards and foreigners alike. I have called this, Milord, a very great error and I should add that it is a ridiculous one as well. This accusation has been made so often and with such an air of smug self-satisfaction and such impertinent pretentions to wisdom, that it is quite clear that the many so-called statesmen who do this do not have even a passing knowledge of our history. They would seem to be the only ones not to know that in former times Spain had as many different constitutions as there were independent states in the Peninsula. I suppose that those who advise us to base a reconstruction of the state on these constitutions would not deny us the right to choose whichever of them seem most appropriate for our avowed aim of establishing and securing our civil and political liberty. Let it be supposed then, that we had revived our ancient right to form a confederacy, or the ancient orders of justices of the realm, or the brotherhoods of Castille. Does anyone suppose that a monarch would look upon these bastions which opposed his rights any more kindly than on the articles of the Constitution of Cádiz.

If we were to have selected any of these institutions, then those who are now caparisoned with the dust and cobwebs of antiquity, who belittle our theories with philosophical superciliousness and who openly call us pedants, would get tremendous pleasure from finding theories to throw in our faces. We would be accused of ignoring utterly the great improvements in social science, of failing to recognise differences in time and circumstances and of being so stupid as to want to clothe present day Spain in the tattered rags of antiquity, condemned to rot in oblivion. In any case this ridiculous question is only of use in drawing-room debates, where the weapons are pen and tongue. When the weapons are politics and the sword, no ruler will give a thought to these idle casuistical arguments concerning history and antiquity. He would consider the resuscitation of these freedoms as an abuse of his right. They had already been smothered by his predecessors and he would crush them under his heel as he has the present constitution, heedless of reason or argument.

Perhaps then, if the Cortes had assembled as did the 'estamentos',* the evils and recriminations which followed would have been completely prevented, or at least their effect mitigated. This is not the case, Milord, for the evils would have been greater and the consequence the same. The two chambers would have been perpetually at loggerheads. Every act concerning public defence would have been obstructed or castrated, and at the end of the struggle the aristocratic estate would have abused its role and sold out freedom and the third estate, just as the 70 dissenting deputies did with the Cortes of the year 1814. And why? Because the upper chamber, or first estate, would be composed of individuals who opposed any kind of Constitution and they would have worked for no other end than the destruction of the representative body of which they formed a part. The decisive proof of this can be seen in what happened in Valencia. There, the balance of political powers could have been restored, had the privileged classes made use of the ample opportunity afforded them of returning to the influential political role which they claimed had been wrested from them. Since the King was dependent upon their judgement and their advice, He could have countered them with neither opposition nor the threat of His displeasure. They had it in their power to effect political reform without annihilating the freedom of the people and their own, yet they did not do so: a tangible proof, if any is needed, that this was of their own choosing. There is no point in keeping any illusions. During this period there were only two political parties in Spain: one wanted a government ruled by a King whose power was checked by constitutional laws,

* The estates composing the Cortes of Aragón.

while the other was composed of those who were at home in a world of arbitrary power and who hated any kind of innovation that would modify and curtail this power. There was no middle way between these two diametrically opposed standpoints and any institution which tried to reconcile them would have encountered the same opposition and suffered the same fate.

Speaking of your King Charles II, David Hume said 'The King was obliged to act as the head of a party, a most disagreeable situation for a King and a perpetual source of much injustice and oppression.' Even if the first part of this statement does not fully apply to our situation, the second part fits with frightening accuracy. For Spaniards, Fernando VII was worth everything that he had cost them, but He placed Himself, of His own free-will, at the head of a party which was by nature intolerant and therefore impossible to deal with. From this point onwards the whole edifice of public opinion which supported the Constitution crumbled into the dust. The Cortes tried in vain to come to terms with the King and to find where He stood on the question of harmonising His rights with the demands of public freedom. It was all futile. Its representations were disregarded and its commissioners were turned away. The orders thundered from Valencia abolishing the Constitution, dissolving the Cortes and out-lawing the government, told the Spanish nation they were to be bound in fetters of ignominious slavery.

It would perhaps be better for me not to mention this evil event here, since the part I played in the calamity would probably condemn my words. However moderate these words of mine may be, they will always seem born of resentment and not of a desire for justice. But I doubt, Milord, whether any future historian, if he weighs up the evidence concerning that terrible period in our history, can tell of them without the greatest of indignation. When the clock struck the hour, the signal was given, and the bailiffs and the soldiers poured into the streets and pounded on the doors. 'Open in the name of the law!', 'Arrested by order of the King!' Doleful sounds in the silence of the night striking fear into the hearts of men and women and children, who were all hearing them for the first time. Very soon there were not enough hands to hold them all, nor dungeons in which to throw them. Presidents of the courts, deputies, ministers, minor officials and political commentators were all swept away by the tide, unprotected by their dignity, their public avowals, their innocence or their service to the nation. This was their reward, the peace they attained, after six years of struggles, torments and sacrifices. They were the most ardent defenders of the independence of Europe in the teeth of Napoleon's tyranny. It was they who kept the flame of national resistance burning bright, and it was they who at long last handed over to their King a crown no longer fraught with perils and joined in alliance with many grateful nations. For the accused, the same man was judge, jury and hangman, and this man had himself been a lukewarm defender of the crown or the accused men's very own friend, who held opinions which were now the pretext for their persecution. If this strange, frightening web of circumstances had been drawn in a novel, it would have been scorned as absurd and impossible. A horrified posterity will find such a concatenation of events, actually attested by history, impossible to believe. And foreigners played their part, with dark hints: they revelled in the imposture and in the insults, accusing us all the more strongly so as to cover up their ugly scheming. Some of them called us deluded, some of them called us rash, some of them called us foolish. They vied with each other to find formulas of scorn and insulting, contemptuous pity. In the free parliament of a free nation one of your very own ministers dubbed us as 'dyed in the wool blackguards'. And who was being treated in this way, Milord? People whose enemies could find no evidence of crime with which to smear them, people who had conducted a political reform which involved not a single drop of blood spilt, nor even a single tear shed.

Silence followed this crushing blow delivered by authority, or rather by injustice. The government of the King found no further obstacles in its march towards absolutism. It possessed an immense moral strength, the means created by the revolution itself and the consent of the theoreticians. Had it wanted to secure the prosperity of the country it could have done so. In the first wave of enthusiasm, the country was willing to accept these things more readily from the King's hand than from the Cortes. If the advantages of a new administration had been tried then, given the rapidity with which despots can do good things when they so desire, the fall of the constitutional system and the victims buried in its rubble would have been forgotten.

But, Milord, the world has never yet witnessed any example in which a ruler wanting to control everything actually produces a better government. Those who had grasped authority had other things to think of; to keep their position they felt it necessary to sow discord and suspicion, to organise denunciations, to sustain political and religious persecutions and to use every means that illegitimate authority has at its command to slander and vilify the true authority. Many aspects of the state of affairs which pertained then were not thought of, or only thought of in passing and without being put into effect: healing the wounds and repairing the disasters of a devastating war, forming a simple financial base for the economy, organising the army and building up the morale of the navy, regenerating industry and internal trade, and disseminating useful knowledge. I will not tire you with the boring details of administration. If I made out a list of its decisions it would be no more than a sickening recital of self-defeating and irrational blunders, condemned long ago by both reason and experience. We can be surprised at no inane decision emanating from men who held as a principle that years mean nothing to a nation and that the clock should be turned back to the time which they knew and loved. Re-establishment of the Jesuits, or of the university colleges, or of the provincial revenues, or of the Holy Office could none of them give us esteem, riches or importance, and even less so the absurd decision to take us back to the year 1808. We were in a fine condition in 1808 to present this as a model! Only cranks could talk in this way. After tremendous sacrifice, our trade with the colonies only made the gulf between us wider, while our trade with Europe was cowardly and inept: small wonder that we gained no profit and reaped only scorn. Each one of us, in his heart, felt the lack of order, peace and confidence. We could see ourselves wasting away and perishing in a time of peace. Ritual rounds of negotiations accompanied ritual sequences of Governments, with the State more and more pitiful and poverty-stricken all the time. In the acts of authority there was only uncertainty, mindlessness and confusion. If by chance some able, upright individual, like Iborra or Garay, rose above the turmoil, then he would have an opponent pitted against him to peck at him and make him fritter away his energy. He would then be ignominiously despatched. 'Nemo in illa aula probitate aut industria certavit: unum ad potentiam iter.'* The man who best knows how to pry and persecute is the man who stays in favour longest. An authority incapable of governing and mindful only of repression harvested only hatred and scorn, which was all it had sown. A change in power was the only logical sequence to a change in public opinion.

The worst aspect of affairs was that no change for the better could be seen in the future. Truth to tell, the King had given His famous decree, offering Spaniards restoration of their Cortes in the form they had had and guaranteeing in law the safety of the individual, justice, freedom of the press and structural re-organisation of the tax system. This offer, made like so many others in this time of crisis to befuddle the simple-minded and facilitate the total destruction of everything the Cortes of Cádiz had done, was clearly going to have no effect whatsoever. In six years, no serious attempt was made to

* Tacitus, *Historia,* liber i, cap. 35.

put the decree into practice and no reference was made to this political decision in any act of authority. The King, His court, His ministers and the majority of His tribunals rejected it. No possibility of action, no right, no legal means, no voice was left to the nation with which to claim this right.

In such a situation, according to some, the determined intervention of a foreign state could have stopped the evil actions which followed. But even given the great difficulties that such interventions cause, it was not to be hoped that those who had allowed Spanish liberty to die in 1814 would really try to re-establish it in 1819. Cold, selfish calculations were the order of the day. Throughout Europe, there was strife between the interests and purposes of the ruling parties and the freedom of the masses. However, it would seem that at various times during this period, attempts were made to get the King to convene the Cortes, or at least to mitigate the violence and oppression of His government. I am unaware of any such attempt: in any case it is unimportant. If there was any note passed to the King, it was as insignificant for those who gave it as for those who received it. When foreigners have tried to intervene in our affairs and, as they say, cure our sickness, their advice has assumed another form and the consequences have been of a very different character.

There remained for the Spanish nation only one recourse: an appeal to its own strength: a line of action both violent and dangerous yet without a shadow of doubt both necessary and just. I know, Milord, that the new politicians, or rather missionaries, will not agree with me on this, yet what are they doing but trying to convert the scientific study of society into an incomprehensible theology, by specious sophistry and pettifogging deceptions? They would doubtless say that we should have been patient, that resignation is the great virtue of the sufferer and that the misfortunes of nations are not to be assuaged by such violent actions. In any case, they would add, we should put our entire trust in God, who always arranges things for the best. This might not have been meant at the time as venomous mockery; it was certainly incredibly stupid. Natural law has a stronger voice than these devil's advocates. It teaches that in questions of self-preservation nations have the same right as individuals. Moreover, it states that no one is forced to sacrifice his well-being or his life on the altar of foreign whim or wickedness. To deny these truths is to deny the evidence of one's reason; to deny that Spain was in this position is to deny the evidence of the facts.

Less than 20 months after the King's arrival, enthusiasm for Him had been replaced by despondency and anxiety. It was indeed bitter to reflect that nothing had changed for the better after such a bloody defence against Napoleon, and after resting plenary power in the King. Spaniards were bound to regret the loss of an order they had made no attempt to preserve, and look back on it with shame and grief. The plot led by Porlier was the first sign of disenchantment. Even though this movement was smothered in its infancy, a recognition of the need for change could be felt in the air. The fact that Porlier died from horrendous torturing did not deter others. Indeed, it seemed to give them more courage and hope in their demands. Porlier was followed by Richard in Madrid, Vidal in Valencia, Lacy in Catalonia and the officers in the port of Santa María awaiting transport to the colonies. It is a moot point whether one should wonder more at the speed with which these futile uprisings followed each other, in spite of the harshness with which they were put down, or at the blindness of the government, which kept its eyes shut tight to every warning. It was clear from the nature of events, that the army was no longer trustworthy, for it seemed to be shame-faced and contrite for having brought the nation to such an ignominious and desperate pass. On the face of it, they wanted to wash away the stain and, in token of their love, hand back the nation's freedom.

One of these plots was so exceptional as to cry out for attention. For Spaniards, the King's person had always been sacred. The base deceits and the vile treachery which disgrace the principle of monarchy and throw palaces into mourning might well be frequent in the history of other nations but not for a very long time have they been known in Spain. Even during periods of great upheaval and in the midst of the whirlwind of civil war, the kings of Spain lived among their people without fear of any such perfidious attacks. Never did Juan II or Henrique IV have to beware of this danger, in spite of being puppets in the hands of factions and pawns in internecine wars. They might both have provoked an attempt on Their lives – the first because of His lack of forethought, the second by His arrant stupidity. Even the implacable King Pedro was safe in spite of his frequent and bloody acts of revenge. It must be said that he set in motion the dismal whirlwind which lost him both life and crown, but he died fighting hand-to-hand in battle against a brother who also called himself King. This catastrophe is the only example of violent death inflicted on any of our Kings in seven centuries. Such an atrocity had never since passed through anyone's mind, until Richard thought of killing the present King. How could such a terrible design be entertained towards a King who was loved and revered and who had cost the nation so much bloodshed? Philosophers would do well to think on this. They can only say that human affairs are indestructibly and irremediably yoked together. They might add

that if Richard's attempted crime had no precedent in the history of
Spain then the dealings of Fernando VII, advised by His courtiers
in the year 1814, had no precedent in the annals of the world.

Such, Milord, was the state of the soul of Spain when the year
1820 began. In this long letter I have tried to point out the causes
of this and to show that the revolution which was about to come
was not born of men but of the irremediable force of circumstance.
However, if one must see the hand of men in this business so that
there is someone to blame, one should look for it neither among the
deputies who created the 1812 Constitution nor the soldiers who
proclaimed it again in 1820. Chance chose the first and ruled that
they be convened by the government to fill the empty seats of the
Cortes. Under the avowal of good faith, they agreed upon everything
which as loyal subjects they both thought and believed did redound
to the good of the state. The second group, impelled by and carried
on by the tide of public opinion, were simply the casual tools of an
irresistible power, as others would doubtless have been had these not
been there. They were not the instigators of the great innovation
that has attracted the attention of the Kings of Europe at the eleventh
hour. There can be no doubt at all that the true instigators are
Carlos IV, with his indolence and profligacy, María Luisa, with her
whims and her scandalous affairs, the Prince of Peace, with His
insolence, greed and incompetence, Napoleon, with his preposterous
invasion, and Fernando VII, the blind instrument of a fanatical
party incapable of governing the nation in harmony with the time
and the circumstances. In competition with each other, they all
helped to break the long-standing springs of authority and power.
Since then no one has been able to furnish another.

(M. J. Quintana, *Obras completas*, vol. XIX, Letter to Lord
Holland, 20 November 1823.)

133

The last footholds on the American continent are lost

1826

'From your crown, my lord, two great and triumphal laurels with
which Cortés and Pizarro wreathed the crown of Carlos I have been
untimely plucked. The Spanish Monarchy has today fifteen million

fewer subjects than it had in 1808. The flag of the Mexican Revolution now flutters over the battlements of San Juan de Ulúa and it is to be feared that that of the rebels in Perú shall soon be flown over the battlements of Callao. In place of the unbounded trade of such vast possessions which fed both the city and the enormous stretches of countryside, there has sprung up paltry coastal trafficking daily molested by pirates from those very countries which learned from Spain the arts of peace and the benefits of civilisation.'

(J. Bécker, *La independencia de América* (1922), p. 103, citing 'Exposición de Don Javier de Burgos, desde Paris, el 24 de enero de 1826 a Don Fernando VII.')

134

Decree of ratification of 29 March on the succession to the throne

1830

'Fernando VII, by the Grace of God, etc.

To the princes, priests, dukes, marquises, counts, peers, priors, and knights-commander of the military orders etc., be it known:

That, in the Parliament held in the Palace of Buen Retiro in 1789, the question of the succession was dealt with on the suggestion of our father, the King (R.I.P.), together with the need and desirability of observing a regular system of succession to the Spanish crown, as laid down by the laws of the Realm and by practice from time immemorial. Seeing that it should be the practice to prefer the elder son over the younger and the male issue over the female – in due order within their respective lines – and keeping in mind the unbounded good which had come to this Monarchy for over seven hundred years from observing these principles, and mindful of the motives and circumstances which eventually led to the reform decreed in the Act passed on 10th March, 1713, Parliament sent a petition to the King, dated 30th September of the same year 1789, mentioning the great profit that had redounded to the Realm, both before and, in particular, after the union of the realms of Castille and Aragón, from the rule of succession outlined in Law 2, Section 15, Part 2, and entreating him to disregard the recent changes brought about by the passing of the Act mentioned above and to see fit to command, by means of promulgating a decree of ratification in the guise of a statute drawn up and passed by Parliament to endorse this decision and to revoke the said Act passed previously, that the method of succession to the throne prescribed by custom dating back beyond memory and attested by the Law we have specified, should be for ever observed and kept.

To this petition, the King, our noble father, deigned to accede, on the entreaty of his realm, giving his decision in writing, which decision his cabinet in Parliament and the Governor and Minister of our Royal Chamber of Castille took with them when they conveyed a petition to Parliament where the decision had been taken to consent to the said appeal. It had been decided however to keep this a closely guarded secret for the moment and in the decree under discussion he had ordered the members of his Council to publish the decree of ratification which is usual in such cases. Parliament, acting through its President, the Count of Campomanes – Governor of the Council, – put a certified copy of the said treaty and other documents bearing on it on the file of classified information, and the decree was announced in confidence to Parliament.

The turmoil which beset Europe at that time and which the Peninsula was to experience later did not permit this important project to be put into effect, for more peaceful times were needed for a move like that. Having, with the help of God's mercy, happily restored peace and good order to our beloved people who needed them so badly, and having examined this grave question and hearkened to the advice of our Ministers, who are so zealous in our service, and having looked to the public good, we have by our royal decree given to this same Council of ours on the 26th of this month ordered that this law be promulgated in the form in which it was sought and granted, together with the original decision of our dear father, the King, in connection with it, and the testimonies of the Chief Clerks of Parliament, whose certificates have been kept with it.

This having been proclaimed in full session of our Council in the presence of our two Attorney-Generals and having been heard "in voce" on the 27th of this same year [sic], the present law has been duly processed and shall be ratified as such. We order therefore that the full substance of Law 2, Section 15, Part 2, be kept, observed, and complied with evermore in accordance with the demands of the Parliament held in our Palace of Buen Retiro in the year 1789, which content is as follows:

[there follows the actual text of the Law and the command that it be respected]

... Given in the Palace, 29th March 1830. – We, the King.'
(M. Ferrer *et al.*, *Historia del tradicionalismo español*, vol. II, pp. 269 *et seq.*)

135

Declaration of Don Fernando VII on 31 December on the succession to the throne

1832

'I, Don Francisco Fernández del Pino, Knight of the Grand Order of the Cross, etc., etc., Secretary of State and of the Department of Justice and Ecclesiastical Affairs and Guardian-in-Chief of Ceremonial, certify and attest that, having been summoned by order of Her Majesty the Queen, His Excellency the First Secretary of State and the Cabinet to present myself this day in the apartments of His Majesty the King, and having been admitted into the Royal Presence at twelve noon, there were admitted along with me the following individuals who had also received the royal summons...

[There follow ministers, grandees of Spain, etc.]

... And in the presence of them all, His Majesty the King handed me a statement written throughout in his own Royal Hand which he ordered me to read out loud so that everyone could hear it. This I did and it is to the letter as follows:

While our mind was disturbed in the throes of a grave illness from which God's mercy has miraculously cured us, we signed a decree revoking the decree of ratification of the 29th of March of 1830, proclaimed by my illustrious father at the instigation of Parliament in 1789, to re-establish regular channels of succession to the Spanish throne. The tribulations and the anguish of our condition in which from time to time it seemed that we were dying would be quite sufficient proof of the hastiness of that act were this not furnished by its very nature and its consequences. As a King we could not destroy the fundamental laws of the realm whose re-establishment we had published, nor as a father could we of our own free-will rob our descendants of their noble and lawful rights. We were surrounded as we lay on our bed with deluded and disloyal men who abused our love and that of our dear wife for the Spaniards and added to the afflictions and bitterness of our state by assuring us that the whole country was against observing the decree and by painting an exaggerated picture of the rivers of blood and the widespread devastation which would result if it were not revoked. These dreadful statements, made at a time when the truth was all the more to be expected from those whose duty it is to tell it us and when we had no time nor any way to find out if they were true, and when we were already weary of spirit, caused us fresh worry and exhausted what little sense we still had, leaving us heedful of nothing but the peace and protection of our people and forcing us to make this great sacrifice in the interest of the peace of the Spanish nation by this very decree.

Perfidy put the finishing touches to the horrible plot set in motion by honeyed words, and that very day notices were posted attesting to what had been done and containing the decree, thereby violating treacherously the secrecy which, both in the decree and in what we had said, we had commanded to be kept until after our death.

Now, having learned of the lies with which the loyalty of our beloved Spaniards – ever faithful to the line of their kings, – has been libelled; convinced that it is not in our power – nor indeed is it our wish – to break with the time-honoured practice of succession which has been established through the course of centuries, sanctioned by the law, made fast by the heroes who have preceded me on this throne, and sought by the unanimous wishes of my people; and free at last from the effects and the exigencies of those sorry times, we solemnly declare, entirely of our own free will, that the decree to which we put our hand during the anguish of our illness was wrung from us while we lay unconscious and that it was one of the results of that unfounded terror which gripped our soul, and that it shall be null and void, being contrary to the fundamental laws of the Monarchy and to the duties which as a King and as a father we owe our proud descendants. In my palace in Madrid, 31st December, 1832.

... So that this ever shall be common knowledge and have its proper result, I hereby witness it. Madrid, the same day, 31st December, 1832. Signed: Francisco Fernández del Pino.'

(M. Ferrer *et al.*, *Historia del tradicionalismo español*, vol. II, pp. 271 *et seq.*)

136
Letter of protest of Prince Carlos

1833

'My dearest brother, my most beloved Fernando, I am delighted to see from your letter of the 23rd that, although you were fully occupied, which fact gives me all the more reason to thank you for writing, you are in good health, as are Christina and the girls; we are ourselves, thanks to God.

... What you want to know is whether or not I plan to recognise your daughter as Princess of Asturias. Oh, how dearly I would love to! Knowing me as well as you do, you must believe me for I speak from the heart, that the greatest pleasure I could know would be to be the first to swear her in and not to cause you this displeasure and other annoyances which might result from this, but my conscience and my honour do not permit me to do so. My claims on the throne, provided that I outlive you and that you leave no male issue, are so lawful that I cannot forswear them; they are rights which God gave me when it was His will that I should be born and only He can take them away by granting you the son which I so earnestly pray for, perhaps even more than you do yourself. Furthermore, in doing this, I am defending the claims of those that shall come after me and so it is that I find myself forced to send the enclosed declaration which I do with all formality both to you and to all those in power to whom I hope you will communicate it.

Farewell, my dearest brother: I shall ever be yours, I shall love you always, and you will always be in the prayers of your most loving brother, Carlos.'

'Sir: I, Carlos María Isidro de Borbón y Borbón, Prince of Spain, persuaded of the lawfulness of my claims to the Spanish throne, provided I outlive Your Majesty and Your Majesty leaves no male issue, declare that I cannot in conscience and honour recognise nor swear support to any other claimant. This is my declaration.
Palace of Ramalho, 29th April, 1833.

Sir: To Your Majesty's Most Gracious Person. Your most loving and loyal subject. Prince Carlos.'

(M. Ferrer et al., Historia tradicionalismo español, vol. II, p. 274.)

137

Letter of Fernando VII to his brother Carlos, condemning him to exile

1833

'Madrid, 6th May 1833. – My dearest brother, my most beloved Carlos... I have ever been persuaded of the love you bear me. I believe that you are persuaded also of the affection I have for you, but I am a father and a king and I must look to my rights, to those of my daughters and to those of my crown. – It is not my wish to make you go against the dictates of your conscience nor am I able to dissuade you from laying claims to rights, which, founded on the decisions of men, you believe only God can revoke. But the brotherly love I have always borne you induces me to spare you the vexations which a country where your hypothetical claims are not recognised would offer, while the duty of a king forces me to exile from the realm a Prince whose claims could be a focal point for the restlessness of malcontents.

Being forbidden to return to Spain for important reasons of state, by the law of the realm which expressly forbids it, and in the interests of your own well-being which I desire as fervently as that of my people, I hereby grant you licence to travel forthwith to the Pontifical States letting me know where exactly you are going and where you finally decide to set up house. One of my warships will put in at Lisbon harbour in the near future to take you ... Farewell, my beloved Carlos: please believe I have always loved you, I still do and always shall. Your most affectionate and constant brother, Fernando.'

(Lafuente, Historia general de España..., vol. V, p. 597.)

Bibliography

i. Bibliography of Source Material

Francisco Barado y Font, *Museo Militar* (Barcelona, 1889).

Jeronimo Bécker, *La independencia de América* (Madrid, 1922).

Fray Nicolás de Jesús Belando, *Historia civil de España y sucesos de la guerra y tratados de la paz; desde el año de mil setecientos hasta el de mil setecientos treinta y tres* (Madrid, 1740).

Carlos Calvo, *Anales históricos de la Revolución de la América* (Paris, 1865).

José Conde de Canga Argüelles, *Documentos pertenecientes a las observaciones sobre la historia de la guerra de España* (Madrid, 1835).

'Carta del Rey al Papa dándole aviso del Extrañamiento de los regulares de la Compañia de Jesús' (MS Bibl. Nac., Madrid, No. 10902).

'Carta del Rey Nuestro Señor Dn. Phelipe 5 escrita al claustro y universidad de Salamanca, en que da quenta de la feliz victoria conseguida en los campos de Almansa el día 26 de Abril de 1707' (MS Bibl. Nac., Madrid, No. 10928).

Pedro Ceballos, *Exposición de los hechos y maquinaciones que han preparado la usurpación de la corona de España y los medios que el Emperador de los Franceses ha puesto en obra para realizarla* (Madrid, n.d.).

El Censor (periódico) (Madrid, 1820).

Colección de los decretos y órdenes de las Cortes generales y extraordinarias (Barcelona, 1820).

Colección de tratados de paz, alianza, comercio, etc. ajustados por la Corona de España con las potencias etrangeras desde el reynado del Señor Don Felipe Quinto hasta el presente. Publícase por disposición de Excmo. Sr. Principe de la Paz ... por orden del Rey, 2 vols (Madrid, 1796–1801).

Copia de carta del rey christianissimo Luis Dézimocuarto, a la Reyna nuestra Señora y Señores del Gobierno (no place of publication and no date).

Correo Universal de Literatura y Política (periódico) (Madrid, 1820).

Manuel Dánvila y Collado, *Historia del Reinado de Carlos III*, 6 vols (Madrid, 1893–1895).

Demostración de la lealtad española. Colección de proclamas, bandos, órdenes, discursos, estados de exército, etc. (Madrid, 1808).

Diaria y verídica relación de las operaciones y sucesos del sitio de la ciudad de Barcelona, desde el día 31 de marzo de 1706 hasta la retirada del enemigo (Barcelona, 1706).

Diario de la Expedición contra la plaza de Panzacola concluída por las armas de S. M. Catolica bajo las órdenes del Mariscal de Campo D. Bernardo de Gálvez (no place of publication and no date).

Diario de la Expedición de las armadas inglesa y holendesa al Mediterráneo, en las cuales se embarcó el señor Príncipe D. Jorge Landgrave de Hassia Darmstatt. Por orden de Su Majestad Católica D. Carlos III. El año 1704 y a continuación sumaria de lo que obraron las dichas armadas hasta el 27 de agosto (Lisbon, 1704).

Diario de Madrid (periódico) 1788–1809.

Diario de todo lo ocurrido en la expugnación de los fuertes de Bocachica, y sitio de la ciudad de Cartagena de las Indias: Formado de los pliegos remitidos a Su Majestad (que Dios guarde) por el Virrey de Santa Fe Don Sebastián de Eslaba con D. Pedro de Mur, su Ayudante General (Madrid, 1741).

Diario di tutto quello successa nell'ultima guerra di Sicilia fra le due armate allemana e spagnuola ... tutte notizie raccolte di molte veridiche Relationi ... Divisa in due parti. In Colonia, 1721.

Albert Du Casse, Mémoires et correspondence politique et militaire du roi Joseph, 2 vols (Bayonne, 1855).

Epistolario Español, ed. Eugenio de Ochoa, Biblioteca de Autores Españoles, 2 vols. (Madrid, 1856–70).

Esteban de Ferrater, Código de Derecho internacional, o sea collección metódica de los Tratados de paz, amistad y comercio entre España y las demás naciones (Barcelona, 1846).

Melchor Ferrer, Domingo Tejera, y José Acedo, Historia del tradicionalismo español, 7 vols (Seville, 1941–5).

Conde de Floridablanca, Obras Originales, Biblioteca de Autores Españoles (Madrid, 1867).

Gaceta de Madrid, 211 vols, 1661–1836.

Gaceta Extraordinaria de la Regencia de España e Indias (Cádiz, 1810–13).

José Gil Fortoul, Historia Constitucional de Venezuela, 2nd ed. (Caracas, 1930).

Gaspar Melchor de Jovellanos, Obras publicadas e inéditas, Biblioteca de Autores Españoles, 5 vols (Madrid, 1858–1956).

Modesto Lafuente, Historia general de España desde los tiempos primitivos hasta la muerte de Fernando VII, 25 vols (Barcelona, 1887–90).

Llantos, pompa funeral exequias que hizo la celeberrima Universidad de Salamanca, dia XV de noviembre año MDCCXXIV a la piadosa memoria y magestad de su amado Rey Luis I de España, Monarca de dos Mundos, n.d. [1724].

Mercurio Histórico y Político, 250 vols (Madrid, 1738–1830).

Fausto Nicolini, L'Europa durante le guerra di successione di Spagna. Con particulare riguardo alla citta e regno di Napoli. Note di cronaca lavorate sugli inediti dispacci degli ambasciatori residenti e consoli veneti, 3 vols (Naples, 1937–9).

Novísima recopilación de las leyes de España. Dividida en XII libras en que se reforma la Recopilación publicada por el Señor Don Felipe II en el año de 1567, reimpresa últimamente en el de 1755. Y se incorporan las pragmáticas, cédulas, decretos, órdenes y resoluciones reales y otras providencias no recopiladas y expedidas hasta el año de 1804. Mandado formar por el Señor Don Carlos IV (Madrid, 1805).

Daniel F. O'Learey, Bolívar y la emancipación de América (Madrid, 1915).

Vicente Palacio Atard, El tercer Pacto de Familia (Madrid, 1945).

Carlos Pereyra, Cartas confidenciales de la reina María Luisa y don Manuel Godoy (Madrid, n.d.).

Pragmática sanción de su Majestad en fuerza de ley para el extrañamiento de estos reynos a los regulares de la compañia, ocupación de sus temporalidades y prohibición de su restablecimiento en tiempo alguno, con las demás precauciones que expresa (Madrid, 1767).

Primera relación extraordinaria de la salida del Rey nuestro Señor Don Felipe Quinto de Versalles para estos sus Reynos, y breves noticias de sus Reales Prendas, assi proprias como adquiridas. Publicada martes el 21 de diziembre de 1700.

Manuel José de Quintana, Obras Completas, Biblioteca de Autores Españoles (Madrid, 1867).

Razones de la guerra del Rey Católico contra el Rey de Portugal, el Archiduque Carlos de Austria sus aliados (no place of publication and no date).

Recueil des actes du Directoire Exécutif publiés et annotés par A. Debidour, 2 vols (Paris, 1911).

Relación de la toma del Castillo de San Felipe en Mahón, campamentos español y frances y aleman de la forma que estaban situados sus ataques y baterías (MS. Bibl. Nat. Paris, Espagne, no. 423).

Relación del auto particular de fe que el Santo Oficio de la Inquisición de esta corte celebró en la Iglesia del convento de Santo Domingo el Real el domingo veinte de este presente mes de febrero de mil setecientos y veynte y quatro y de los reos que salieron en el, Madrid, n.d. [1724].

Relación diaria de todo lo sucedido en Madrid desde el día 20 de agosto hasta el día 3 de diciembre de este año de 1710 en que Su Majestad entró en su corte, Madrid, n.d. [1710].

Relación verdadera y circunstanciada de todo lo acaecido en la ciudad de Zaragoza desde primero de abril de este año de 1766 hasta quince del mismo, sacada de Cartas y Relaciones enviadas a Madrid a Personas de dignidad y respeto, Madrid, n.d. [1766].

Vicente Riva Palacio, *México a través de los siglos*, 5 vols (Barcelona, 1883–90).

Duque de Rivas, *Obras completas (Colección de Escritores Castellanos)*, 7 vols (Madrid, 1894–1904).

Vicente Rodriguez Casado, *Política marroquí de Carlos III* (Madrid, 1946).

Enrique Rodriguez Solis, *Los guerrilleros de 1808. Historia popular de la guerra de la Independencia* (Madrid, 1930).

Federico Carlos Sáinz de Robles, *Historia de Madrid* (Madrid, 1934).

Salvador Sampere y Miquel, *Fin de la nación catalana* (Barcelona, 1905).

Conde de Toreno, *Historia del levantamiento, guerra y revolución de España* (Madrid, 1835).

'Trasumpto de la carta que escribió al Nuncio de España el Srio. de Estado de Su Veatitud. Año de 1759' (MS. Bibl. Nac., Madrid, No. 10893).

Antonio de Ubilla y Medina, *Juramento y pleyto omenage que los Reynos de Castilla y León por medio de sus Capitulares y los Prelados, Grandes Títulos y otras personas hizieron el día 8 de mayo de 1701 en el Real Convento de San Geronimo de la villa de Madrid a el Rey Nuestro Señor Don Felipe V que por orden de Su Magestad escrive* (Madrid, 1707).

Juan Francisco Yela Utrilla, *España ante le independencia de los Estados Unidos* (Lérida, 1925).

ii. General Bibliography

(a) POLITICAL

M. Artola Gallego, *La España de Fernando VII* (Historia de España, ed. R. Menéndez Pidal, vol. 26) (1968).

A. Baudrillart, *Philippe V et la Cour de France*, 5 vols (1890–1900).

R. Bouvier et C. Soldevila, *Ensenada et son temps* (1941).

C. Corona Baratech, *Revolución y reacción en el reinado de Carlos IV* (1957).

A. Danvila, *El Reinado relámpago: Luis I y Luisa Isabel de Orléans, 1707–1742* (1952).

H. Kamen, *The War of Succession in Spain, 1700–15* (1969).

H. Kamen, 'Melchor de Macanaz and the Foundations of Bourbon Power in Spain', *Engl. Hist. Rev.* (Oct. 1965) pp. 699–716.

J. Lynch, *Spanish Colonial Administration, 1782–1810 : the Intendant System in the Vice-Royalty of the Rio de la Plata* (University of London Hist. Studies, no. 5, 1958).

B. Moses, *Spain's Declining Power in South America, 1730–1806* (New York and London, 1965).

C. Petrie, *Charles III of Spain* (1970).

A. Soldevila, *Historia de España*, vols 5 and 6 (2nd edn, 1963–4).

(b) SOCIAL, CULTURAL AND ECONOMIC

H. Berindoague, *Le Mercantilisme en Espagne* (1929).

J. Carrera Pujal, *Historia de la economía española*, 3 vols (1943–7).

G. Delpy, *L'Espagne et l'esprit européen, l'œuvre de Feijóo 1725–60* (1936).

A. Domínguez Ortiz, *La sociedad española en el siglo XVIII* (1963).

J. de Entrambasaguas, *El Madrid de Moratín* (1960).

E. J. Hamilton, *War and Prices in Spain, 1651–1800* (1947).

E. J. Hamilton, 'The Decline of Spain', *Econ. Hist. Rev.* viii (1938) pp. 168–79.

E. J. Hamilton, 'Money and Economic Recovery in Spain under the First Bourbons', *Journal of Modern History*, xv (1943) pp. 192–206.

J. O. McLachlan, *Trade and Peace with Old Spain, 1667–1750* (1940).

P. Mérimée, *L'Influence française en Espagne au XVIIIe siècle* (1936).

J. Sarrailh, *L'Espagne éclairée de la seconde moitié XVIIIe siècle* (new edn, 1964).

M. Soria, *Art and Architecture in Spain and Portugal and their American Dominions, 1500–1800* (Pelican History of Art, 1959).

J. Vicens Vives, *Historia económica de España* (1959).

Index

288

69652